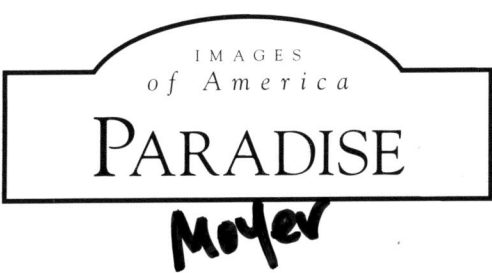

Moyer

ON THE COVER: Harvest fairs have a long tradition in Paradise, dating back to the late 1880s when they were held in the old community hall at Clark and Elliot Roads in Leonard's Mill or Old Paradise. The festival in this photograph is at the Woodman's Dance Platform at Olive Street and College Avenue in 1912–1913. Dressed up for "going to town," these people inspect a variety of produce from boxed fruit to canned preserves. (Courtesy Lois McDonald.)

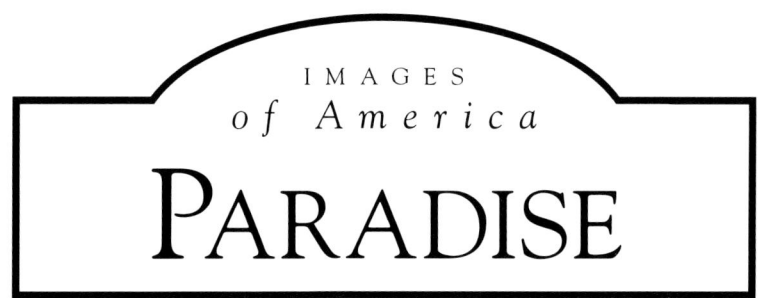
IMAGES
of America
PARADISE

Robert Colby

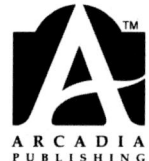
ARCADIA
PUBLISHING

Copyright © 2006 by Robert Colby
ISBN 0-7385-4675-5

Published by Arcadia Publishing
Charleston SC, Chicago IL, Portsmouth NH, San Francisco CA

Printed in the United States of America

Library of Congress Catalog Card Number: 2006927527

For all general information contact Arcadia Publishing at:
Telephone 843-853-2070
Fax 843-853-0044
E-mail sales@arcadiapublishing.com
For customer service and orders:
Toll-Free 1-888-313-2665

Visit us on the Internet at www.arcadiapublishing.com

Last year, we lost a great historian, Lois Halliday McDonald. For over 30 years, Lois researched, wrote, and taught the history of the Paradise Ridge and Northern California. Lois undoubtedly was the person most knowledgeable about the history of Paradise and adjoining areas. A considerable amount of information and a number of photographs came from Lois's files and her 2000 book, This Paradise We Call Home. *Take it from one who knows—especially after doing the Images of America volume* Paradise—*she is missed as a historian, mentor, and friend. In 1998, Lois said, "When I look at our area I don't see what is, I see what it used to be." The author has attempted to present this view to the reader.*

Contents

Acknowledgments 6

Introduction 7

1. First on the Ridge 11
2. Leonard's Mill, Old Paradise 15
3. Orloff, New Paradise 39
4. Apples, Timber, and More 57
5. Water and Power 75
6. Roads, Rails, and Aeroplanes 83
7. "Modern Times" 95

Acknowledgments

An important source of information and photographs was the files and books written by the late Lois McDonald. Another major source of material was *Tales of the Paradise Ridge*, for over 46 years the biannual journal of the Paradise Historical Society and now the Gold Nugget Museum and History Center in Paradise. The museum collection of photographs exceeds 3,000 in number, all of which were made available to me. I especially want to thank Connie Rogers, executive director, for scanning some 200 of these photographs, as well as the rest of the museum staff for just putting up with me. The Paradise Genealogy Society and their Florence Styles Collection was another great source of photographs and information; thank you to the staff for your help. The multitude of unnamed people that donated their photographs to these institutions also deserves a heartfelt thank you.

Others who helped with photographs, information, and/or were kind enough to do such chores as reviewing or proofing the text are John and Jean Heinke, Tobias Palmer, Chuck Smay, Pat Berry, Ken Gardner, Rodger and Frank Green, Kent Stephens, Pat Brice, Colleen Murto, Jim and Laurie Noble, Jack De Coup–Crank, Rick Riddell, George Bille, Loretta Griffin, Norma McKillop, Linda Kautter, Jim McAfee, Michelle Shover, Bill Shelton, Nick Becker, George Barber, Janeece Webb, Doug Flesher, Johnnie Spreen, June Van Gooden, Joan Dresser, Wayne Stout, Alberta Tracy of the Butte County Historical Society, Bill Jones of CSU Chico, Meriam Library Special Collections, and Glenda Chombeau of the Stirling City Historical Society for the Velma Butler Collection. I give my apologies to anyone whom I may have overlooked.

Finally there is my editor, Hannah Clayborn, at Arcadia Publishing and my wife, Patsy, for listening to me grouse about the computer and the book numbering system that do not work like I think they should.

INTRODUCTION

"Boys, this has got to be Paradise." So said William "Uncle Billy" Leonard as he leaned back, relaxing in the shade of a ponderosa pine. He and his crew had just driven their wagons up the ridge from Oroville in the heat of a summer day. Is that how Paradise got its name? Could be; it's as good a tale as any. Uncle Billy was not the first to settle in what became known as Leonard's Mill, but around his sawmill formed the first community of any significance. Today it would be at the intersection of Clark and Elliott Roads.

Another oft-told tale about the name is that there was a "watering hole" called the Pair 'O Dice Saloon. Apparently there was such a saloon, but pioneer Francis "Fannie" Breese said the story that the saloon was the inspiration for the town's name is not true.

The community officially became Paradise in 1877 when it got a post office. Later when a new "center of town" sprang up around the railroad depot to the west, the original community became known as Old Paradise or Old Town.

The term "the Ridge" often refers to the geographic feature starting below Paradise, where the foothills meet the flat Sacramento Valley and extend at least up to Inskip, 20 miles above Paradise. However, in this book it is arbitrarily placed at the upper boundary where the northern Paradise town limit abuts Magalia. The eastern limit is the west branch of the North Fork of the Feather River, aptly called the West Branch. The western limit is Butte Creek Canyon. The reader should be aware that this is less than a comprehensive history of Paradise; coverage depended upon the available photographs and space.

For perhaps 10,000 years, the Paradise Ridge was home to the Maidu Indians. They lived in autonomous groups best referred to as tribelets. A tribelet usually had a major camp site and seasonally ranged over an area up to 50 miles in extent, determined by food sources and water. The Maidu were hunter-gatherers whose survival depended on their understanding of nature. They lived on the Paradise Ridge during the summer and fall when acorns, grass seeds, insects, deer, and small game were plentiful. They left limited physical evidence that they were here.

In 1808, the Spanish passed through Butte County, and by 1829, American trappers were exploring the foothill streams. In 1849, the gold rush changed the county and state forever. Even though it was in the midst of the northern mines, Paradise played a minor role in the gold gush. There was gold in abundance above Dogtown and in the canyons on both sides but virtually none in Paradise. One just passed over the Ridge on the way to the mines.

In the 1850s, there was a trading post and ferry at Nelson Bar on the West Branch. Below the Ridge in the Mesilla Valley, Manoah Pence built a ranch, hotel, and store. In Butte Creek Canyon there were Diamondville, Centerville, and other mining camps.

In the 1850s, Sam Neal blazed the earliest primitive road up the Ridge, from his Mexican land grant in the valley to his sawmill along Little Butte Creek, about a mile south of Dogtown. By the mid-1850s, Oroville-Honey Lake Road passed through Pence and climbed the east flank of the Ridge to Dogtown and beyond. It was later called Pentz Road in Paradise.

It was not until the mid-1850s and early 1860s that people started to settle in the area that would become Paradise. Initially these were miners who did not strike it rich. Giving up gold mining for farming, John Ware and his wife, Hannah, were among the first to homestead land. Farming and harvesting the Ridge's dense forest became the local occupations of choice. Every family raised vegetables, fruits, and grains, along with hogs, a cow or two, and a few chickens for their own use. Any excess was bartered to neighbors or sold to the miners.

Uncle Billy Leonard's sawmill, near the Oroville-Dogtown Road in the vicinity of today's Clark and Elliott Roads, is the best-remembered mill and the early community was called Leonard's Mill and later Old Paradise or Old Town. The road was renamed for Elisha D. Clark, who operated the first stage line on the route to Dogtown (Magalia in 1863), Lovelock, Powellton, and Inskip and on to Susanville.

Leonard's sawmill was used as a refuge for neighboring families during the Indian conflicts of the 1860s. In a desperate attempt to reclaim their traditional lands and to avenge violence done to them, Native Americans resorted to theft, arson, and murder. The whites reacted by killing virtually any Native Americans they could find, guilty or innocent. Both sides believed retaliation was morally justified.

Charles Delaplain, another early settler, is best remembered for the land he donated in 1861 for the first schoolhouse and the ditch he dug from Little Butte Creek to his 160 acres south of Dogtown. Brothers William and James Dresser and their families came in the 1860s. Letters written by James provide a window into what life was like in early Paradise. Dresser descendents still live in Paradise, but James moved on when freezing weather, and later drought, killed his crops.

By 1877, Leonard's Mill had about 80 residents and got a new post office named Paradise. John Strong, of another pioneer family, was postmaster. People continued to move onto the Ridge, one of the more notable being William E. Mack, M.D., who besides being the Ridge's doctor, first recognized that the soil and mild climate would support commercial agriculture. In 1877, he planted 65 acres of olives and built a processing plant. His Highland brand of olives and olive oil was produced into the 1940s.

At that time, people in other parts of Butte County considered the settlement as just a place (sometimes referred to as Poverty Ridge) a person traveled through to get to the mines and timber at higher elevations. Living may not have been easy, but the people who lived here did not consider themselves especially poor. They liked the climate and the isolation.

In 1902, strangers were quietly buying land on and above Paradise Ridge. Residents were blissfully unaware that the Diamond Match Company planned to build a town and sawmill above Magalia along with a railroad up the Ridge, just west of the current Paradise. Diamond Match feared that if the landowners knew their plans, prices would dramatically escalate. By 1903, the secret was out, as surveyors examined the right-of-way for the Butte County Railroad. Construction started on a depot about a mile west of the current center of town in 1904. Even though the old community had a community hall, a schoolhouse, a couple of hotels, a one-room Congregational church, a saloon at various times, numerous homes and ranches, and a general store housing the Paradise post office, the railroad still named the new depot Paradise.

As businesses started up along Olive Street, opposite the new depot, the area became known as "New Paradise." In 1905, the nascent new town applied for a post office. Old Paradise was using the name Paradise so the name Pinedale was submitted. Orloff was the name selected. Why Orloff? It was first name of the son of the railroad station agent, George Miller, and was submitted apparently as a joke. Pinedale was already in use, so Orloff became the name of the post office that opened in a store on Olive Street across from the depot.

When the depot opened, the Ridge and New Paradise (Orloff) gained significance for other county residents. The same year that construction on the depot began, a subdivision had been approved across the tracks to the east, and a Chico real estate developer, Roland Diller, laid out "downtown" streets. Almost overnight it became "a town with a future," to use the appellation coined by a real estate broker. A boom was underway, and by 1908–1909, the Sierra Park, Oakdale Farms, and Chico Heights subdivisions were the places to buy. However, the boom petered out around 1910, when it was realized that there was little employment on the Ridge aside from jobs in agriculture.

Confusion remained about the name of the town. Was it Orloff because of the post office or Paradise because of the depot? Any confusion was resolved in 1911 when the post office on Clark Road closed and the name was transferred to the Orloff post office across the street from the depot.

Isaiah Horace Cook was a virtual "one man Chamber of Commerce" for Paradise. A successful life insurance salesman, he discovered Paradise on his sales trips around Northern California. Perceiving a great opportunity, he bought 400 acres at "dirt cheap" prices in 1911. He started a ranch and opened a real estate office from which he advertised the virtues of Paradise. Cook next built a sawmill, a planing mill, and a box factory near the intersection of today's Pearson and Sawmill Roads. By 1916, he had bought and sold over 4,000 acres. Still traveling through California and Nevada selling insurance, he continued to extol the advantages of Paradise. People listened, and by Cook's account, at least 50 families "pulled up stakes" and moved to the Ridge at a time when there were maybe 800 people living there.

That the Paradise Ridge had agricultural potential was well known. After all, a freight carload of Paradise pears had sold in Los Angeles for $100 a ton. But there was a big problem—the lack of a reliable water supply during the growing season. Lucky farmers had streams or springs on their property, but often these sources were reduced to a dribble in the summer. Since the 1950s, ditches had crossed the Ridge to bring water to mines as far away as Table Mountain near Oroville. Sometimes Ridge farmers used this water "without so much a by your leave." Other farmers, notably John Ware and Charles Delaplain, dug their own ditches to carry water from Little Butte Creek to irrigate their crops and provide for everyday living. Still, the supply of water was anything but sure.

The answer came in 1916 with the formation of the Paradise Irrigation District (PID). It built Magalia Dam on Little Butte Creek, adjacent to the old mining town. As the dam was being completed, the United States entered World War I and PID could not buy steel pipe to carry water to the orchards. They had to use pipe fashioned by binding redwood staves bound with steel wire. Within 15 years, leaks were a major problem. Probably as much water was lost as was being delivered. In 1941, PID started replacing the original pipe with steel, only to be frustrated by steel shortages during World War II. In 2006, PID is still replacing substandard World War II pipe.

When PID brought water to the Ridge, one would think that the farmer's problems were solved. Not so. The "solution" to the water problems actually worsened conditions for a large number of farmers. Even though they now had water and the demand for their produce was high, their orchards were just beginning to produce, and they did not have a marketing system. The PID taxes still had to be paid, and many farmers lost their land for unpaid taxes. The Great Depression made the situation still worse. At one time PID is said to have owned 60 percent of the land in the district. Eventually federal government programs created during the Depression helped destitute farmers buy back their land and helped PID pay off delinquent bonds and repair the deteriorating water system.

With a reliable water source on the Ridge, commercial agriculture "bloomed" when the Butte County Railroad, now owned by Southern Pacific, brought transportation to remote markets. In 1909, farmers organized a Fruit Grower's Union to jointly market their pears, apples, plums, peaches, olives, nuts, prunes, grapes, red potatoes, and strawberries. They set up a sorting and crating service near the depot and even built a small building next to it to display their produce to travelers.

In the 1920s, farmers formed the Paradise Farm Center, which worked with the University of California at Davis Farm Extension Service to develop seeds and fertilizers suited to the red, volcanic soils of the Ridge. The center provided lectures and demonstrations on all phases of farming, and it publicized Paradise as a place to live.

Paradise harvest fairs began with the Paradise Harvest Festival of 1889. They reached their peak in 1938, when Paradise was selected as the site of the Butte County Fair. Today's annual Johnny Appleseed Days in Paradise is a reminder of these bygone festivals.

Apples were the most important produce, and there were over 50 orchards on the Ridge. The taste and color of Paradise apples benefited from the soils and the cold, fall weather. Most of them were shipped to such western markets as Denver, San Francisco, and Los Angeles. Until the 1960s, fresh apples from the Ridge had a competitive edge, as they were marketed slightly before those from Washington and Oregon. However, faster transportation and improved refrigeration eventually gave apples from these areas the advantage. Most of the orchards were gone by the early 1980s. Today only the Noble Orchard is still in production.

In the 1950s, the population of the Ridge steadily grew. In response, PID built the Paradise Reservoir above the Magalia Reservoir. Schools, churches, and all varieties of businesses multiplied along with the population, all of which continue to grow today. Yet, as more people came, many of them retirees, tracts of homes replaced the orchards. By the 1970s and 1980s, farms were scarce on the Ridge.

The first road was oiled in 1910; now most are paved. Although not the first newspaper on the Ridge, the *Paradise Post* started in 1945 and remains to this day, outlasting a number of other papers. Skyway, a major new road from Chico, opened in 1952. In 1951, a tax-supported fire district replaced volunteer firemen, and the town incorporated in 1976.

Real estate developers of the early 1900s would not believe the growth of Paradise in the last 50 years. The "town with a future" really lived up to the old advertising slogan. In 2006, it is appropriate that the Town of Paradise is building a park centered on the old Butte County Railroad depot and that the Gold Nugget Museum and History Center is planning a museum in the restored depot building to preserve the history of Paradise Ridge.

One

FIRST ON THE RIDGE

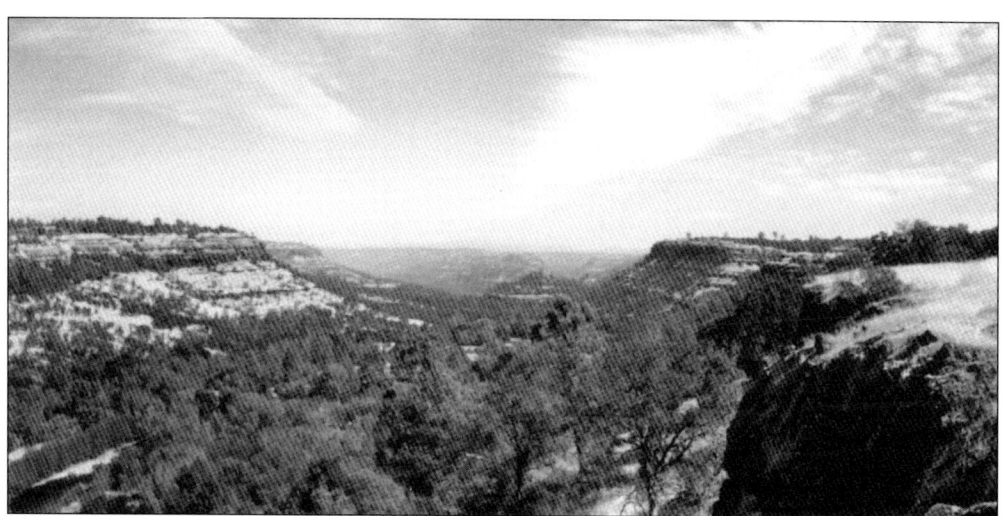

Four million years ago, an 11,000-foot volcano existed near Butte Meadows, 25 miles northeast of Paradise. It spewed forth massive mud flows and intermittent, dense, gray sheets of basalt to form layers between the flows of mud and boulders. The Ridge was inundated with hundreds of feet of volcanic rock. These bedded volcanic rocks are evident in this view of Butte Canyon, the western boundary of the Paradise Ridge. (Courtesy author.)

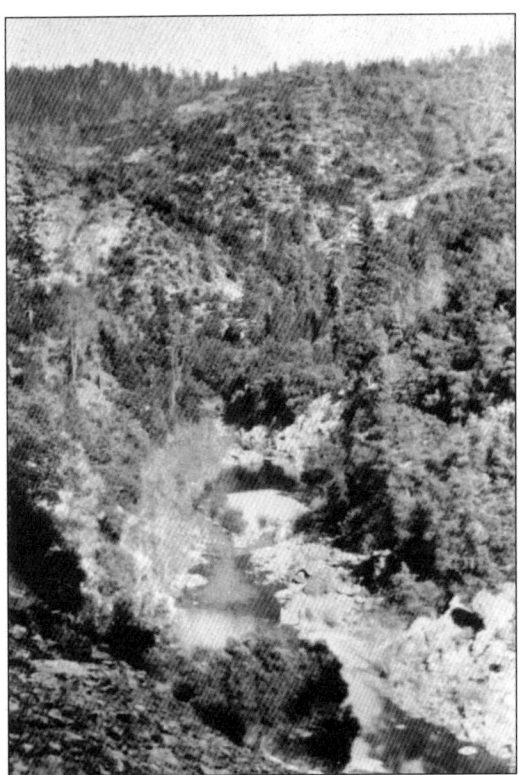

Incised deeply into the granite of the Northern Sierra Nevada, the West Branch of the Feather River provided gold in abundance. It is the eastern limit of the Paradise Ridge. Gold also was plentiful from Dogtown/Magalia northward. On the Ridge itself gold was absent, the surface covered by a deep red soil, volcanic in origin. But this made little difference to the Native Americans and the later white settlers. (Courtesy Lois McDonald.)

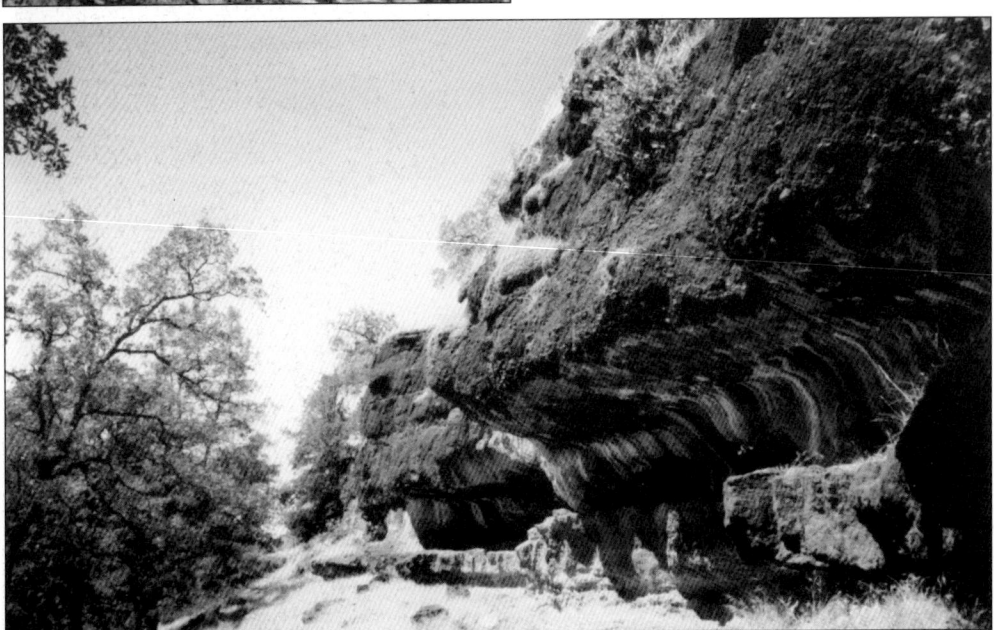

Eroded by the elements into a volcanic tuff formation, these caves often were enlarged by the Native Americans who sheltered in them. Overlaid by massive, volcanic mudstones, some caves go many feet back into the hillside, and the ceilings are high enough for one to stand upright. These caves are found high on the walls of canyons and buttes, and those on a butte south of Paradise are called Robber's Roost. (Courtesy author.)

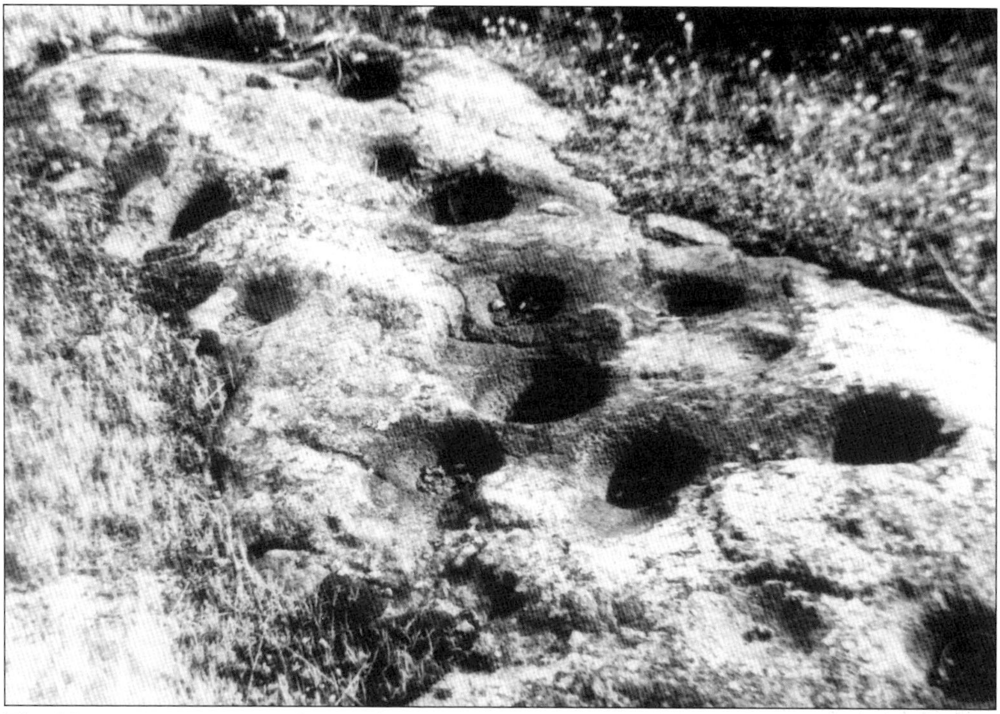

This Native American grinding rock near Neal Road is a site where Indian women gathered with their children to socialize and grind acorns from oak trees and seeds into meal from which they baked bread. The rocks were typically under a tree for shade. The Native Americans normally resided on the Ridge during the spring and summer, subsisting on acorns, seeds, berries, fish, and game. (Courtesy Gold Nugget Museum.)

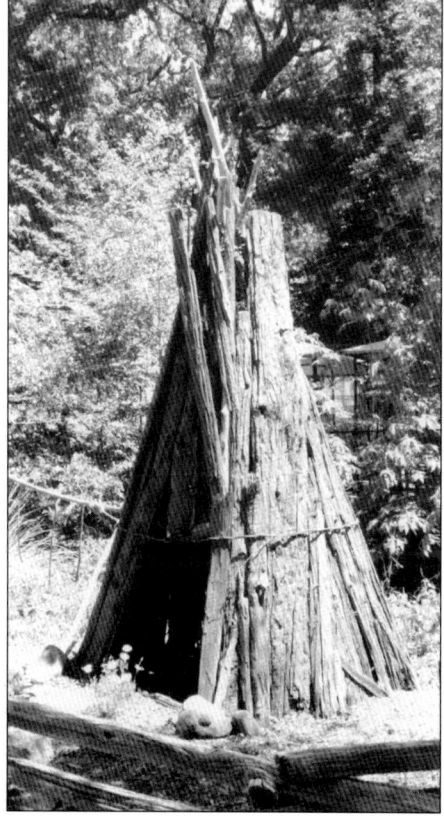

Aside from grinding holes, relatively few artifacts were left behind by the Maidu tribelet that occupied the Ridge during the spring and summer of each year. This photograph, though, shows how one of their temporary shelters may have been constructed. It is built of pieces of bark cut from the cedar trees, which are plentiful in the area. This structure is at the Gold Nugget Museum. (Courtesy author.)

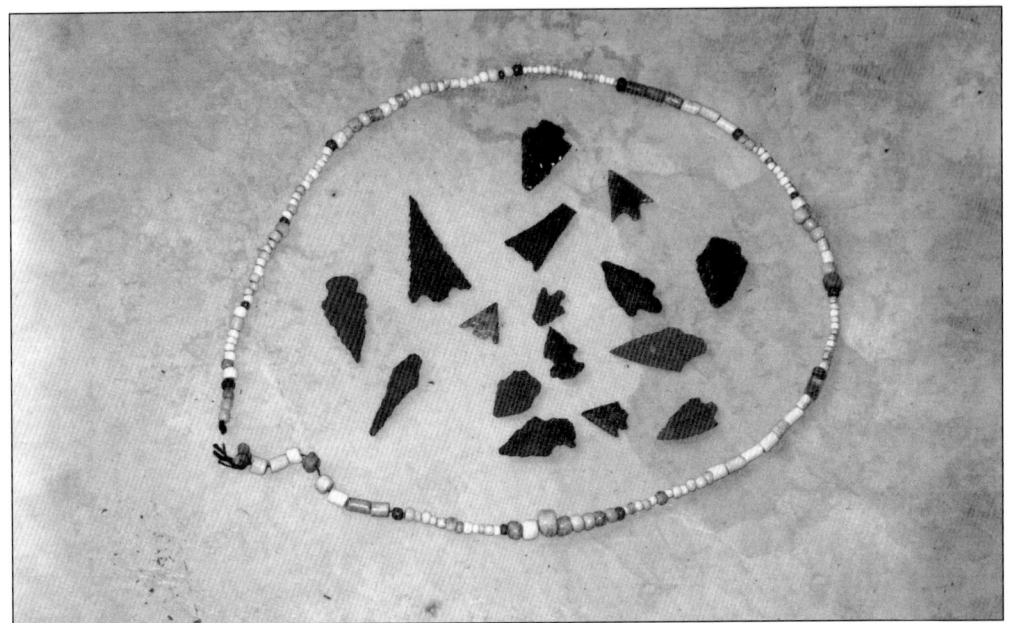

These arrowheads and beads were found near the Nimshew School about 80 years ago. (Nimshew is four miles northwest of modern Paradise on the ridge above Butte Canyon.) After school, the boys often looked for arrowheads next to the school grounds. The shell beads were found separately and strung together later. The pristine condition of the arrowheads and the beads may indicate a Maidu burial site. (Courtesy author.)

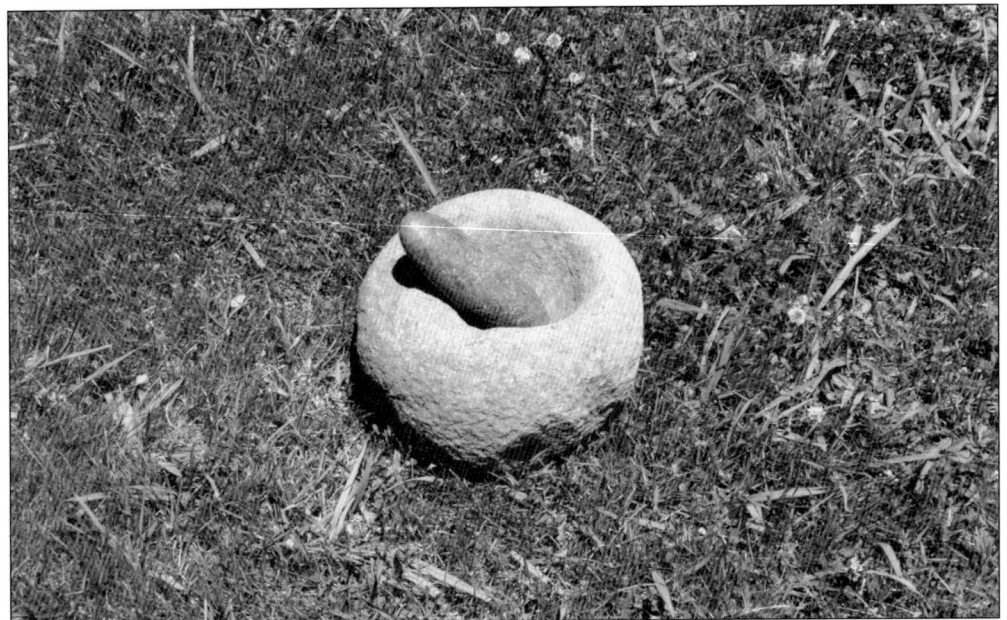

This Maidu stone bowl mortar was found in May 2006 while digging a grave in the southwest section of the Paradise Cemetery. The pestle was found separately in the cemetery. Years ago, another melon-shaped mortar was found a quarter mile south when the Seventh Day Adventist Church was being built. This one is about the same size and shape but has decorations cut into the exterior and a lid. (Courtesy author.)

Two
LEONARD'S MILL, OLD PARADISE

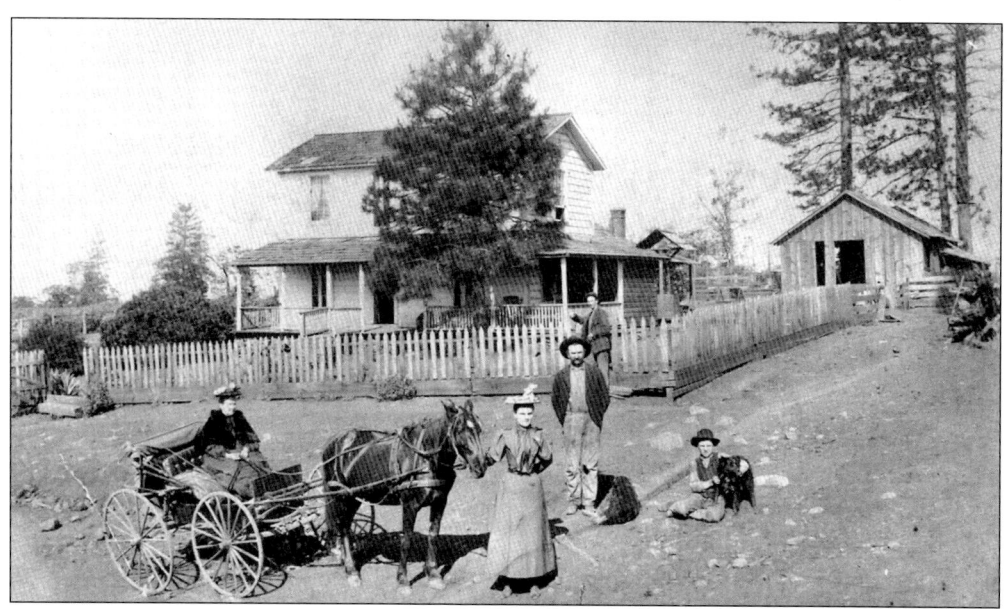

Pictured here c. 1900, from left to right, at the Ware home on Neal Road are Hannah Ware, granddaughter Pansy, her father William, and her brother Raymond. Pearl Stetson, also Hanna's grandson, leans on the fence. Hannah's husband, John, came for gold in 1852, went home to Indiana in 1856, and returned to Butte County before 1860. John and his family were the first permanent settlers and farmers on the Ridge. (Courtesy Gold Nugget Museum.)

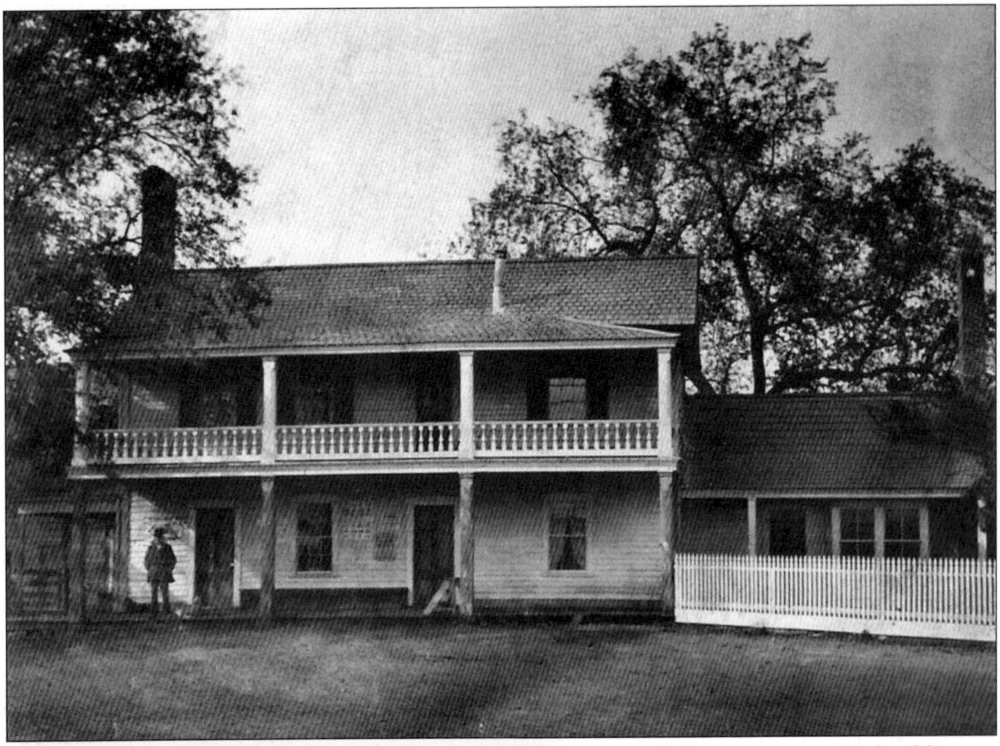

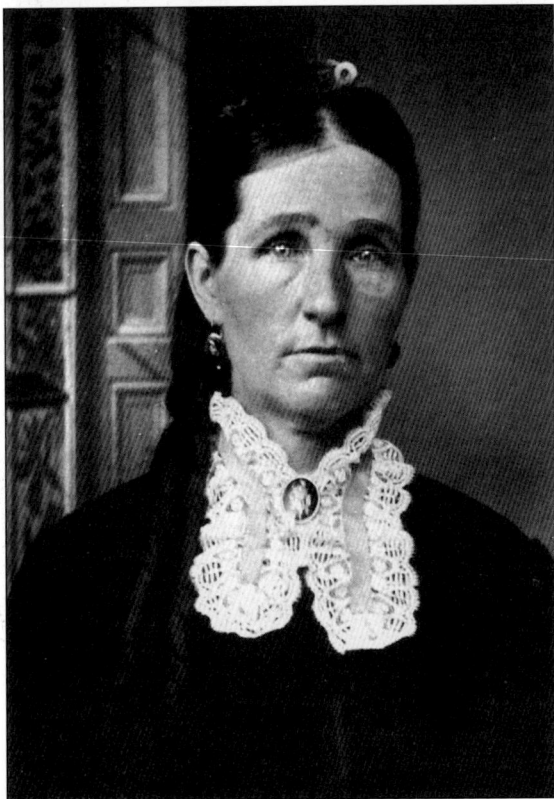

Manoah Pence came to find gold in 1849 and found that "there's more money in selling shovels than using them." He purchased 400 acres in Mesilla Valley below the Ridge, opening a tent-store and bar. He built a home and a hotel and became a prosperous farmer and renowned Native American fighter. He died in 1882, after a road and post office were named for him but spelled Pentz. (From the Sophia Pence Album.)

Widow Sophia Finn came to California and married Manoah Pence in 1856. She helped him build a prosperous ranch and bore him a son, Watt. Widowed a second time in 1882, she and her son moved to Paradise where she used her considerable skills as a writer to advocate women's rights through newspaper articles and poetry. Ridge husbands were not happy with the women's discussion group she started. (From the Sophia Pence Album.)

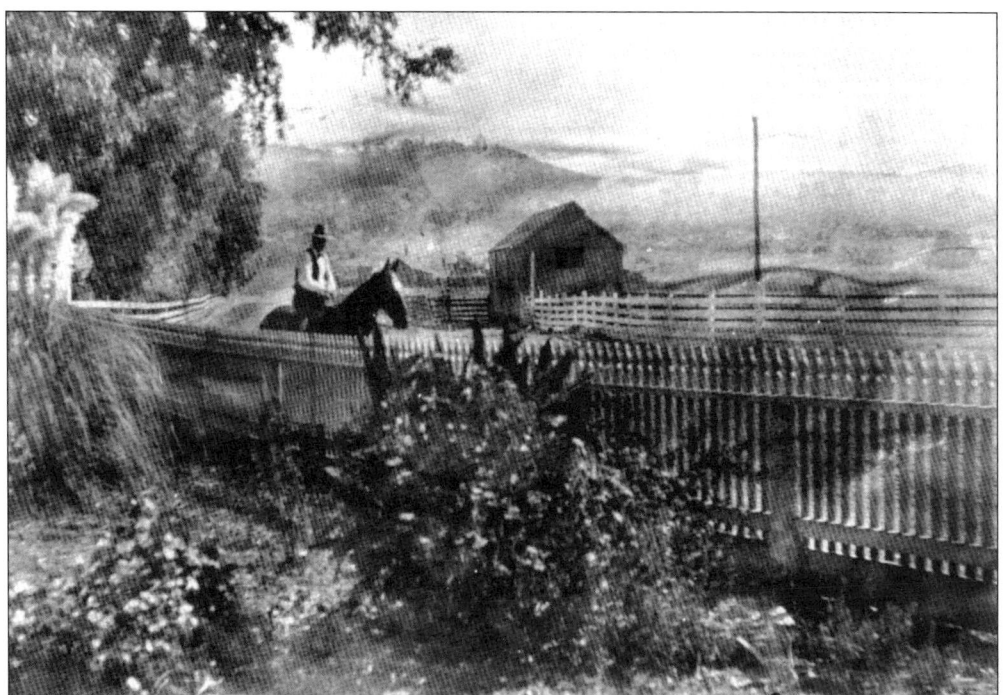

Here is Manoah Pence's son Watt on horseback in front of the Pence home and hotel. The view is northward over the Messilla Valley toward the Ridge. In 1892, after Watt's divorce from a spendthrift wife, he and his mother, Sophia, left the ranch in Mesilla Valley and moved to Paradise to a small home off Clark Road above Pearson Road. (From the Sophia Pence Album.)

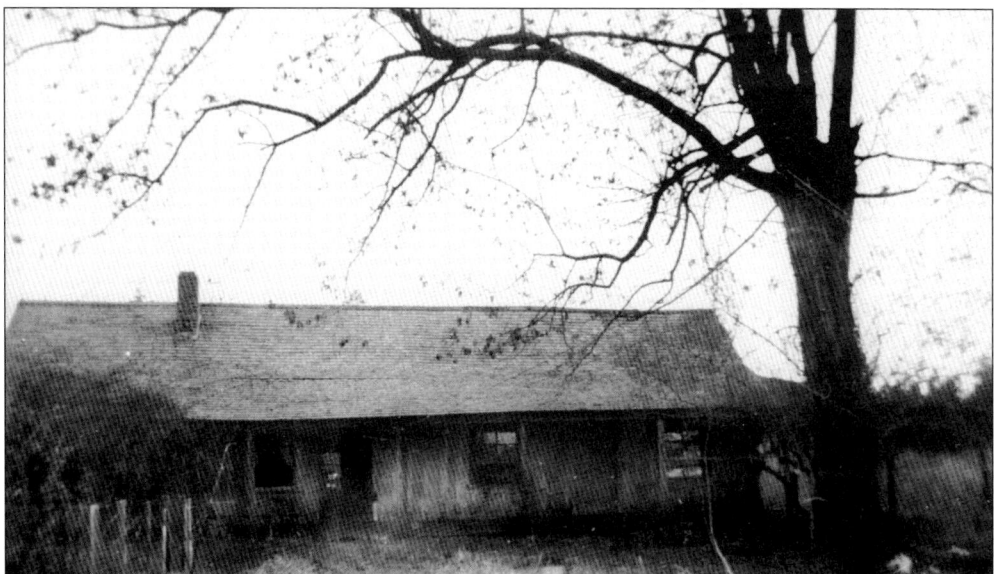

This is an undated photograph of the stage station in Leonard's Mill. It was located on Clark Road near today's Lovely Lane, a half mile north of the center of town. In later years, lumber from the building was used to construct a home on the same site for Goldie Langberg. In 1973, it was the residence of Michael Wines. (Courtesy CSU, Chico, Meriam Library, Special Collections, Plumas County Museum.)

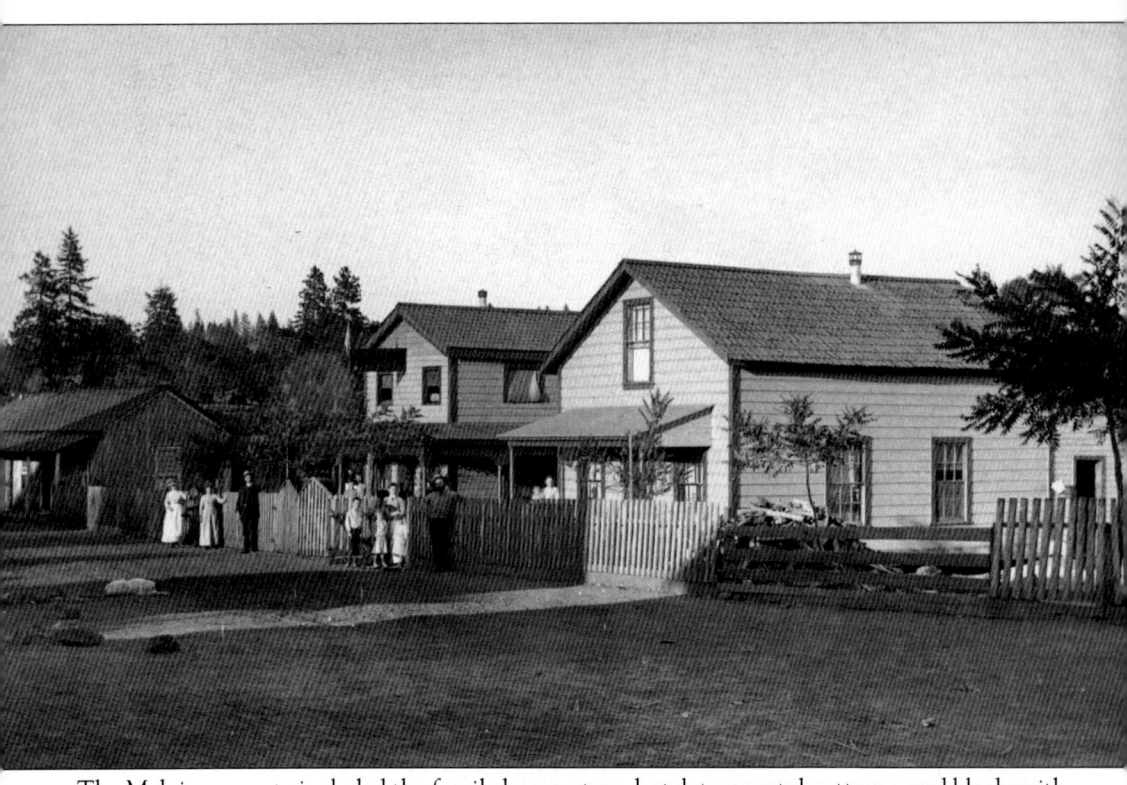

The Melvin property included the family home, store, hotel, two rental cottages, and blacksmith shop. William Lord Melvin, his wife, Mary, and eight children came to Leonard's Mill in 1881. He had been a successful farmer and butcher in Colusa County before "retiring" at age 47 to Paradise. He bought five acres on the east side of Clark Road, south of what became Elliott Road. Neighbors thought Melvin a bit "high hat" as he preferred to be called Lord rather than William. Moreover, he and his family did not attend worship services and were suspected of being spiritualists. Sumner and Georgiana Skillin and their family moved to Leonard's Mill in 1878 and bought 160 acres of land. Their eldest daughter, 14-year-old Mabel, fell in love with the oldest Melvin boy, Eugene. Violently opposed to marriage because of Mabel's age, the Skillins forbad her seeing Eugene. The fact that the elder Melvin referred to himself as Lord impressed them not one bit, and with him being a spiritualist, it was too much. On Christmas night 1882, the Good Templars gave a ball. It was well attended, and Eugene and Mabel used it as cover to elope. Ridge families speculated that the Melvin family had staged the elopement and their reputation did not help. It was plain that somebody had taken Eugene and Mabel to Oroville, where they caught the train to San Francisco and were married aboard the steamship *Eureka*. There were rumors that Skillin might be out for Melvin's blood. However, in 1884, a grandson was born to the young couple, doing much to reconcile the grandparents. Remember Lord Melvin's rental cottages? In 1902, men were seen continually going to one of them. Charged with running a brothel, Melvin was found not guilty by the Kimshew Justice Court. (Courtesy Gold Nugget Museum.)

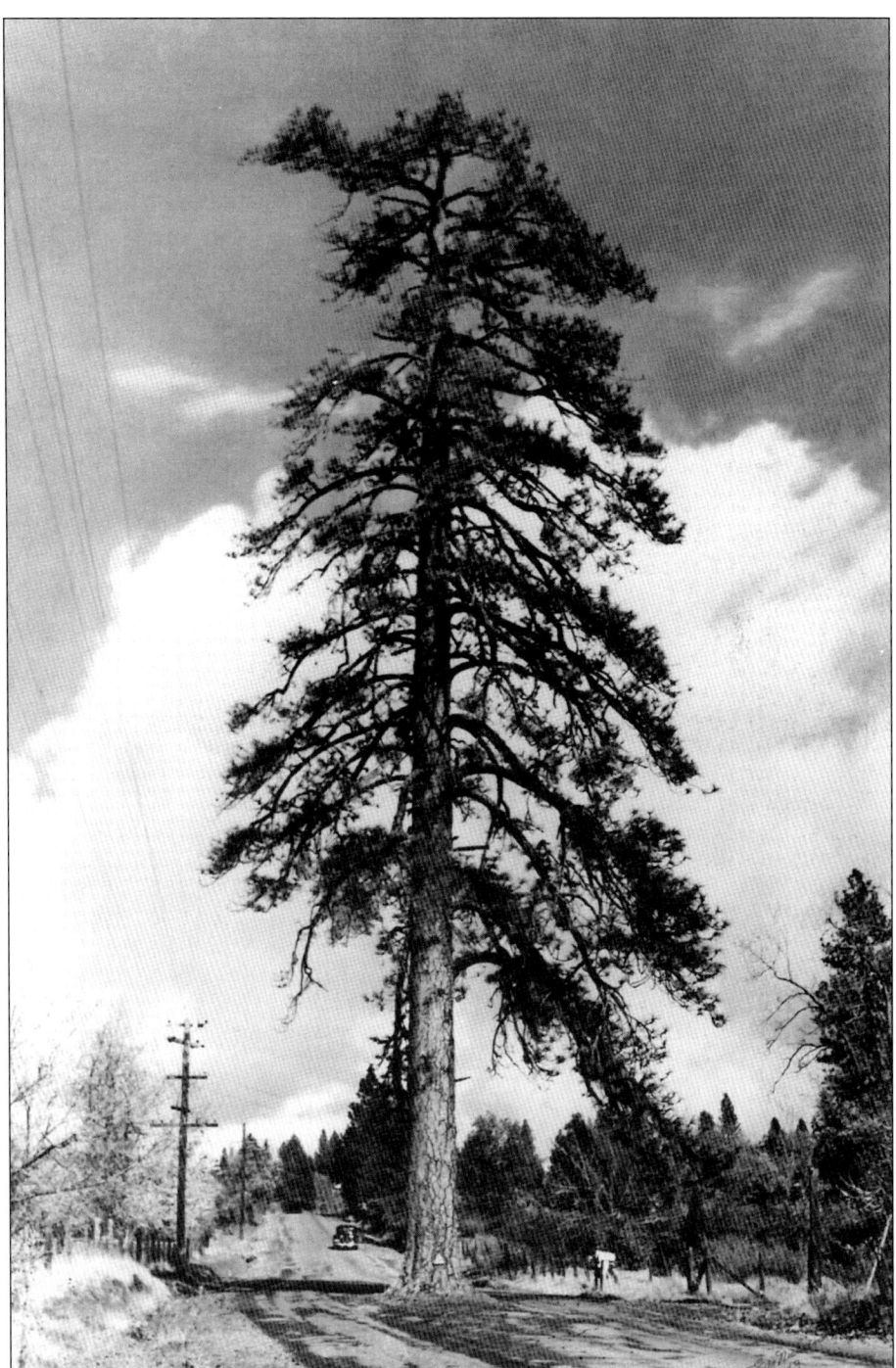

This large ponderosa pine (yellow pine), considered by some as the icon of Paradise, stood in the middle of Clark Road at today's Lovely Lane. This is about a half mile north of the intersection of Clark and Elliott Roads, the center of Leonard's Mill. This photograph, looking north up Clark Road, was taken in 1943, two years before the landmark died and was cut down. (Courtesy Josie E. M. Nielsen.)

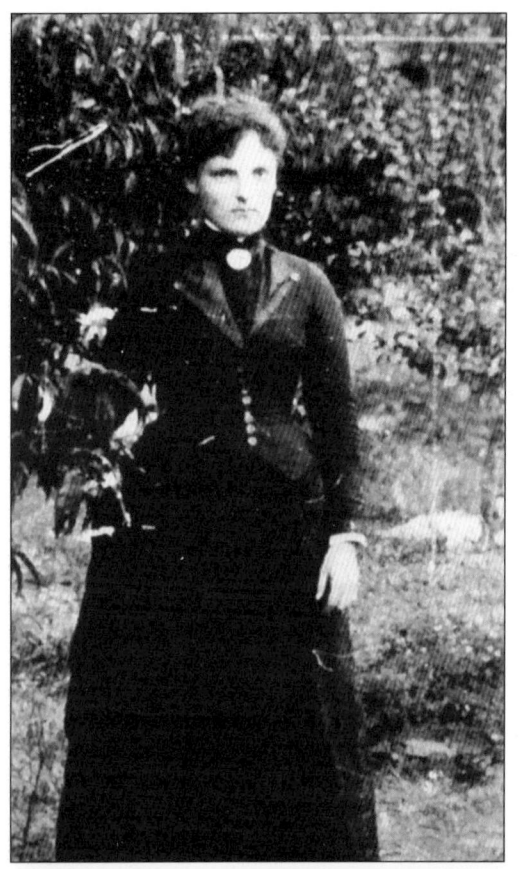

People were buried in what became the Paradise Cemetery before 1860, but without Frances "Fannie" Breese, the cemetery known today might not exist. In 1884, Fannie's uncle Miles H. Strong offered to sell three acres for a cemetery for $41. The Good Templars Lodge put up $21.50 and Fannie, just 17 years old, raised $21.50 from 28 citizens who contributed from 25¢ to $2.50. Wood and labor for fencing was contributed. By 1892, fires and wandering stock had taken their toll. Again Fannie raised the money, this time for a wire fence. After her death in 1950, the Frances Breese Gate was erected at the Elliott Road entrance to the cemetery to honor Fannie for her efforts. In 2005, the gate was moved to the "old section" of the cemetery. On the left is a picture of Fannie Breese in 1877. (Courtesy Paradise Genealogy Society and Marygrace Colby.)

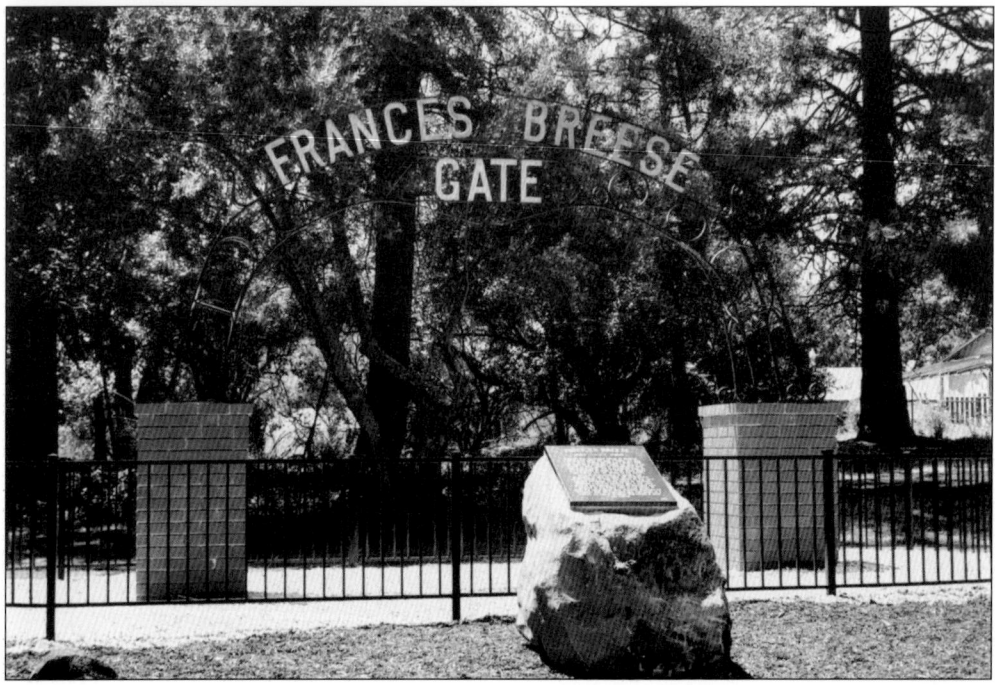

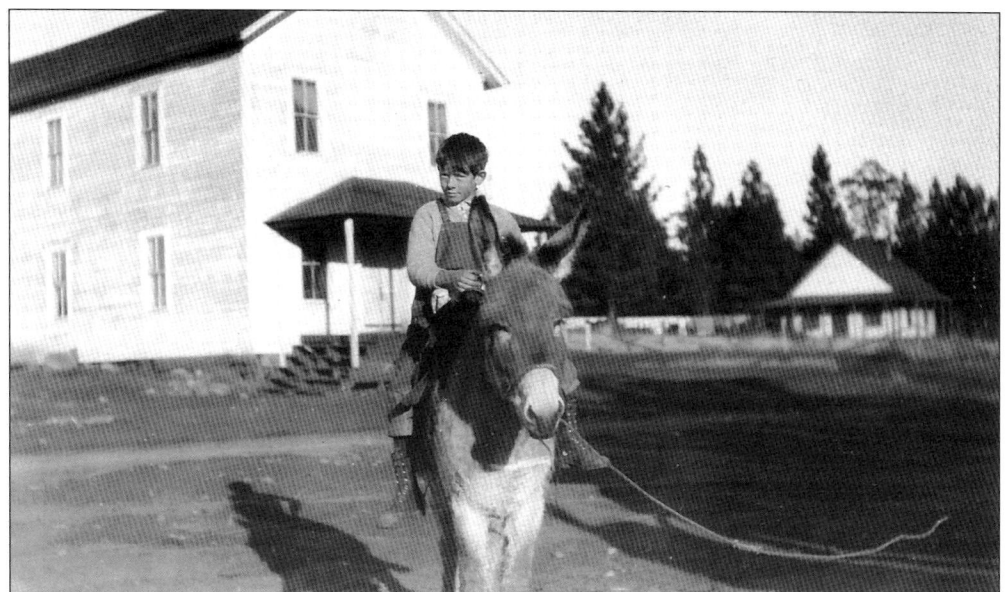

The top photograph shows the two-story Good Templars Lodge on the southwest corner of Clark Road and Cemetery Lane, later Elliott Road, sometime before 1888. The Good Templars were the first public service organization on the Ridge and their lodge was used for weddings, dances, church services, and meetings. The redoubtable Fannie Breese helped raise funds to build the lodge. In 1888, the building burned, supposedly "torched" by a customer of a saloon across the street that objected to the noise of temperance meetings. Sometime later, the saloon owner sold his building to the community. It was moved to the site of the former lodge and served as the Community Center for 80 years. During remodeling in the early 1900s, the second story was removed as is evident in the photograph below. (Above courtesy Paradise Genealogy Society; below courtesy Gold Nugget Museum.)

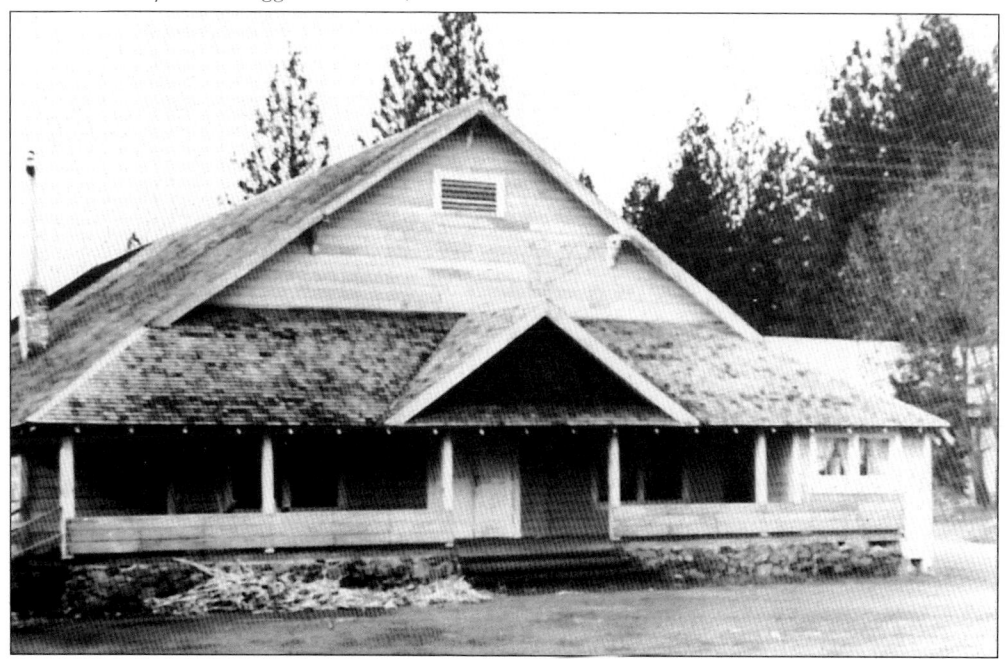

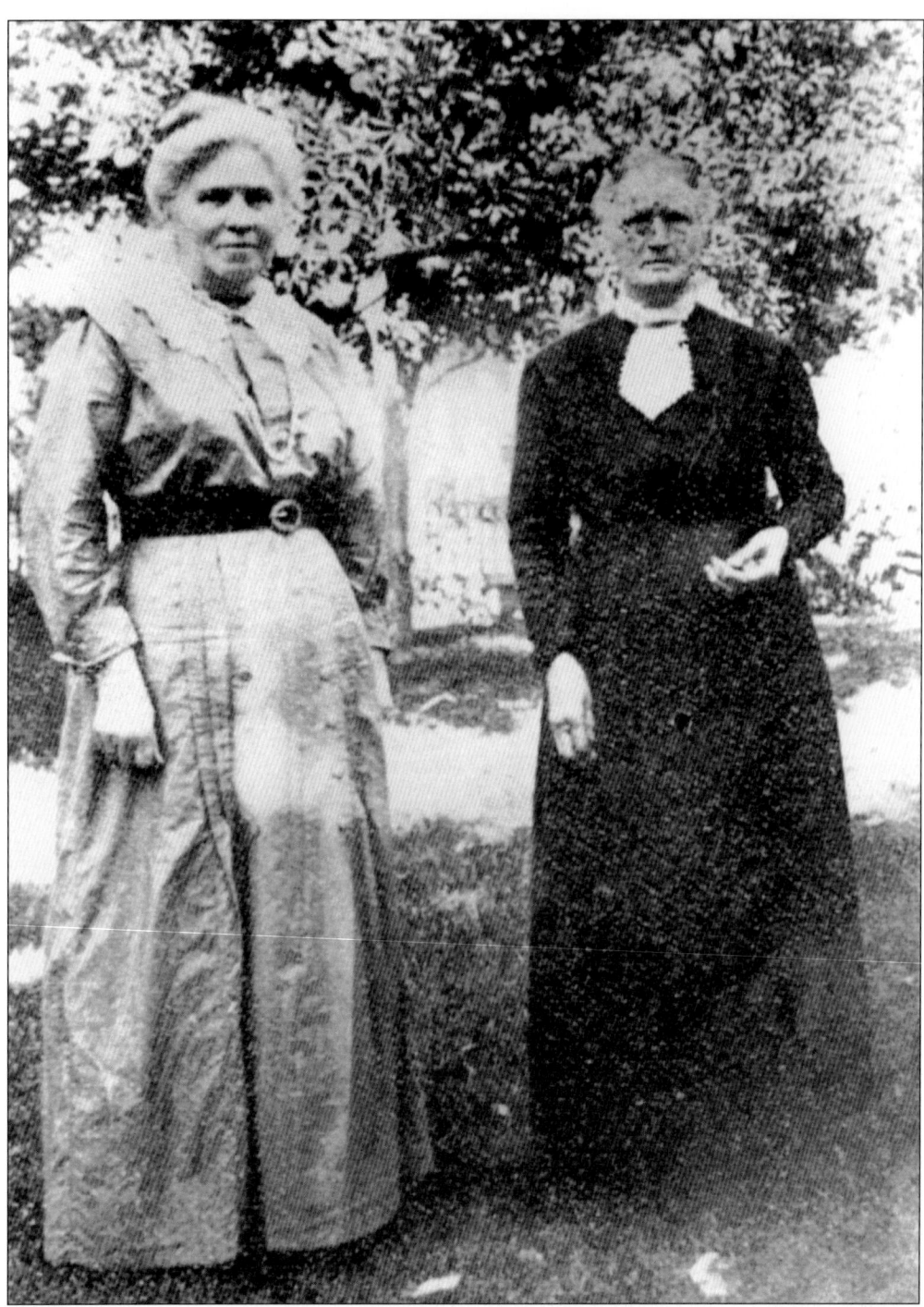

In July 1863, as the Lewis children walked home from school, Jimmy was shot dead by Mill Creek Indians at Little Dry Creek. The Native Americans took 10-year-old Thankful and Johnny Lewis with them and later killed Johnny. In Big Chico Creek Canyon, Thankful escaped and made her way to the Thomasson place. This photograph of Thankful Lewis Carlson and Mrs. Thomasson was taken 50 years later. (Courtesy Paradise Genealogy Society.)

Perkin's Rock is west of Bille Road. A seaman since age 13, George Perkins jumped ship during the gold rush, and while mining in Little Butte Canyon, carved his name on the rock. In 1869, he was elected U.S. Senator from California; in 1879, governor of California; and in 1893, was appointed senator to replace the late Leland Stanford. Perkins retired in 1915. Ann and Archie Smith sit on the rock. (Courtesy Lois McDonald.)

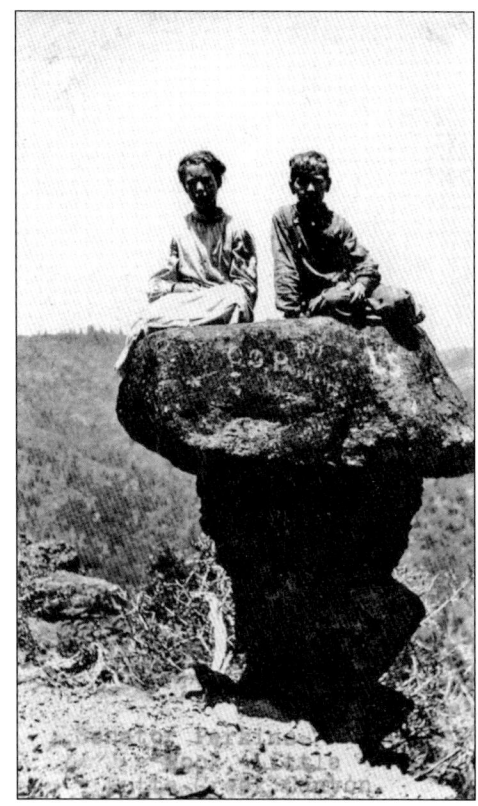

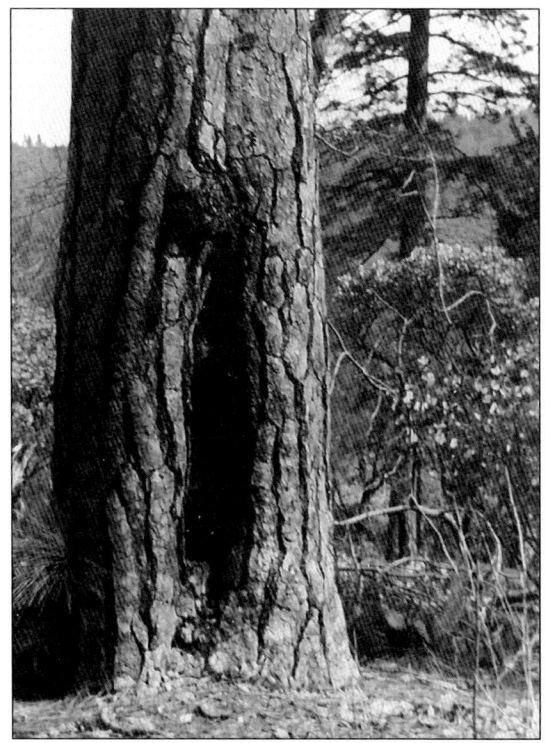

In the age of wooden ships, the Union Navy needed turpentine and most of it came from North Carolina. However, the Civil War forced the Union to look for other sources, and the Ponderosa Pine in Butte County became a primary source of pitch from which to make turpentine. Deep scars from tapping the pitch are evident today in trees remaining on the Ridge. There were numerous distilleries on the Ridge; William Chapman's located a short distance east of Leonard's sawmill. (Courtesy Velma Butler.)

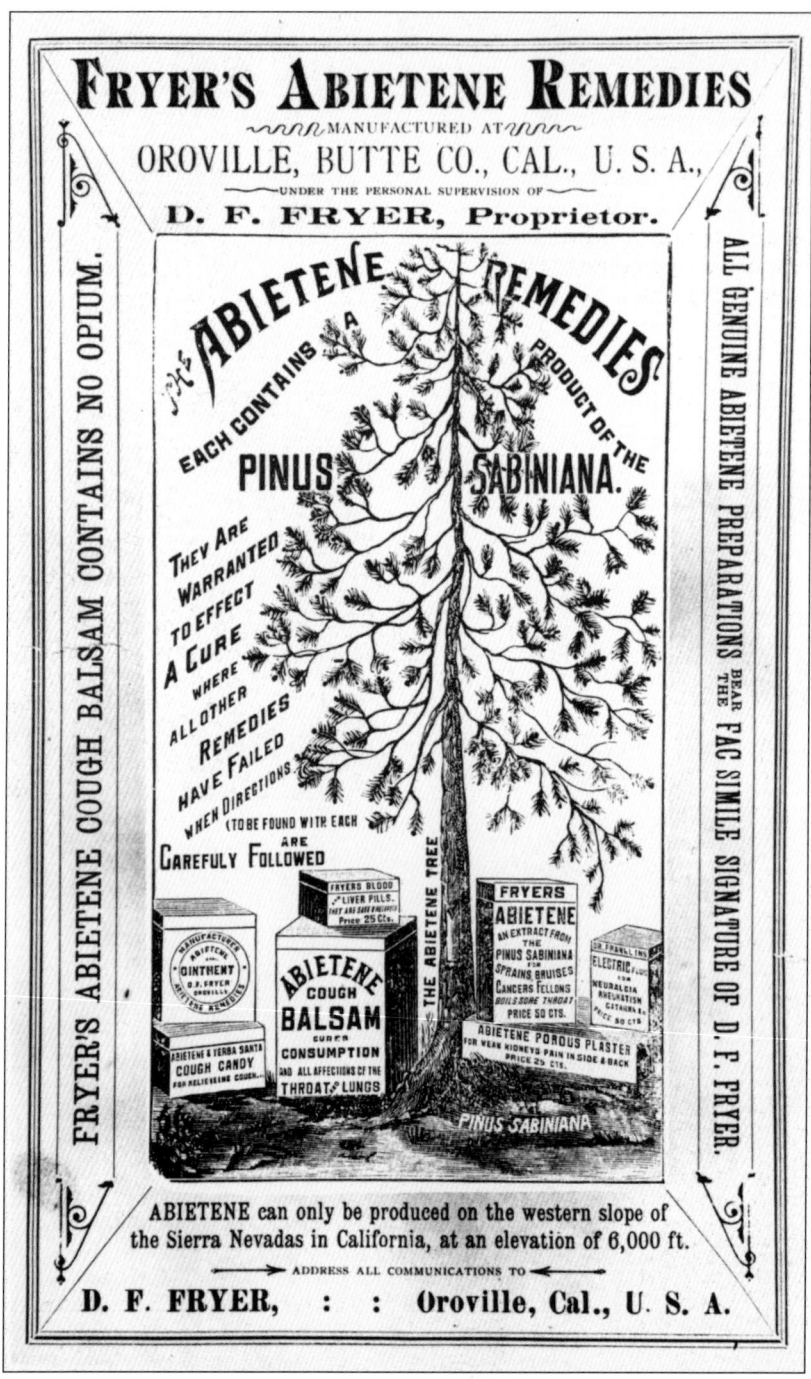

Abietine was accidentally discovered when a turpentine distiller in Pence nearly blew up his still. He thought he was processing pitch from ponderosa pines, but the pitch actually came from Jeffery pines, which produced a lighter, much more volatile distillate. Soon it was sold as Abietene, a patient medicine that cured everything from sprains and bruises to rheumatism and lung and kidney complaints as shown in this 1886 advertisement in a Butte County pamphlet. (Courtesy Jesse Wood.)

James and Joanna Dresser came to Leonard's Mill, or Old Paradise, in 1863. James, a prolific letter writer, exchanged numerous letters with their two married daughters and families back East. James, a farmer, actively participated in the community. His letters paint a detailed and interesting photograph of life on their farm, which he called Pleasant Hill, and in the community during the 1860s. (Courtesy Gold Nugget Museum.)

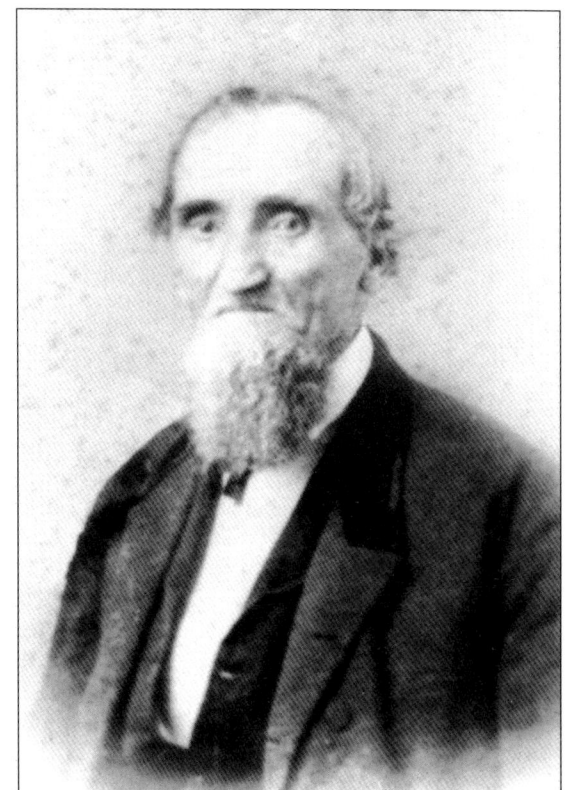

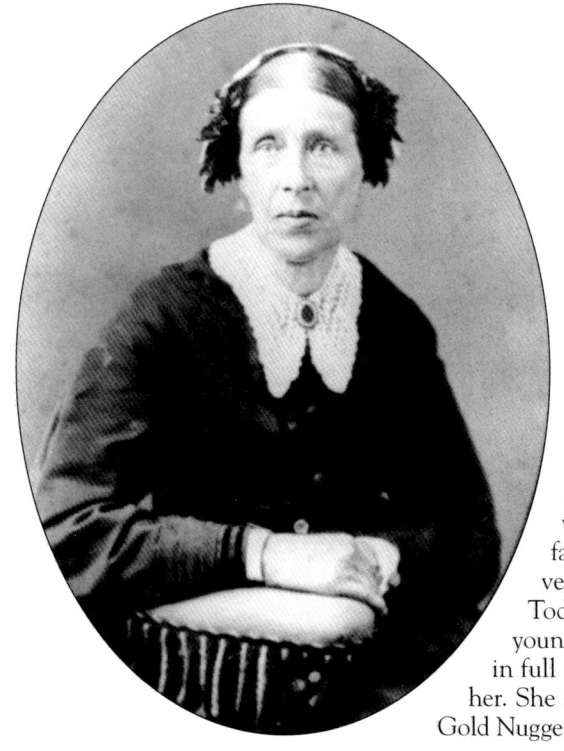

James Dresser was the letter writer, but his wife, Joanna, was an equal partner in their farm. He wrote, "Gardening, raising fruit and vegetables is a very profitable business here. Today for $5 per dozen Mother sold 1 dozen young roosters not full grown. Mother, I think in full as good health & strength as you ever saw her. She is quite fleshy and works hard." (Courtesy Gold Nugget Museum.)

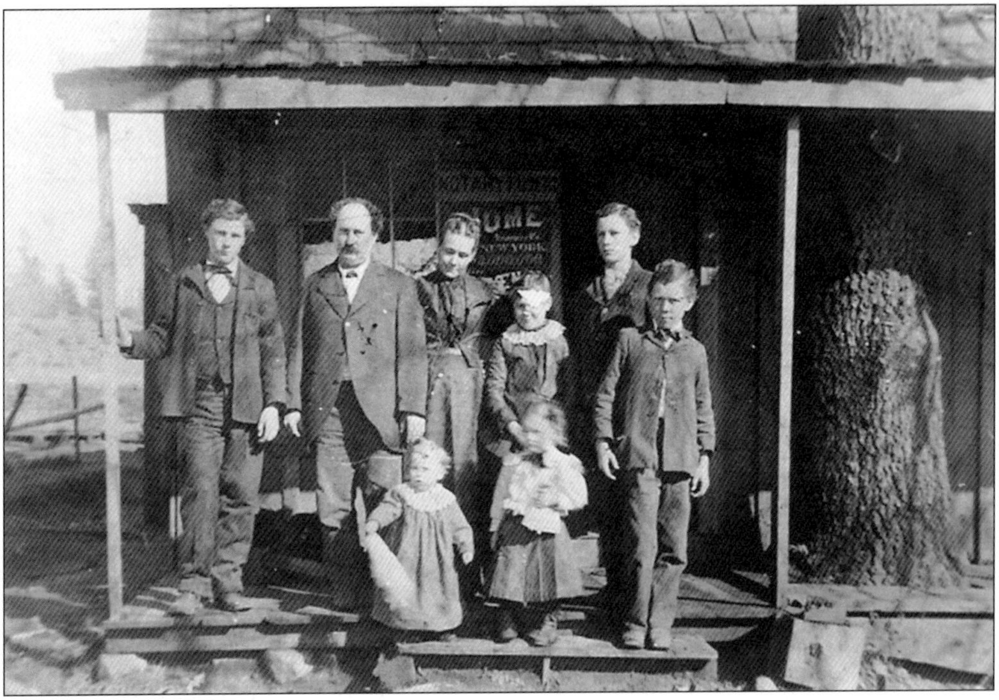

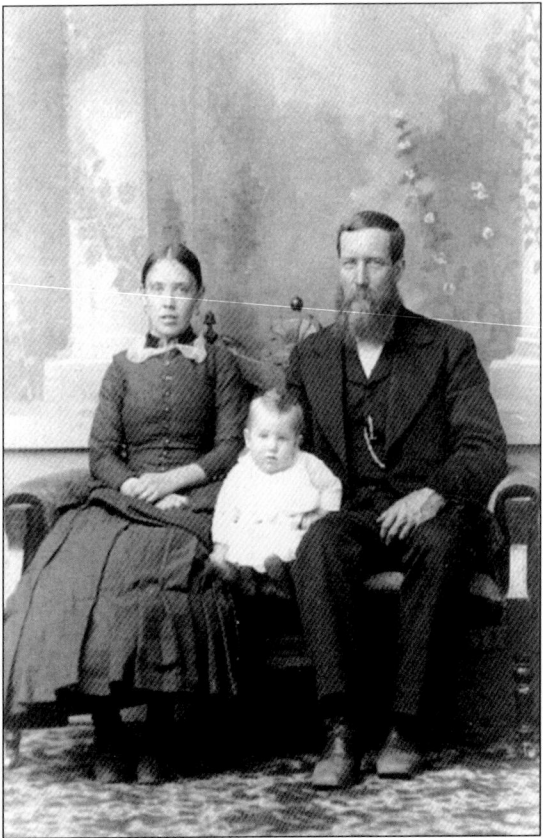

James Nunneley and his family came from Oregon around 1872. Northeast of Leonard's Mill, Nunneley bought 500 acres of railroad land at $1.25 an acre and traded a span of mules and a buckboard for another 300 acres. The Nunneleys were early founders of the Seventh Day Adventist Church on the Ridge, and Nunneley Road was named after them in 1921. (Courtesy Gold Nugget Museum.)

This photograph of Lucy Elliott Foster, Charles Foster, and their son George was taken around 1886. Lucy was born in 1865 on the journey from Missouri to California; Charles came to the Ridge in 1871 from Maine. In the 1880s, he acquired a quarter section of land south of what would become Orloff. Foster Road is named for George Foster. (Courtesy Paradise Genealogy Society.)

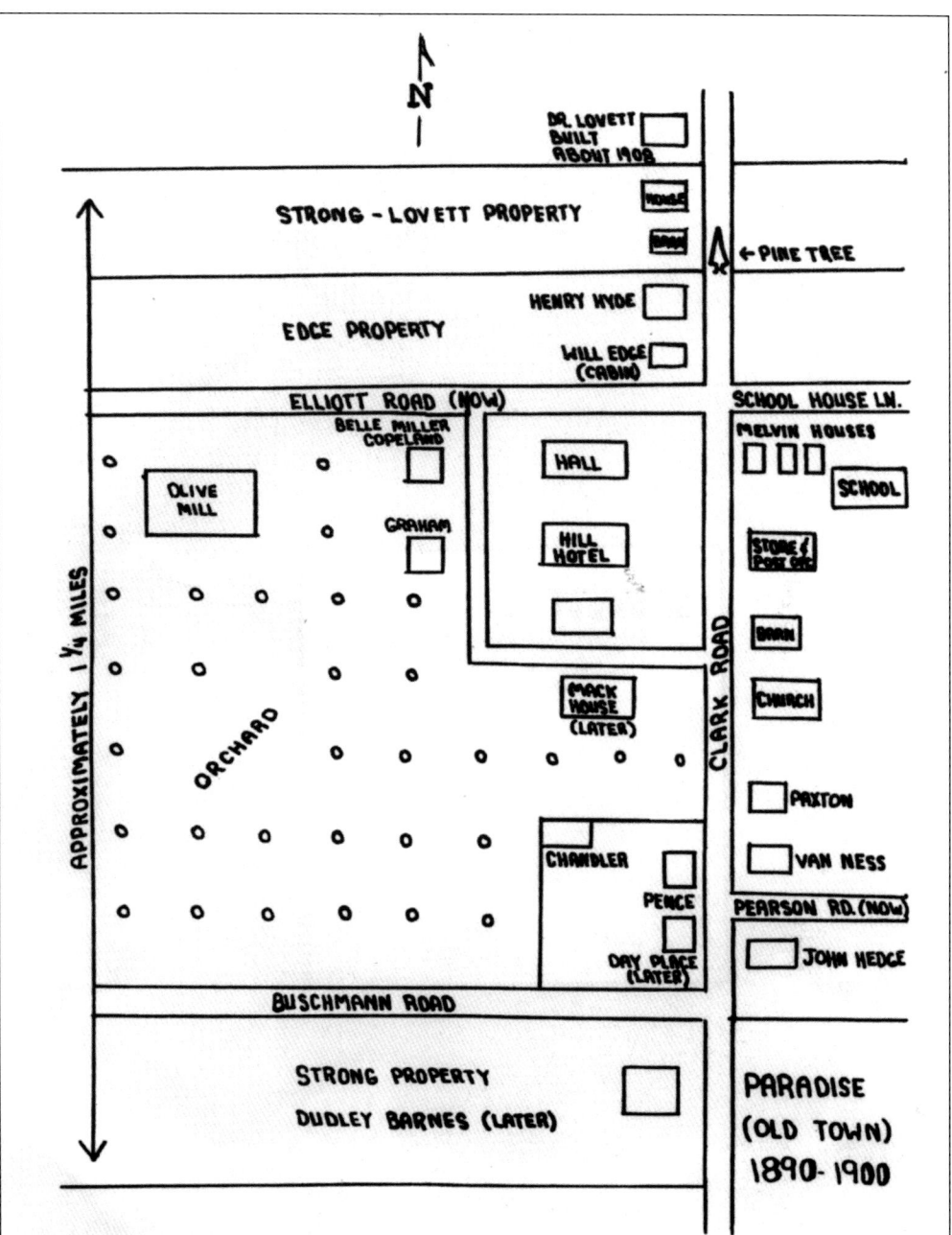

Leonard's Mill was sometimes referred to as Old Paradise or Old Town, especially after 1904 when a business center grew around the new Butte County Railroad depot a mile to the west of what, by then, was Paradise. The map is based on the recollections of Winslow Lovett, son of Dr. William and Abbie Lovett. The family moved here in 1895 and bought the Strong Place. (Courtesy *Tales of the Paradise Ridge*.)

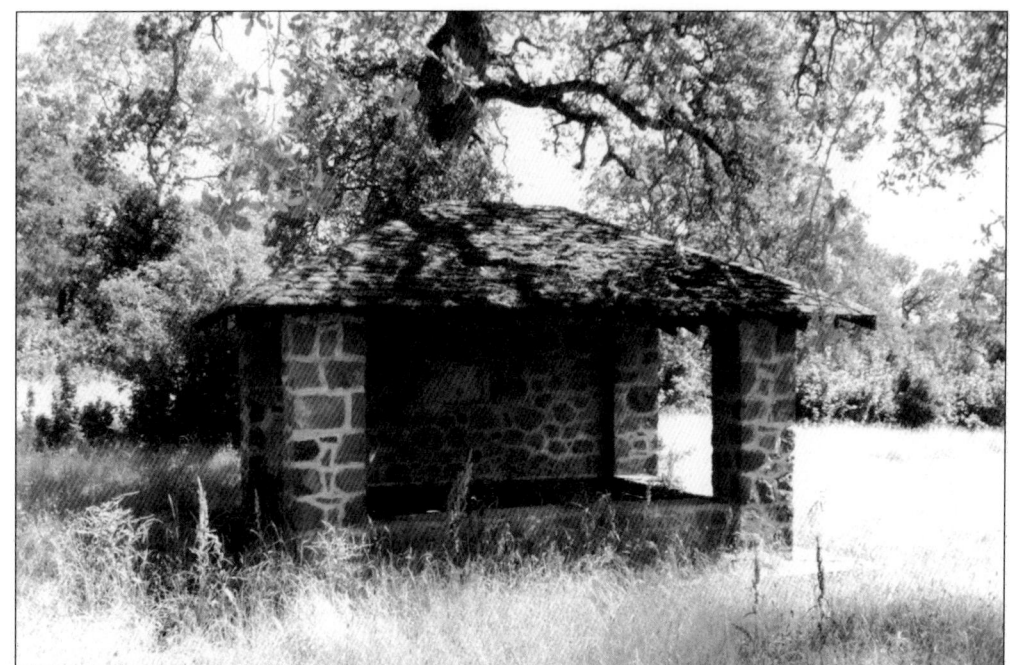

In 1879–1880, Alexander Elliott built a home on lower Neal Road on land that he and his older brother Jacob were raising cattle on. He piped water from a spring down to a wood springhouse on Neal Road for the convenience of travelers. The Elliott home is long gone, but around 1950, this stone springhouse was built, apparently as a memorial. A century and a quarter later, the spring still flows. (Courtesy author.)

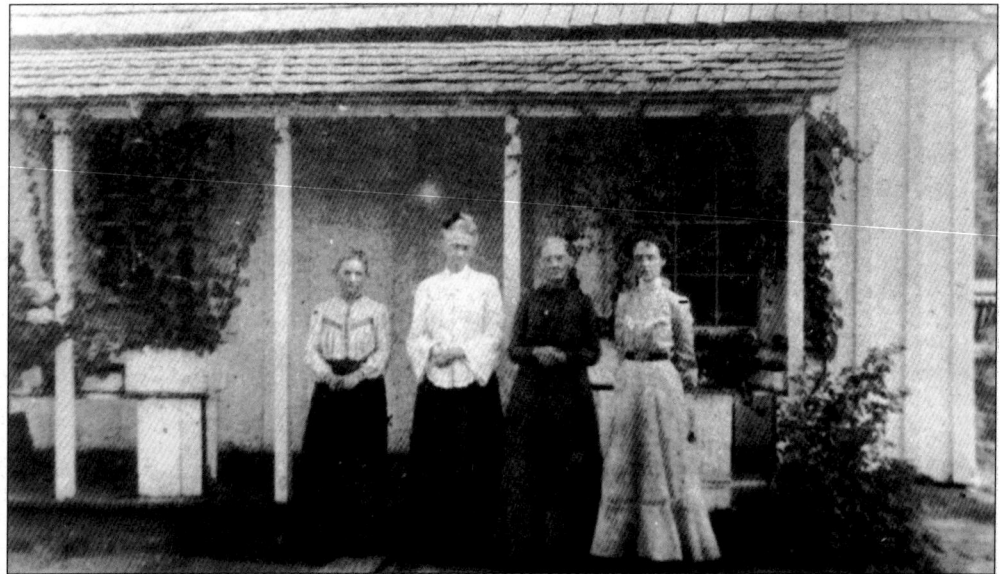

Alexander Elliott later built a home on Cemetery Lane about where the Paradise Cemetery is today. It burned around 1890. His entire family, by then greatly augmented through his children's marriages, got together and built the smaller house shown in this photograph. His wife, Margaret, is second from the left. Cemetery Lane was renamed Elliott Road in 1921. (Courtesy Paradise Genealogy Society.)

As a boy, Frank Knox came to California before 1880 by wagon train. While on the Plains, a Native American offered to buy his mother, Catherine, and, not wanting to offend the man, Frank's father, Tom, told him he would take 25 horses for her, thinking that was way too many horses for the man to obtain. The Native American returned with the horses, but Tom got out of the deal by saying Catherine had a fever. Five generations of Knoxs lived on the Ridge. (Courtesy Gold Nugget Museum.)

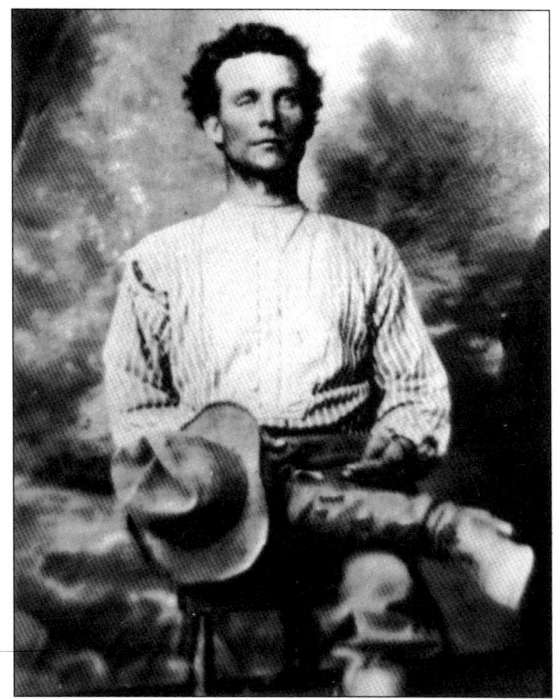

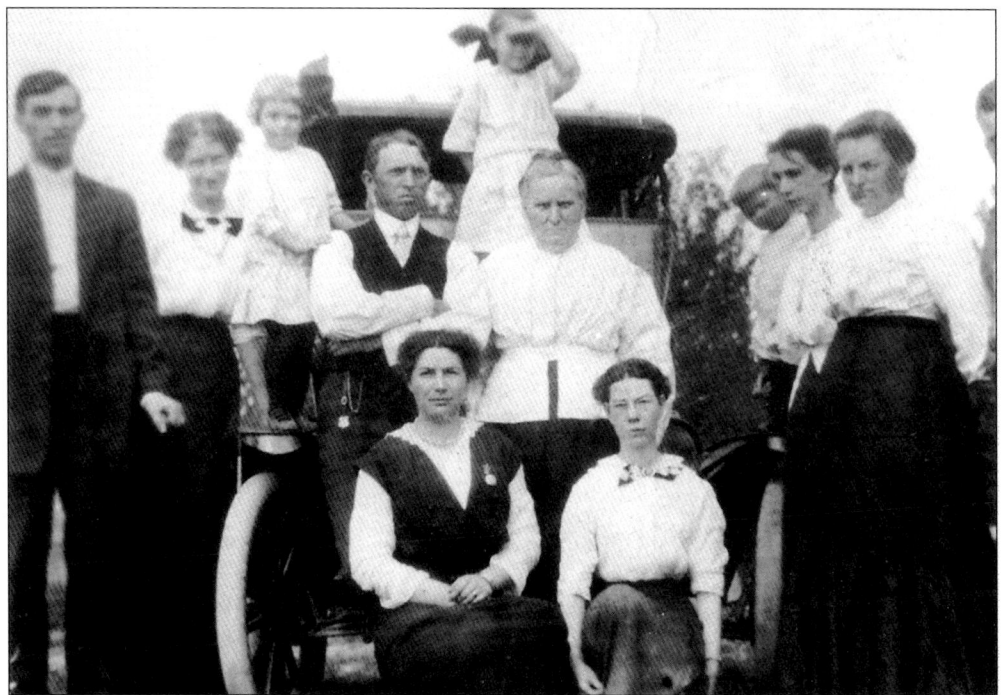

This *c.* 1915 photograph of the Strong family also includes members of other pioneer families—Bishop, Moore, Bell, Cory, and Shawkey. Two Strong families and one unmarried brother came to Leonard's Mill in 1875–1876. Having tried gold mining and other occupations at one time or another, most went back to what they knew—farming. Typically they married into other pioneer Ridge families. (Courtesy Gold Nugget Museum.)

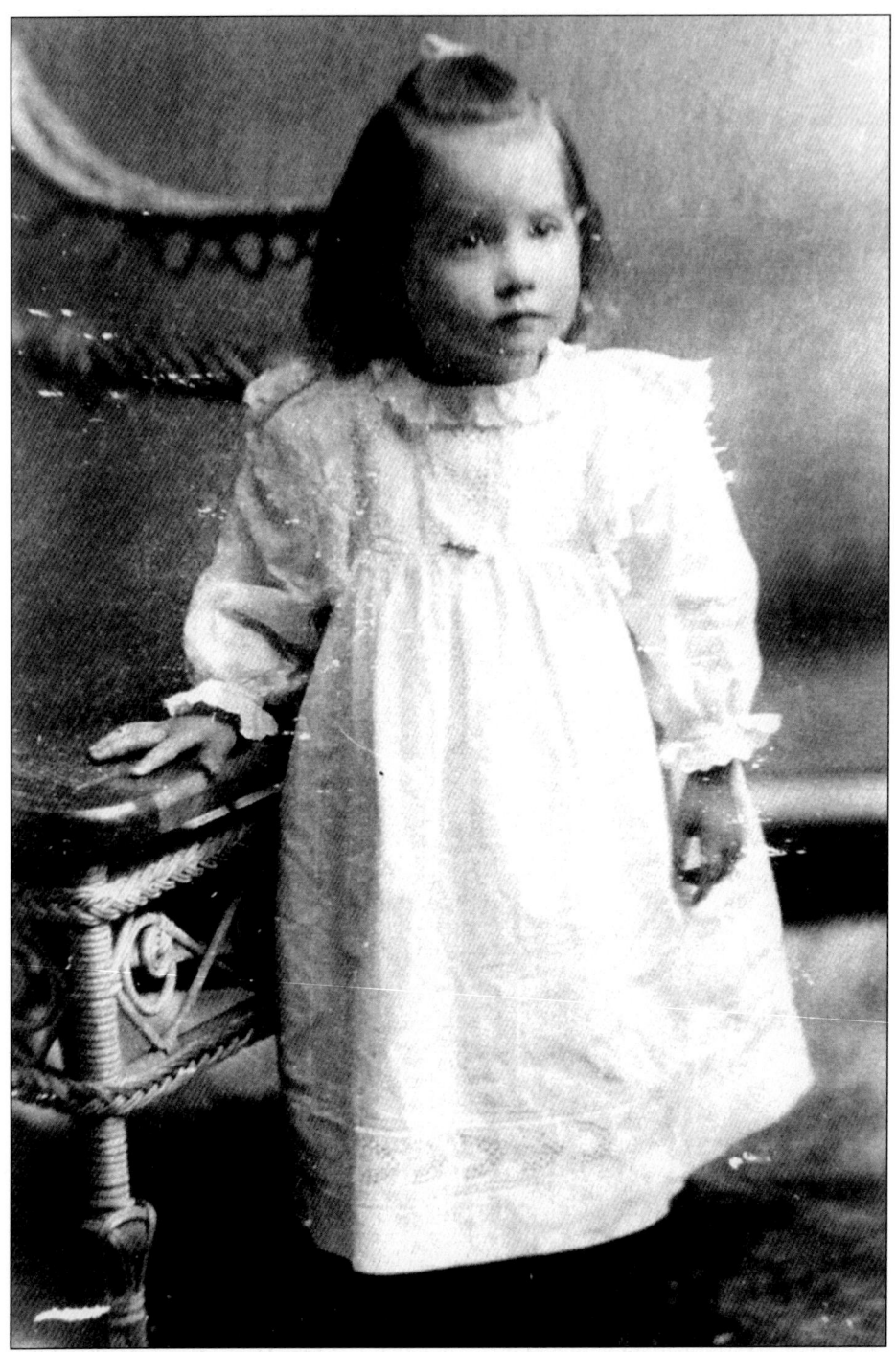

Pictured here at age two, Clara Foster was born in 1896 in Paradise, the daughter of Charlie L. Foster and Lucy Fairlee Elliott, who was born in 1865 on a wagon train from Missouri. Clara's brother George started the Paradise Telephone Company that served the Ridge until the 1950s. Clara married Don Brown and was operator for the phone company for 30 years. (Courtesy Paradise Genealogy Society.)

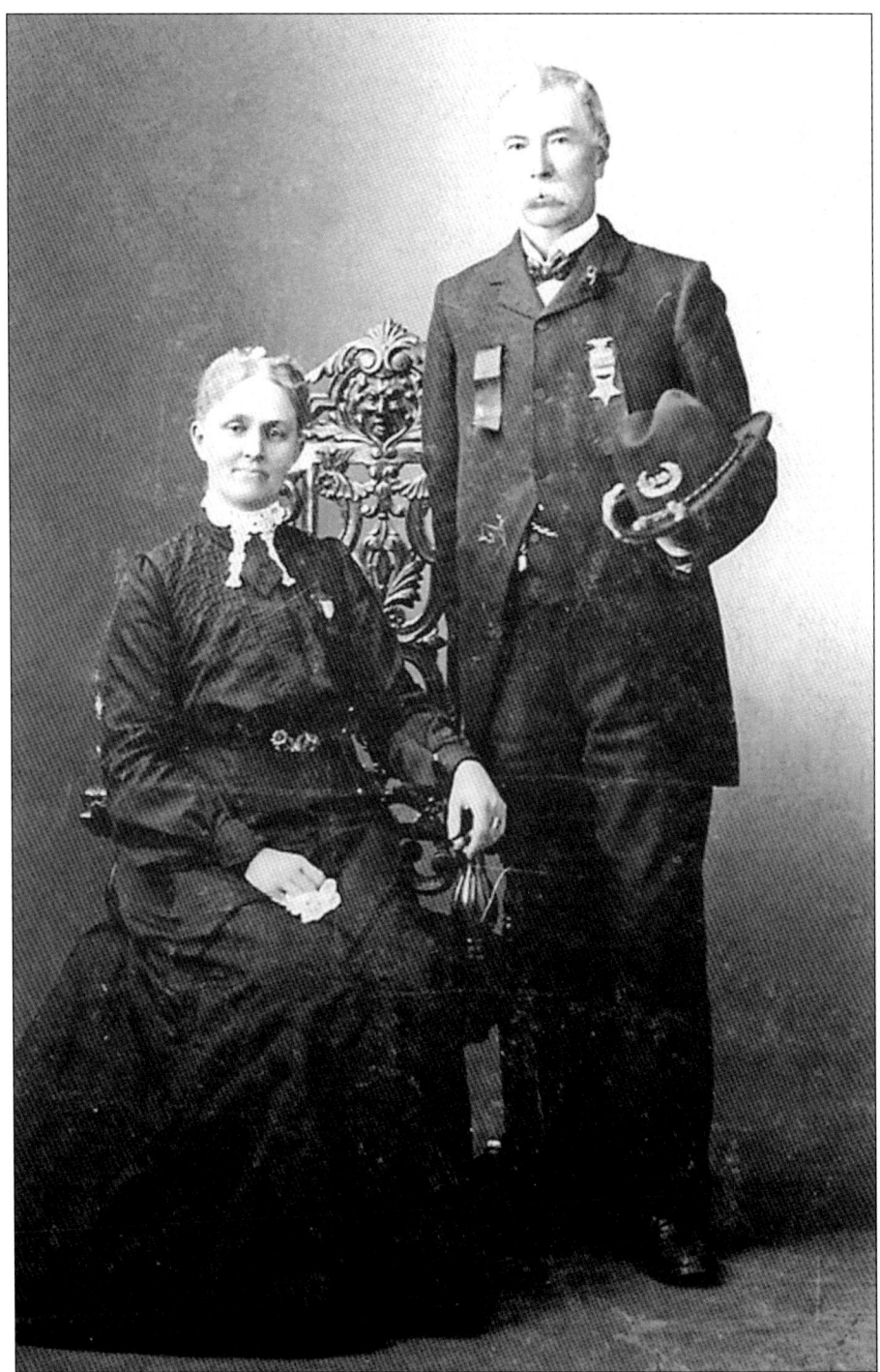

When Dr. William Lovett, his wife, Abbie, and their three children moved to Paradise, he established a horse-and-buggy medical practice that covered from Magalia down to Clear Creek below the Ridge. A cash-poor area, he often received his fee in barter: vegetables, fruit, dairy, and poultry products. This photograph was taken in 1900, five years after the Lovetts came to Paradise. (Courtesy Gold Nugget Museum.)

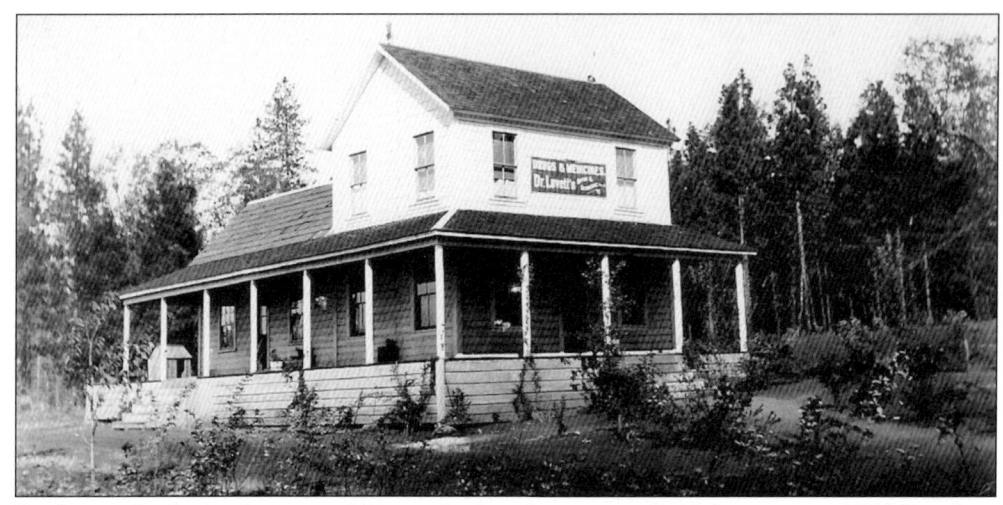

Dr. Lovett built this home on 80 acres he bought just north of the center of Old Paradise. He practiced medicine from the home and had a drugstore in town, but because dispensing drugs was a 24-hour business, he constructed another building near his home to use as a drugstore. The Lovetts also planted a large variety of fruit trees on the property. (Courtesy Gold Nugget Museum.)

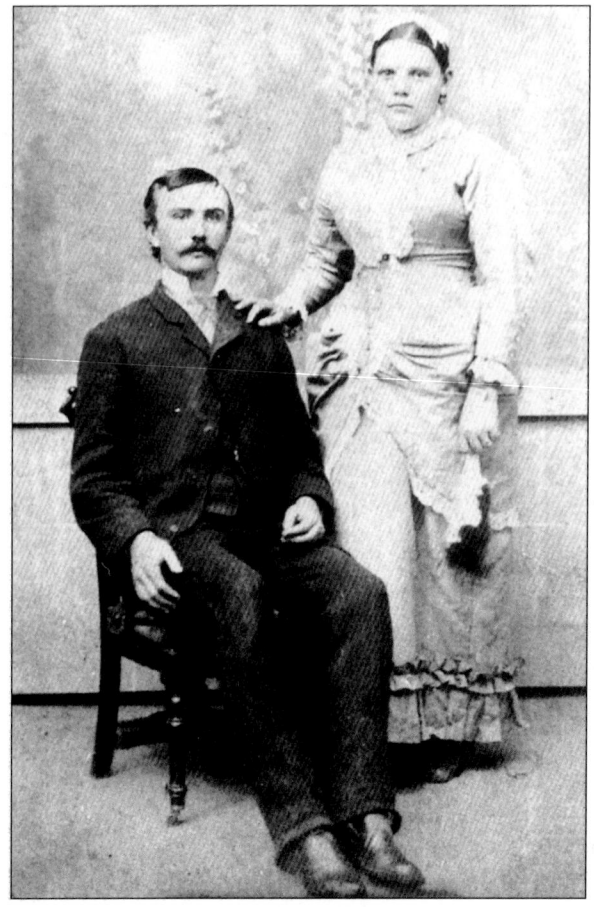

William Ware, pictured here with his wife, Mary E., was the last of John and Hannah Ware's children, probably the best known because he served as constable for Kimshew Township, which includes the Ridge, for 30 years. He sometimes kept and fed prisoners in his home overnight before transporting them to the jail in Oroville the next morning. (Courtesy Gold Nugget Museum.)

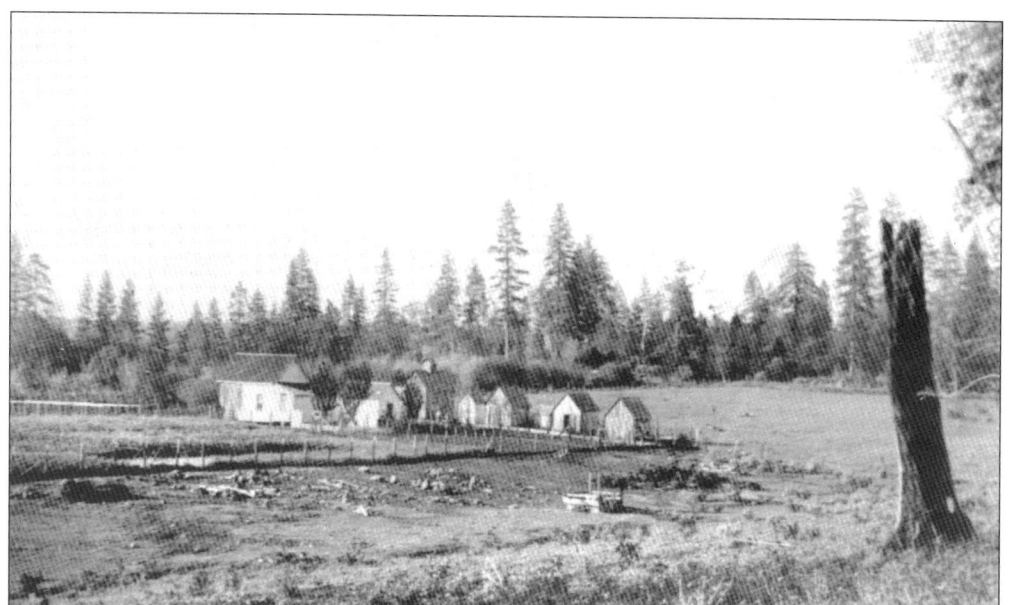

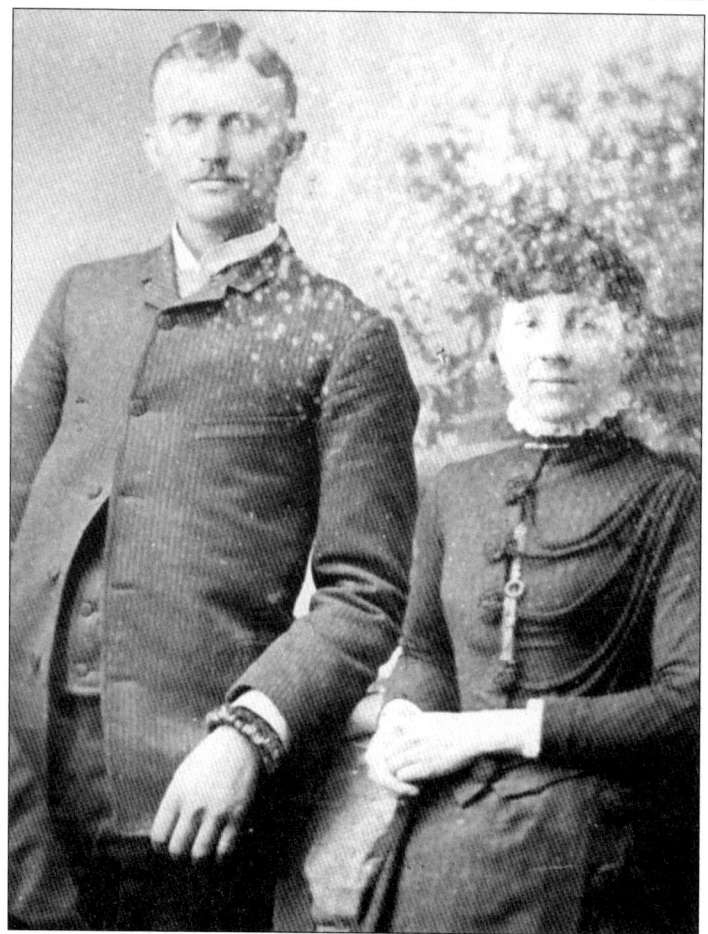

It took a lot of effort to clear the forest, as the above photograph of James and Mary Jane Wagstaff's ranch shows. In 1890, the Wagstaffs bought a section of land, and in 1910, bought another 160 acres northwest of Old Paradise in the area of what became Wagstaff Road. The Ridge was heavily timbered, and it is said that the timber has been harvested at least seven times. This is hard to believe when looking at the size of trees that are currently standing. On the right are John and Mary Jane Wagstaff. It is rather surprising that virtually no information exists on the Wagstaff family, especially since a major road in Paradise is named after them. (Both courtesy Paradise Genealogy Society.)

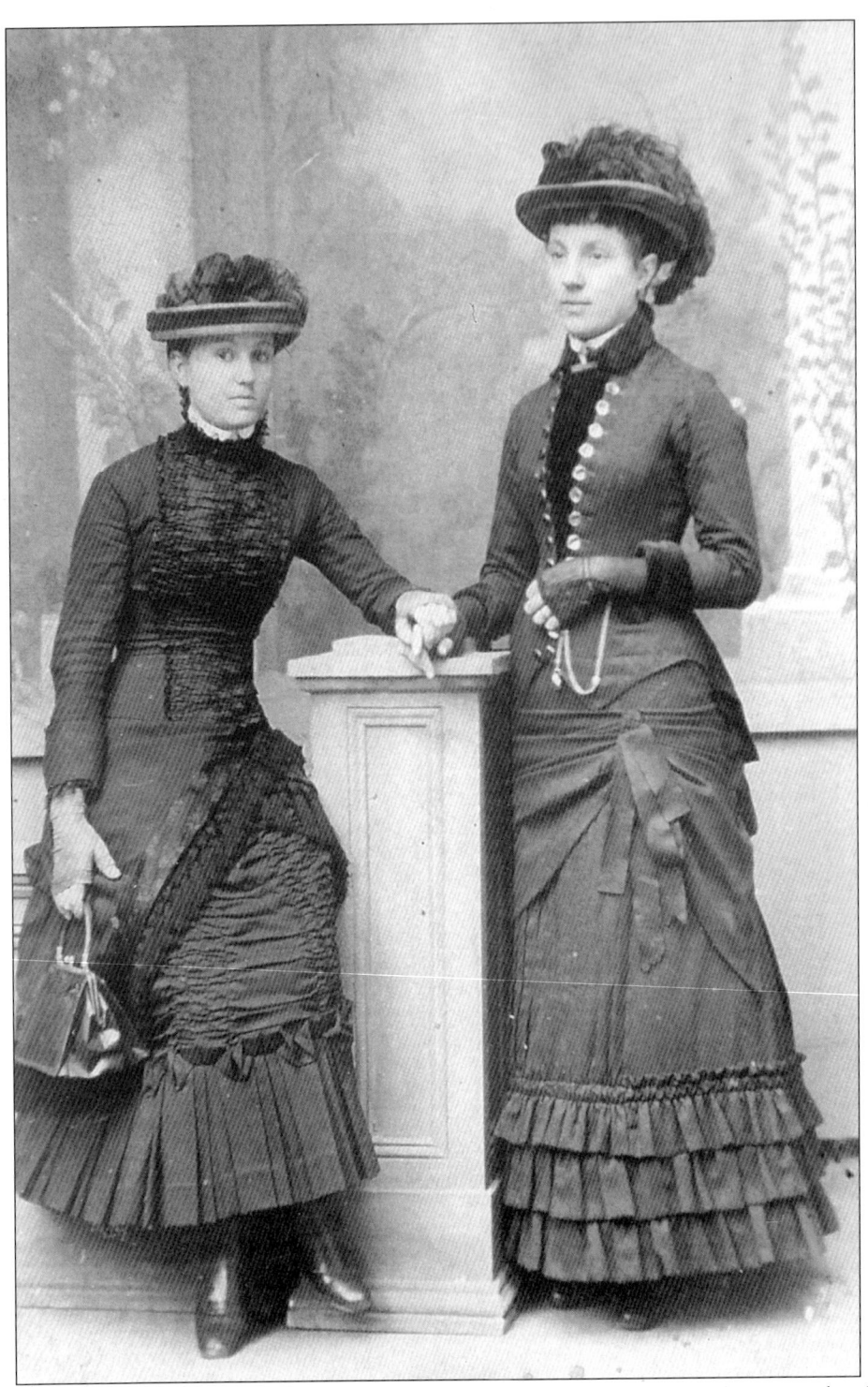

Mary Jane Wagstaff, left, and her sister, Eliza Stone, demonstrate that even if a woman lived on the very rural and rustic Paradise Ridge in the late 1800s, she could be a fashionable lady when it came to her attire. (Courtesy Paradise Genealogy Society.)

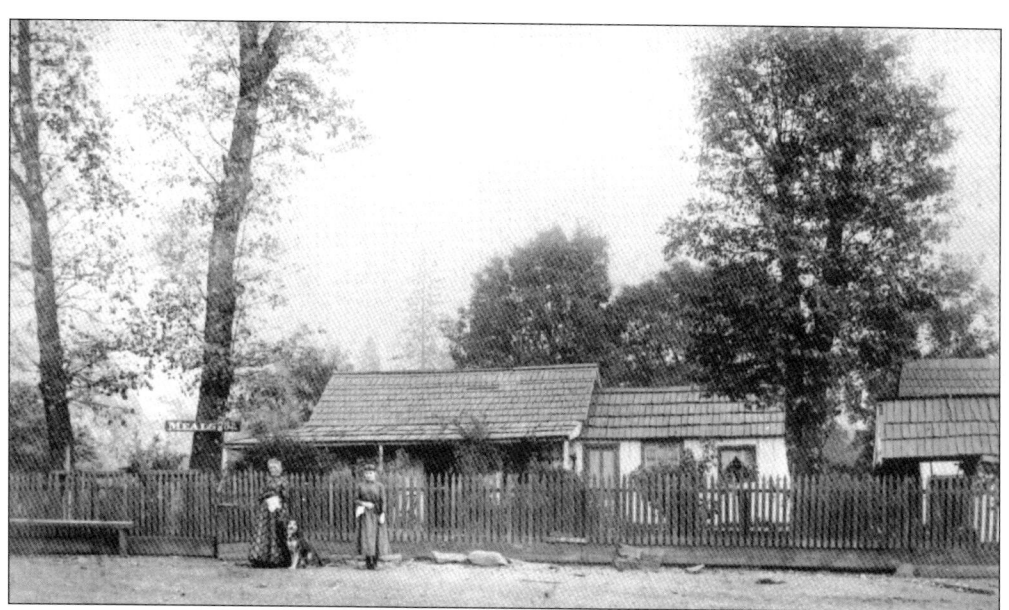

Horace Wilder's home was located east of Neal Road and south of the intersection with Maxwell Drive. His wife cooked for passing travelers, miners, and most anyone with the money for a meal. In this c. 1888 photograph, "Grandmother" Wilder is standing with her dog Carlo, and to the right stands Abbie Wilson, who lived with Grandmother Wilder before she was married. (Courtesy Gold Nugget Museum.)

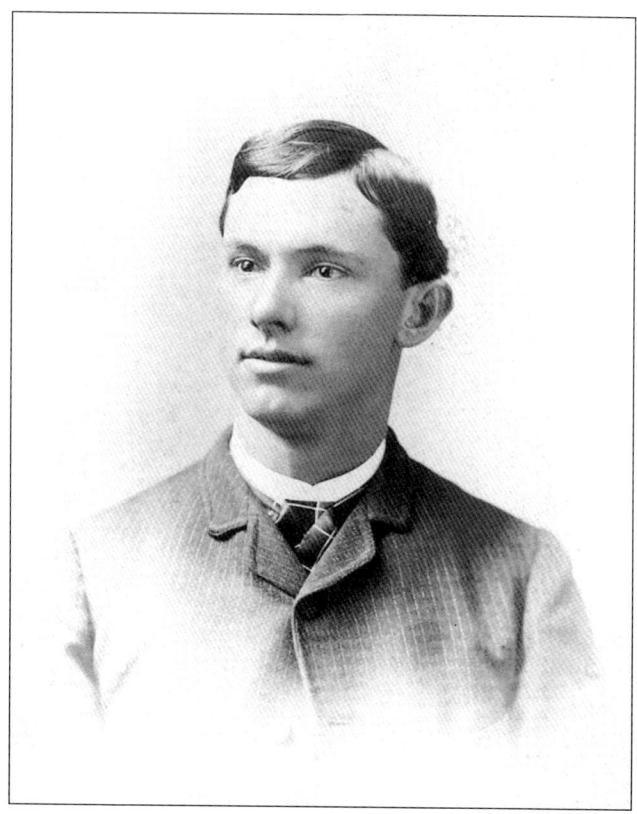

In 1884, J. E. "Edward" Rutherford came from Wyandotte, south of Oroville, to teach school in Leonard's Mill. In a letter to his mother, he wrote, "I have about 40 scholars, and they seem to behave well, but are awful backward in their studies." Giving up teaching, he operated a store in Mountain House on the Oroville-Quincy stage road, later moving back to Wyandotte to manage the family ranch. (Courtesy Gold Nugget Museum.)

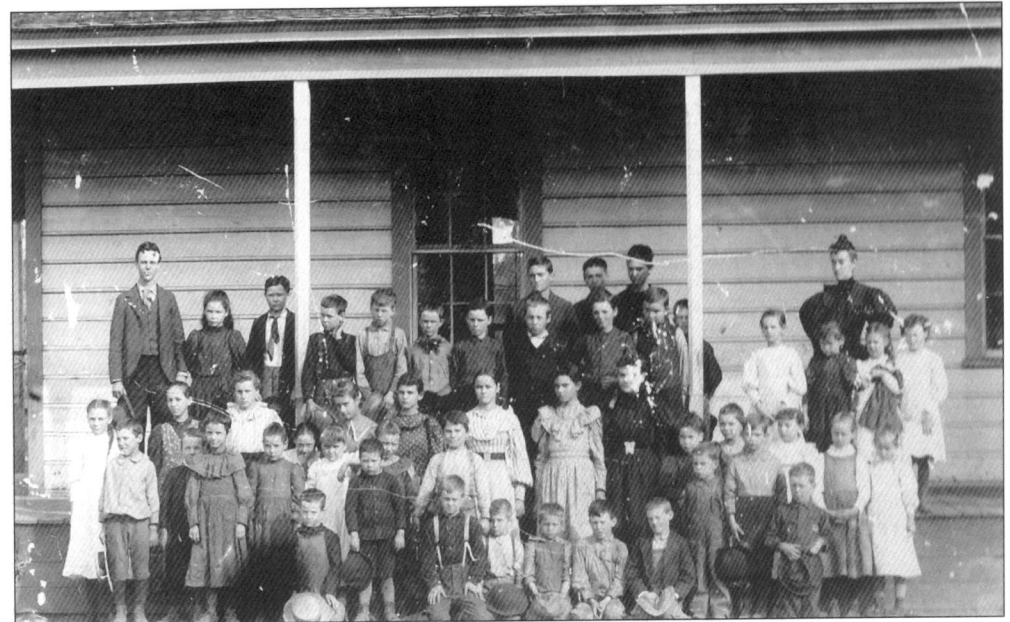

The first school in Leonard's Mill was the Delaplain School, named for Charles Delaplain, who donated the land for the school in 1861. In 1883, a new school was built on School Lane (now Elliott Road, east of Clark) in what had become Paradise. This photograph shows the students and their principal, Mr. Skinner, on the left. (Courtesy Gold Nugget Museum.)

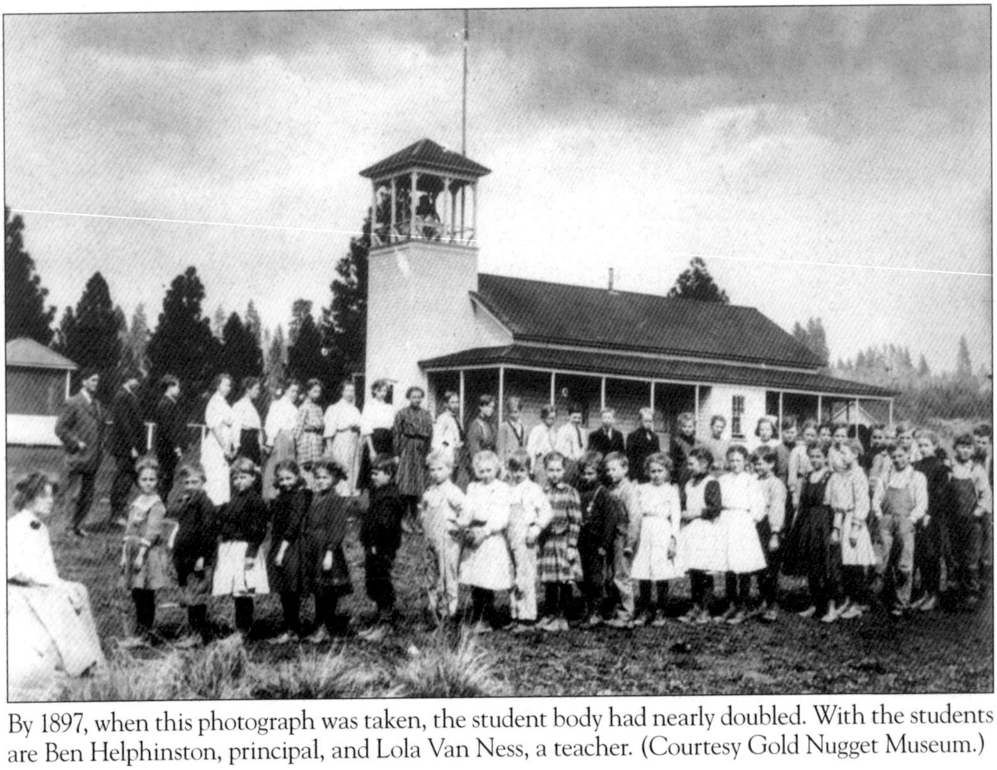

By 1897, when this photograph was taken, the student body had nearly doubled. With the students are Ben Helphinston, principal, and Lola Van Ness, a teacher. (Courtesy Gold Nugget Museum.)

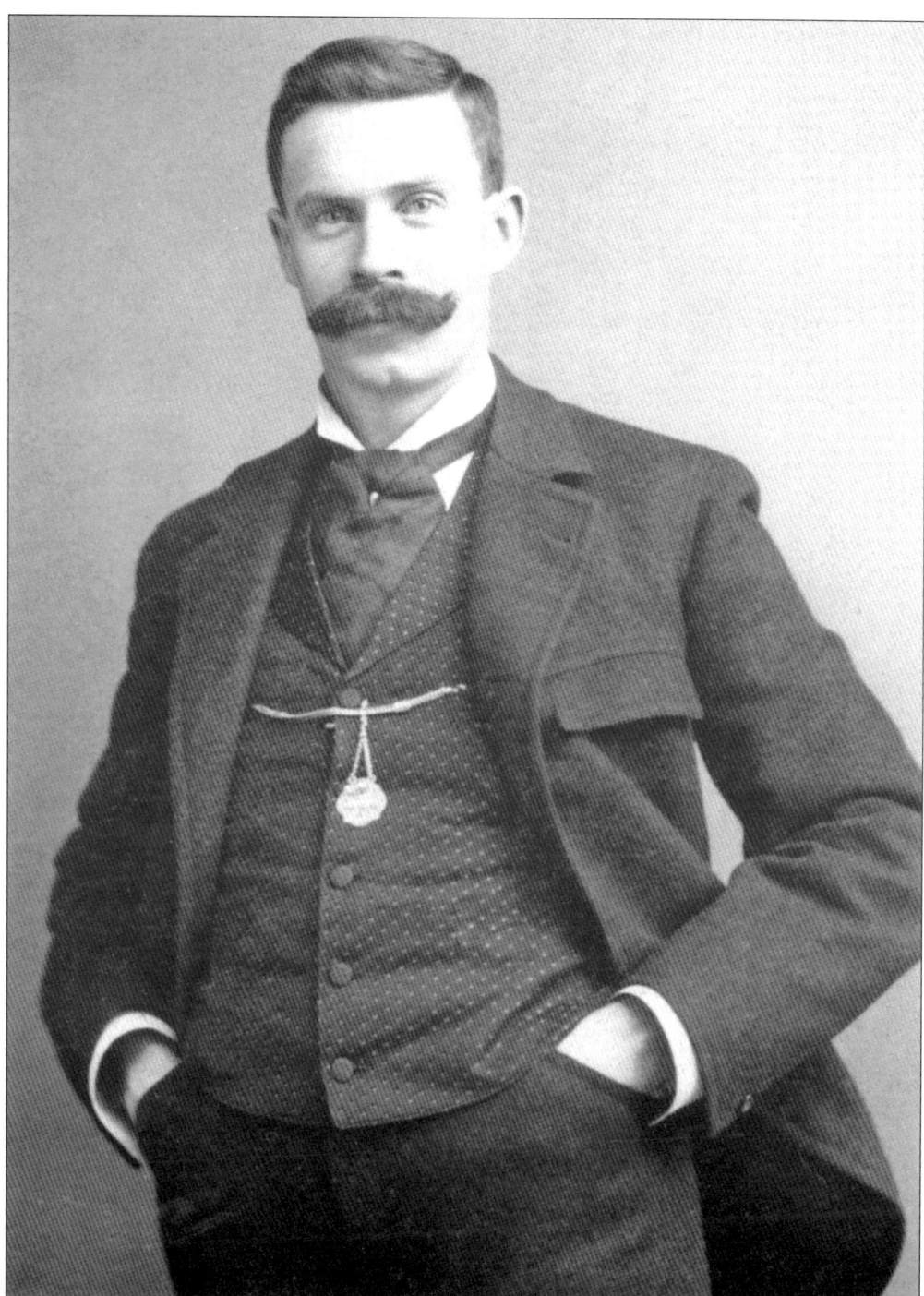

A man of many interests, Dr. William Mack was the only doctor on the Ridge for several years. Every family grew crops for themselves, but he reasoned that the Ridge had potential for commercial agriculture. He proved this by setting out an olive orchard and building a processing and packing plant. The popularity of his Highland Brand olives and oil proved that he was right. (Courtesy Gold Nugget Museum.)

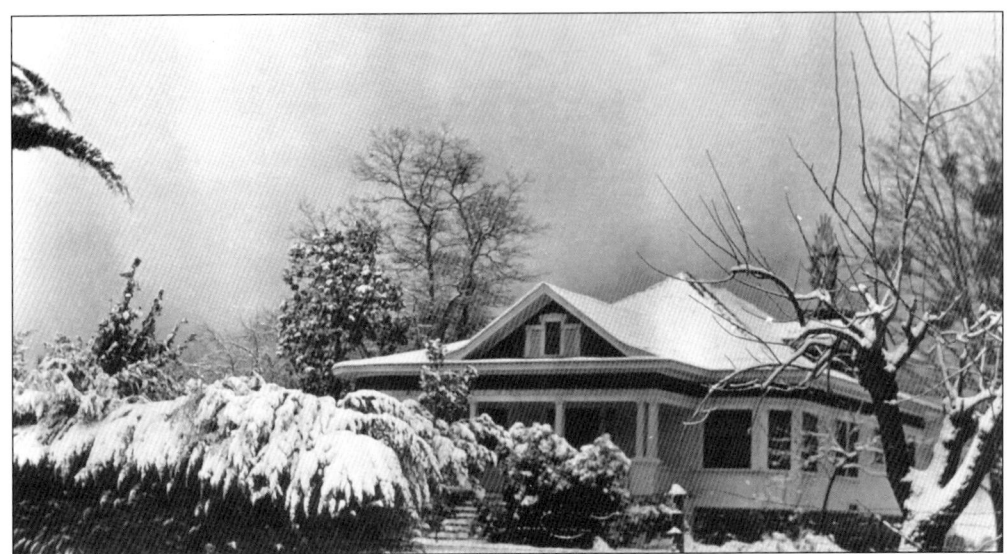

This is the Mack's second home as it looked in 1914; the original home was a small cottage that was on the property when he bought it. In 1937, he would donate land just across Clark Road from his home for the Masonic Lodge. Although not all that often, it does snow in Paradise. (Courtesy Paradise Genealogy Society.)

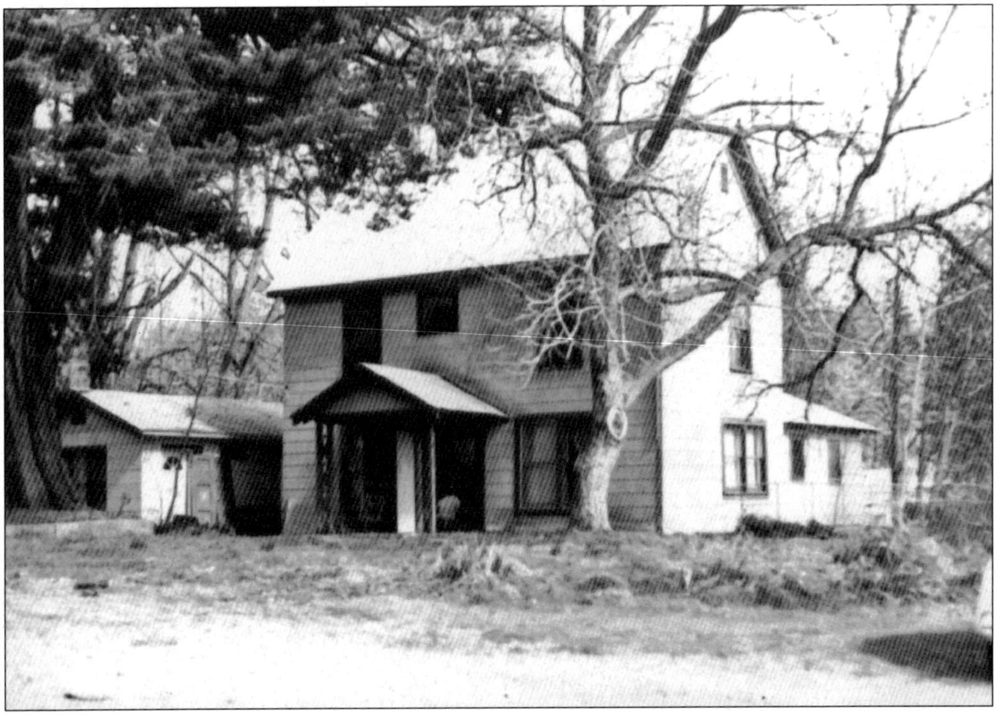

Few buildings from Paradise's early days exist now. The 1880s Walter McDowell home is, if not the oldest, then one of the oldest homes still standing on the east side of Clark Road above Wagstaff Road. In the 1940s, Ben and Jean Filer started their Cypress Acres Convalescent Home here. When a new facility was constructed, the building was relegated to a storage facility. (Courtesy Gold Nugget Museum.)

Three
ORLOFF, NEW PARADISE

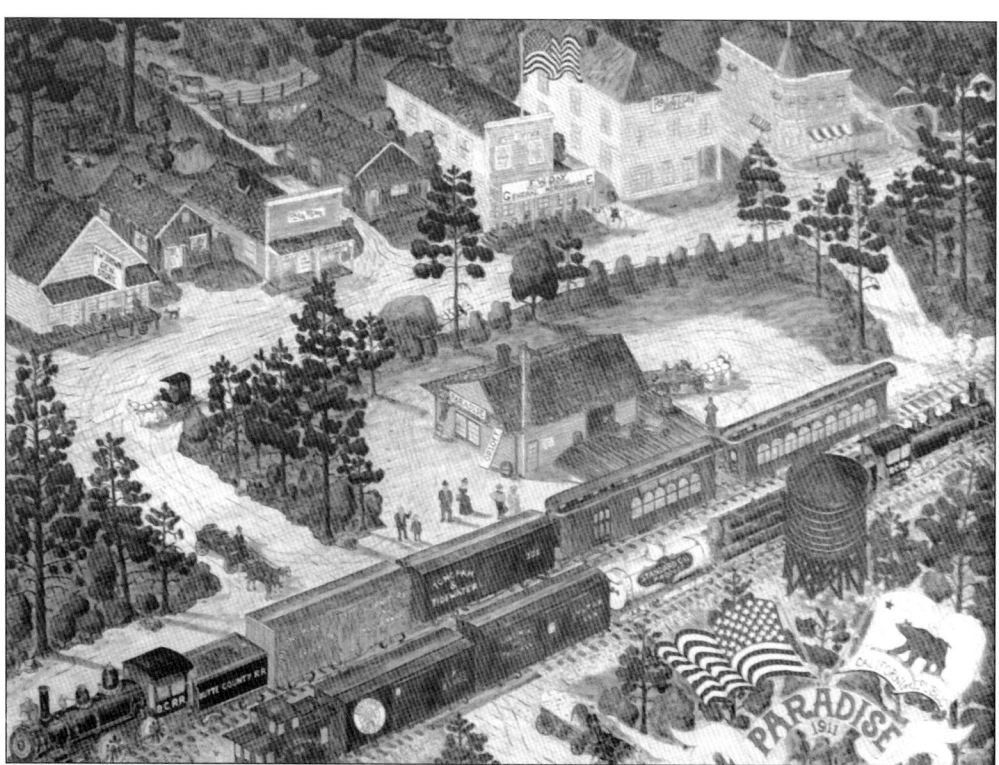

Orloff or Paradise? From 1905 until 1911, the name of the post office was Orloff and the name of the depot Paradise. Thereafter both were known as Paradise. Fred Green's bird's-eye painting of "New Paradise" shows the depot and the businesses that quickly sprang up around it. The Orloff sign leaning on the end of the depot is wrong—the name of the depot has always been Paradise. (Courtesy Fred Green family.)

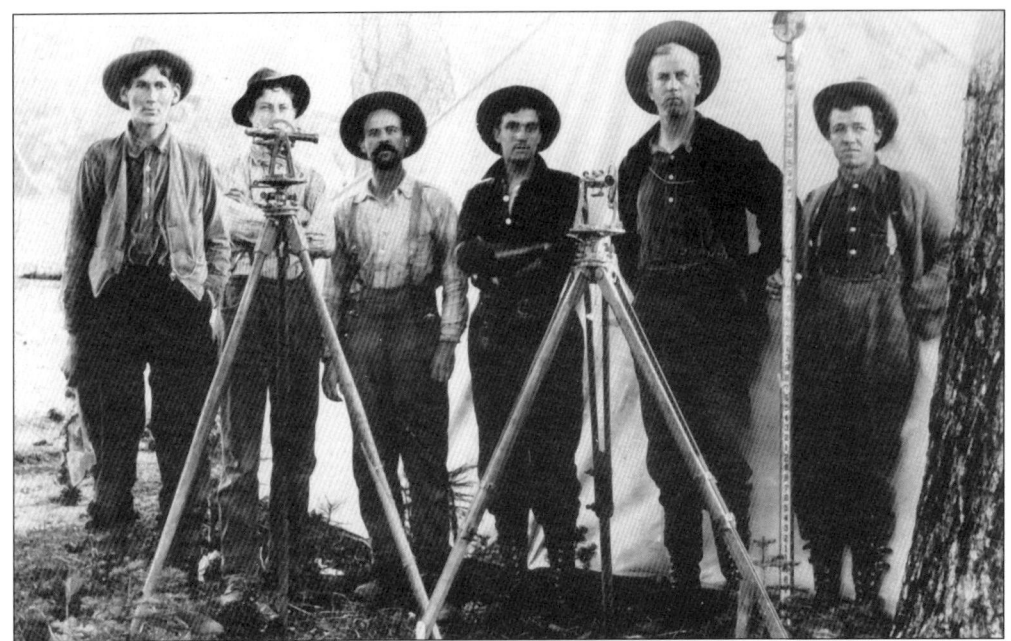

When Frank Compton's survey crew arrived in 1902, the locals learned why strangers were buying parcels of land on the Ridge. The Diamond Match Company was entering the lumber and match business in California and building a facility in Chico and a sawmill town, Stirling City, in the mountains above Paradise. A railroad with several depots would connect the sites. Frank Compton is pictured second from the right. (Courtesy Gold Nugget Museum.)

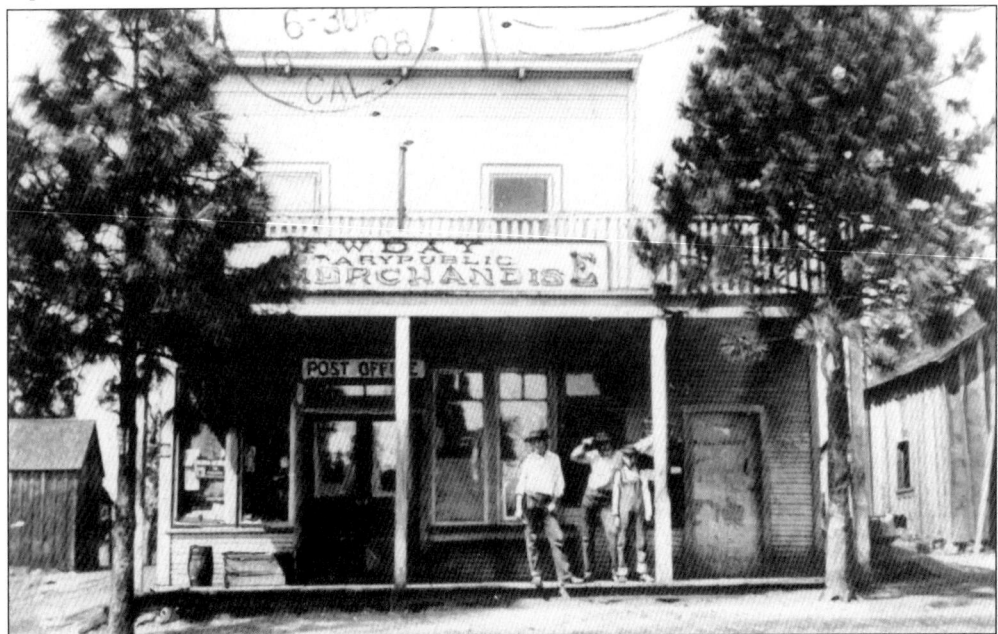

R. M. Brown, the first postmaster, owned this store in 1905 when the Orloff Post Office was first housed here. In 1906, he sold to Fred Day, who then became postmaster. When the post office, a mile to the east in Old Paradise, closed, Orloff became Paradise. The store and post office were across Olive Street from the railroad depot that had always been called Paradise. (Courtesy Lois McDonald.)

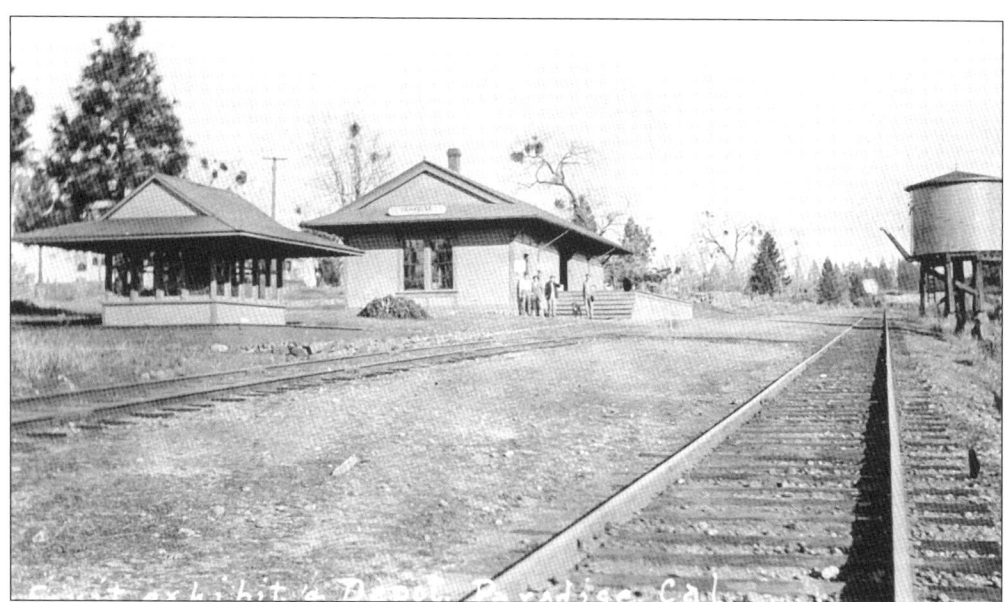

This is a northward view of the Paradise Depot and Fruit Growers Union Exhibit Building before 1914. Some of the businesses on Olive Street are barely visible on the left. Below is the depot, a Southern Pacific (SP) design, in 1916. Basically only a baggage room, there is neither a station agent's office nor living quarters in the building. Typically, if SP thought that the agent might have difficulty finding local lodging in a community, a two-story station with living quarters on the second story was built. Diamond Match is supposed to have built the railroad and sold it to SP, however, there is some thought that it was an SP job from the start. (Above courtesy CSU, Chico, Meriam Library, Special Collections, and Tehama County Library; below courtesy Kent Stephens and Southern Pacific.)

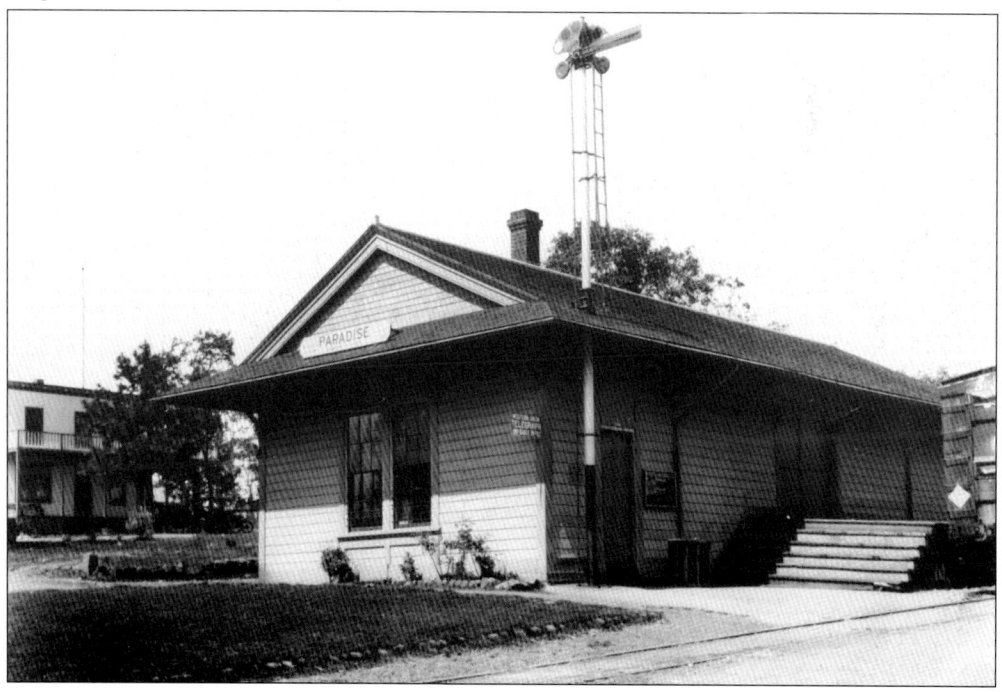

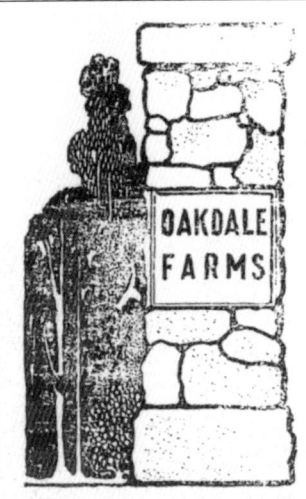
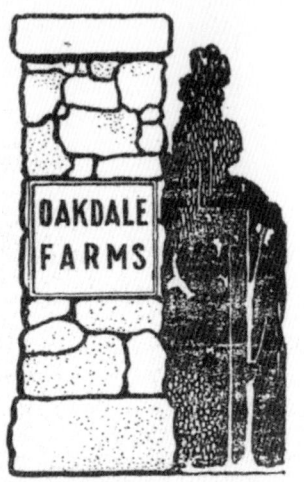

This Is The Portal to Prosperity

OAKDALE FARMS comprises 320 acres of the finest soil in the frostless belt of Paradise. Pre-eminently adapted for ALMONDS and TOKAY GRAPES.

How would you like to have a steady income of from $800 to $2000 per year? Or a country home among the Oaks and Pines?

Five, ten, and twenty-acre tracts, from $15.00 to $50.00 per acre; one-half cash, balance at your pleasure.

PARADISE REALTY CO.
ELKS' BUILDING   PHONE RED 31   530 SECOND STREET, CHICO

When the railroad arrived in 1903, real estate promoters changed Paradise (or Orloff according to the post office) from a village to a town. Real estate investors, speculators, subdividers, and just plain folk wanted to invest in Paradise. In 1908, the Paradise Realty Company assured buyers that Oakdale Farms on Neal Road, a mile and a half south of the depot, was "the" place to invest. Cleared land sold for $50 an acre and uncleared for less, with the terms of one-half cash down and the balance due at the buyer's pleasure. "Paradise—The Town with a Future" became the slogan according to the *Chico Record*. Across the railroad tracks on College Avenue, Sierra Park was another 1908 subdivision. Advertising extolled the fertile soil, beautiful scenery, healthful climate, higher educational opportunities, and no saloons. The Sierra Polytechnic Institute is visible at the end of the avenue. (Courtesy Gold Nugget Museum.)

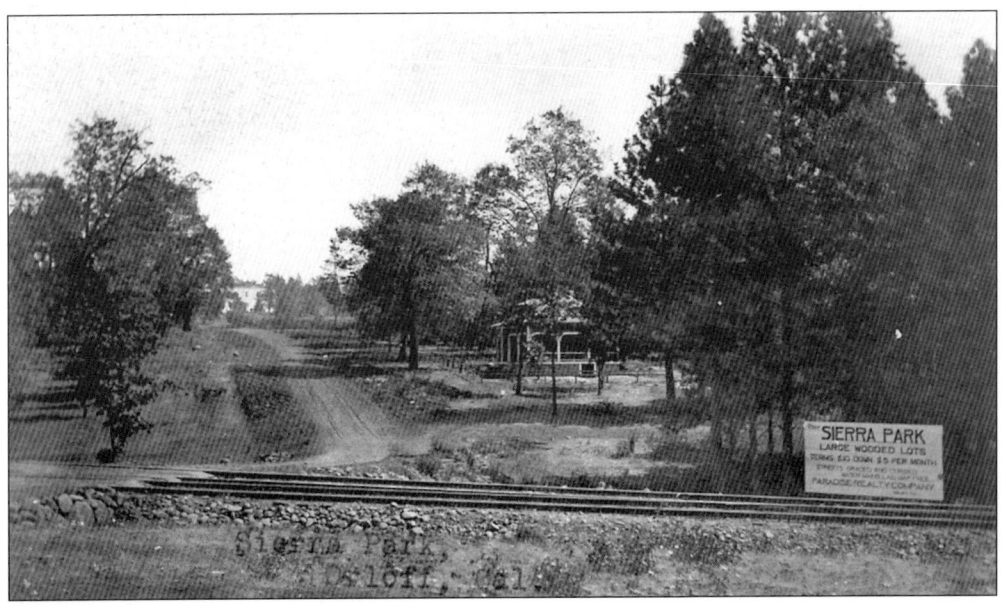

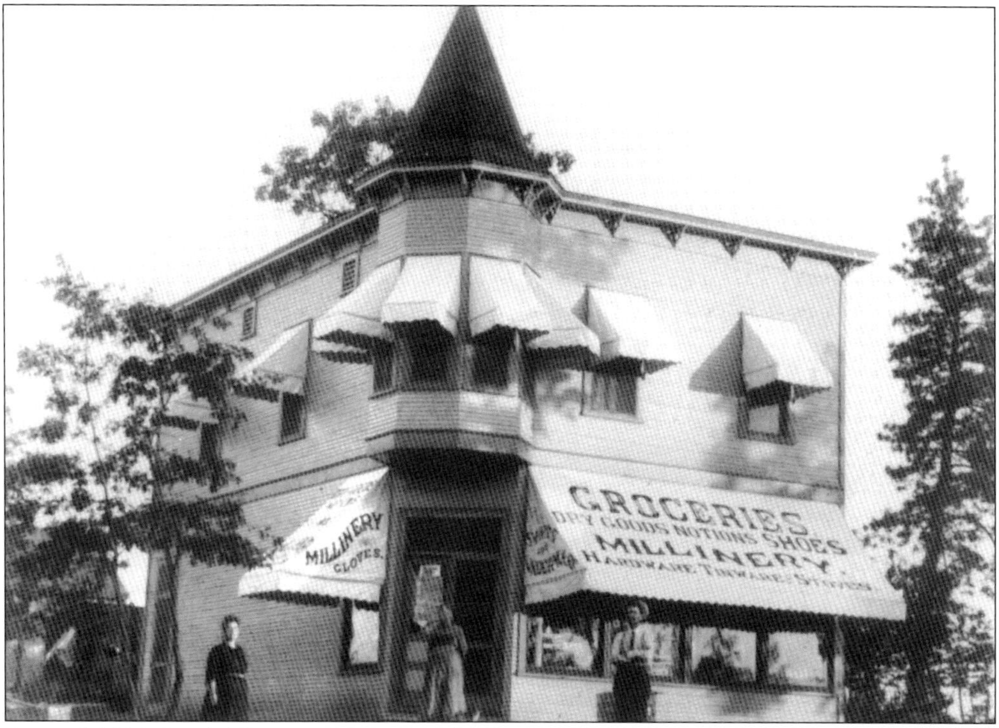

Around 1906, Jacob Thramer constructed this classic Victorian building at Birch and Olive Streets across from the Paradise Depot. He was a member of the Dowieites religious sect that erected several buildings in the "downtown" area. Thramer sold to Dr. William Lovett, who had a pharmacy and store downstairs and a residence upstairs. The building has had many owners since and was demolished in 2005. (Courtesy Gold Nugget Museum.)

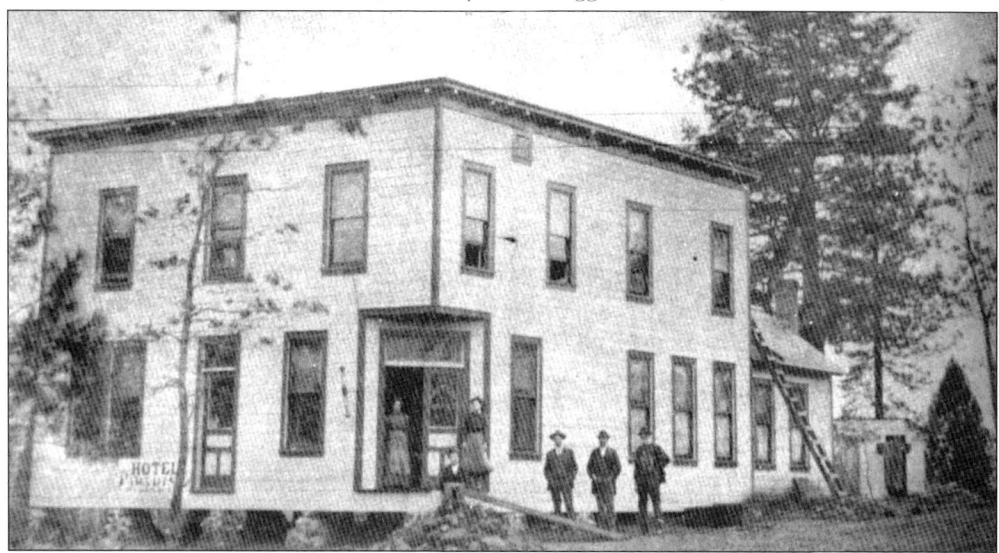

On the corner of Birch and Olive Streets, across from the depot, Joseph R. Miller built this hotel in 1904. In 1906, he sold it to the Brown brothers, who then sold it to Jefferson and Edna Ralston in 1910. They operated it as the Ralston Hotel until 1919 when it burned, taking three other buildings with it. By at least 1916, a front balcony had been added. (Courtesy Paradise Genealogy Society.)

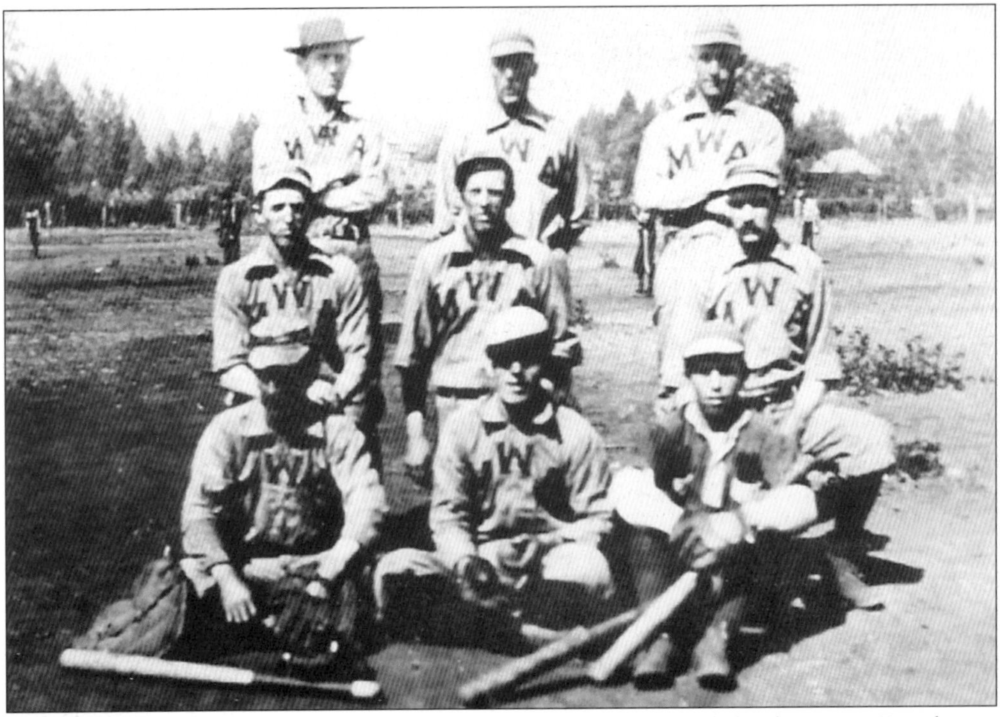

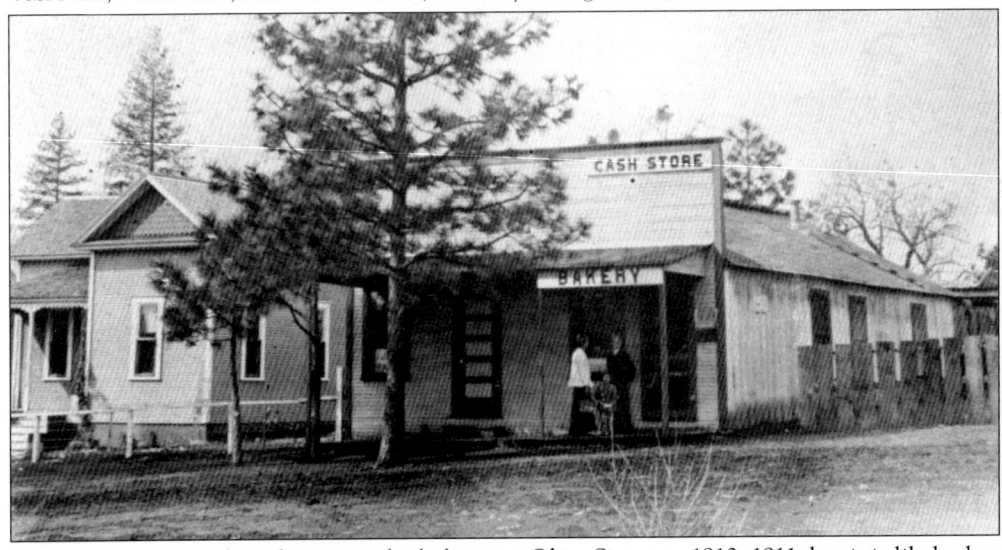

In 1909, some may have wondered whether the community around the depot was Paradise or Orloff. These men had no such problem, however. They were members of the 1909 Orloff baseball team. Pictured here, from left to right, are (first row) Frank Buschmann, Oscar Moore, and Mudd Tilton; (second row) George Strong, Harry Graham, and Billie Wilson; and (third row) Leon Van Ness, ? Crawford, and Chet Clark. (Courtesy George Bille.)

It may have been cash-and-carry at the bakery on Olive Street in 1910–1911, but it is likely that farm produce also was accepted as payment. By 1937, Nena Burkhalter's beauty shop shared the building with a barber; Nena lived in the back of the building. Hot water was still heated on a wood stove. The house to the left may have been M. V. Roe's home and funeral parlor. (Courtesy Paradise Genealogy Society.)

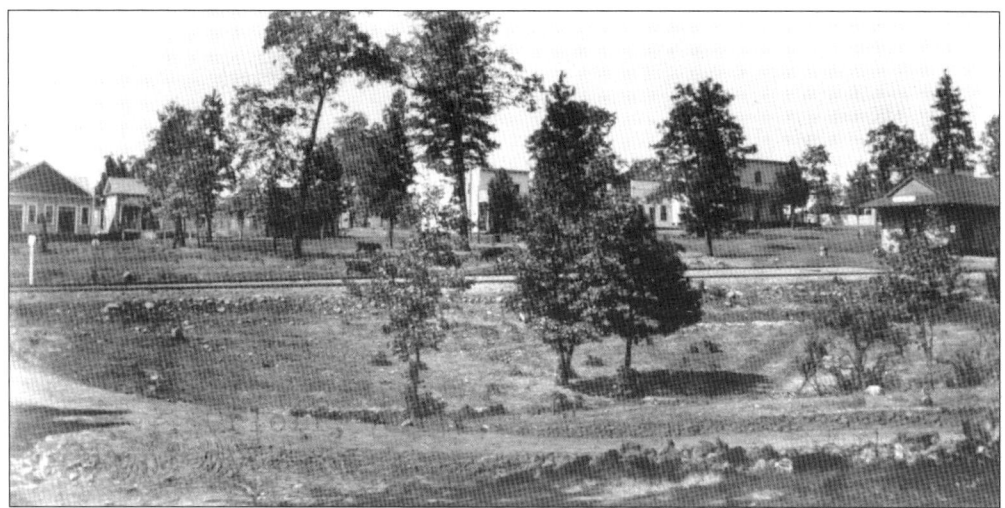

That Paradise was a rural, farm community is obvious from this 1910 photograph, as cows graze between the railroad tracks and Olive Street in downtown. As far as is known, no train collided with a cow. The Paradise depot is on the right. (Courtesy Lois McDonald.)

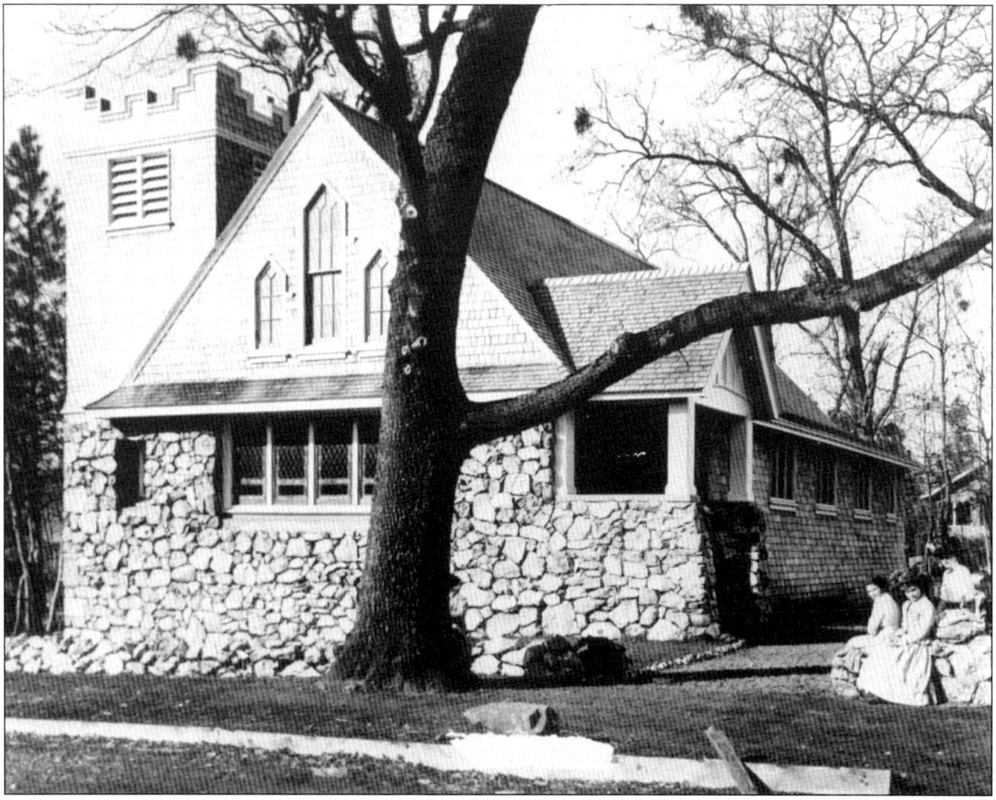

In 1879, the Union Congregational Church, pictured here around 1910, organized and met in the Good Templar's Lodge in Old Paradise. In 1888, a church was built on Clark Road about where the Paradise Library is today. Renamed the First Congregational Church of Paradise, it burned in 1909. A new building was erected at today's Pearson and Scottwood Roads in Orloff and was renamed the Craig Memorial Church. (Courtesy Gold Nugget Museum.)

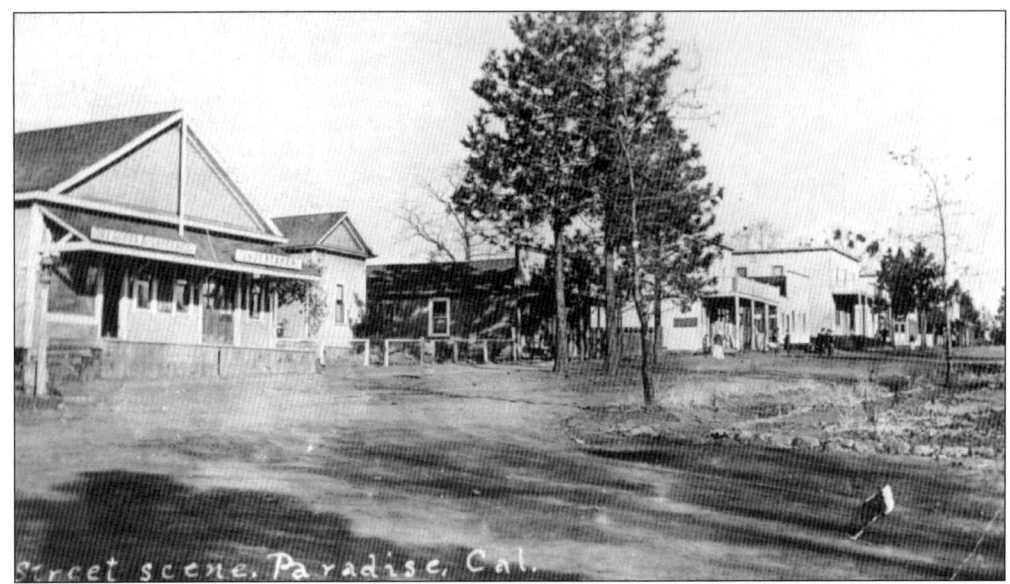

This is Olive Street before the 1919 fire that started at the Ralston Hotel, pictured here on the right with a balcony. From left to right, the businesses are a dry goods store, owned by Wyatt Brown, and M. V. Roe's undertaking business (both in the Roe Building, later Hamma's mercantile in 1920), Roe's residence, a bakery, R. M. Brown/F. W. Day store, the Orloff Post Office, and the Ralston Hotel. (Courtesy Gold Nugget Museum.)

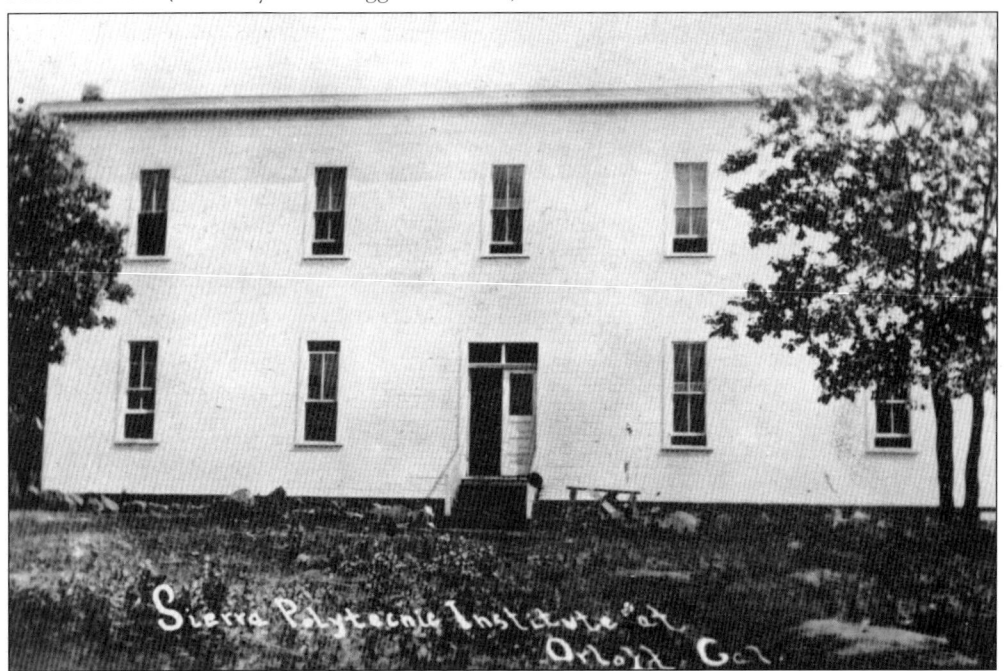

New Paradise had a college of sorts, the Sierra Polytechnic Institute, located on what became known as College Hill at the end of College Avenue (later Pearson Road). It opened in 1906 with great hopes but never was able to find the funds to sustain its curriculum and closed its doors in 1910. One president even mortgaged his home for money to pay teachers' salaries. (Courtesy Lois McDonald.)

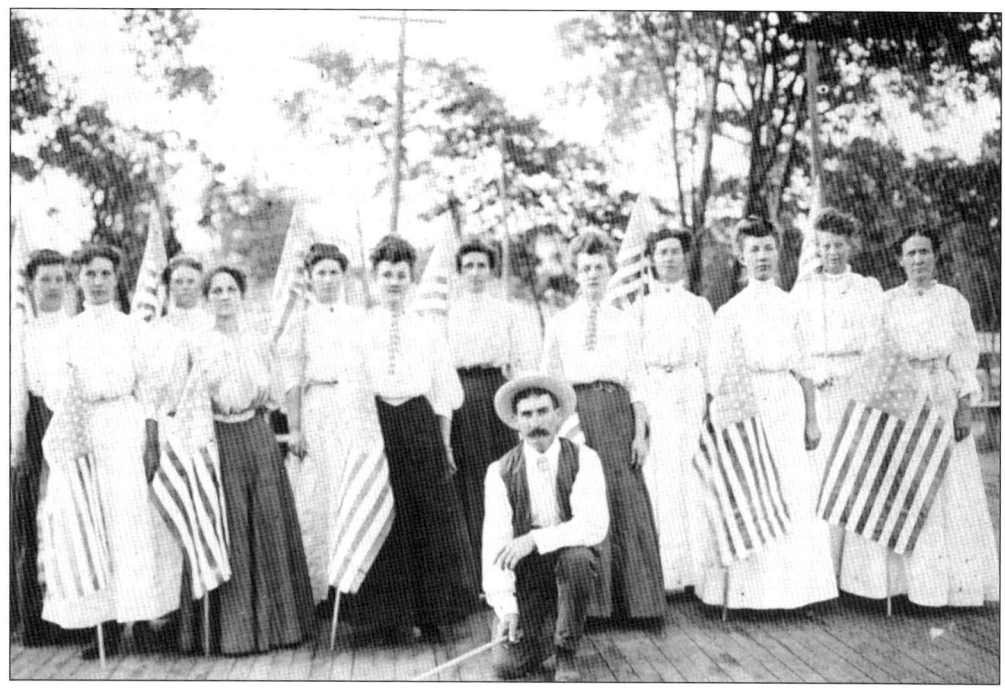

This photograph shows the faculty and students of the Sierra Polytechnic Institute around 1906. Although sometimes called a college, it was not really one. During the late 1800s and early 1900s, communities like Paradise that had no high schools sometimes had preparatory schools, called institutes or academies. They taught classes from ninth to 14th grade, and graduates could go on to complete college in two years. (Courtesy Ruby Swartzlow.)

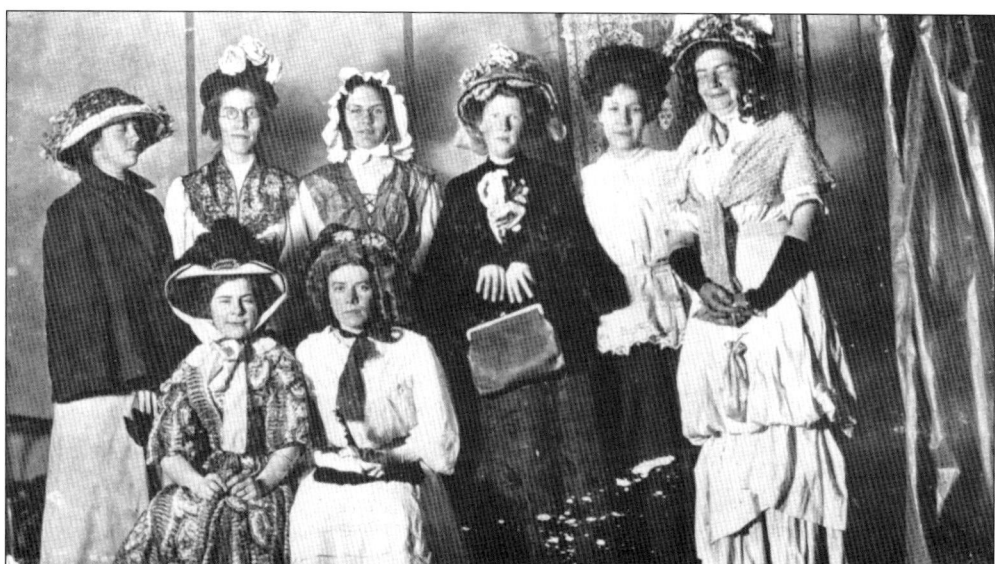

These ladies from the drama group of the Congregational Church put on a play at the Sierra Polytechnic Institute c. 1913. Pictured, from left to right, are (first row) Fern Ralston Harvey and Mabel Robinson Burkett; and (second row) Elsa Bille Edwards, Eva Stearns Weahunt, Lida Stearns, Francis Burkett, Edna Ralston, and Irma Pettite. (Courtesy Ethel Bornefield.)

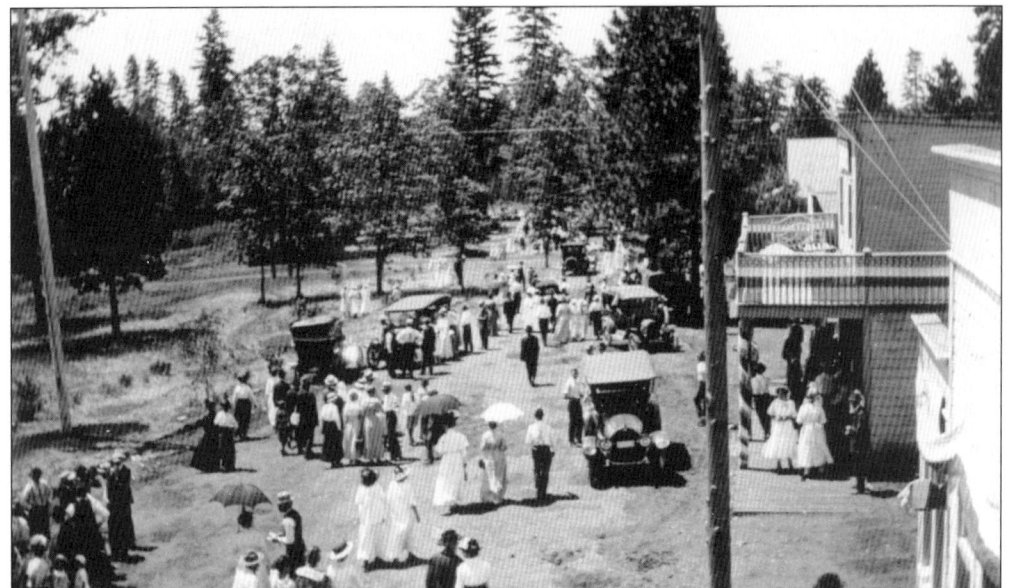

The Fourth of July was a big holiday in small communities. This view of ladies and their gentleman promenading on Olive Street in 1916 was taken from the balcony of the Ralston Hotel three years before it burned. The building on the right with the patriotically decorated balcony is Day's Mercantile and the post office. The Paradise depot is out of sight on the left. (Courtesy Lois McDonald.)

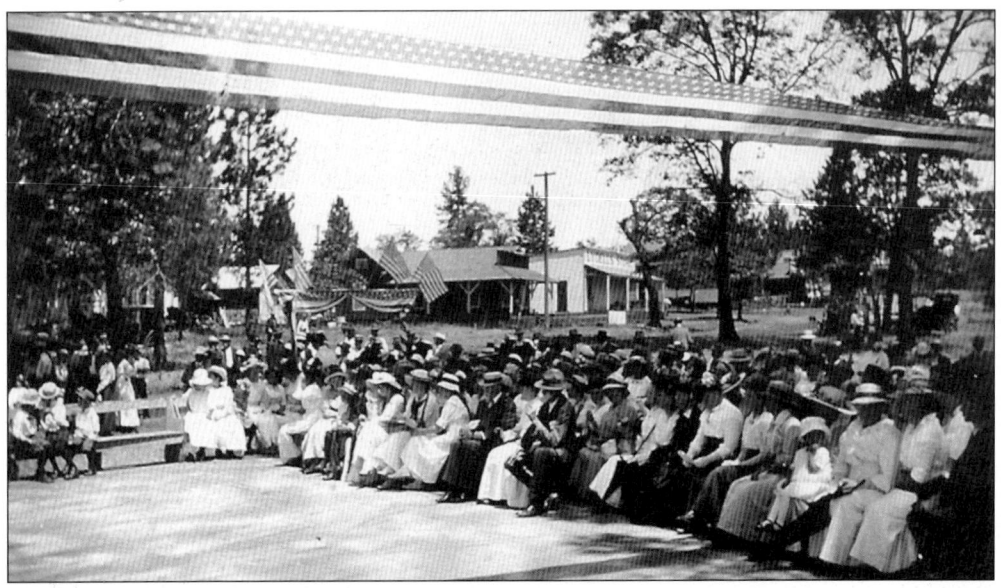

The Modern Woodman Lodge of Chico built a dance platform and bandstand on the southeast corner of Olive Street and Manzanita Road. (Olive Street is in the background.) This photograph, taken on the Fourth of July in 1916, shows the holiday crowd socializing and waiting for the festivities to start. Many activities were held here, including dances, lectures, concerts, and harvest festivals. (Courtesy Gold Nugget Museum.)

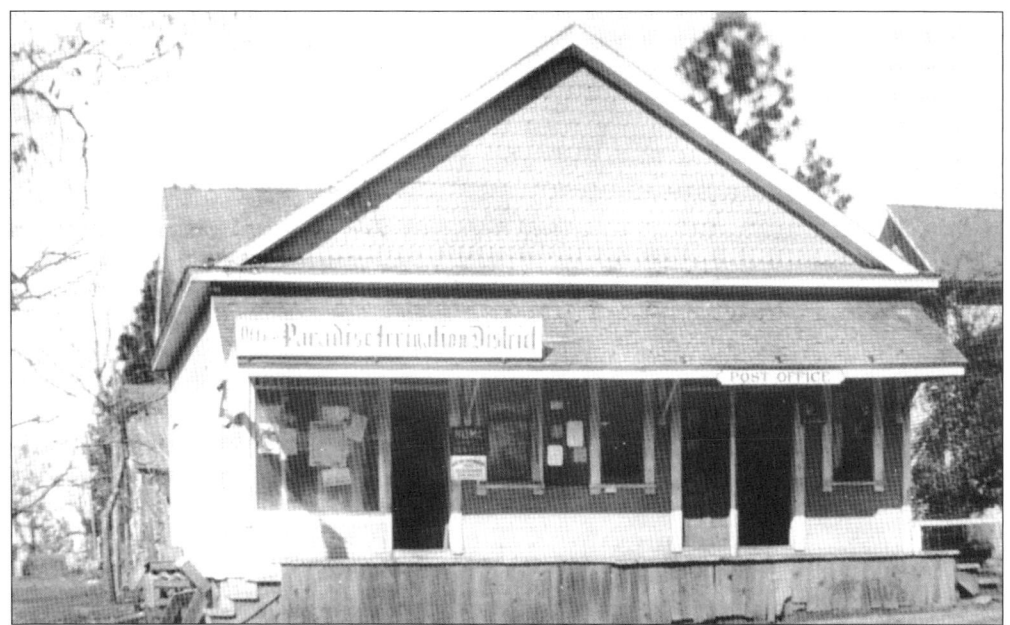

The Roe Building, apparently named for the undertaker who owned it and had his funeral parlor there, was on the northwest corner of Olive Street and College Avenues (later Pearson Road). It was PID's first office in 1916 and housed the post office. In 1917, Wyatt Brown had his store there, and in the 1920s, I. G. Hamma opened his mercantile in the building. (Courtesy Paradise Irrigation District.)

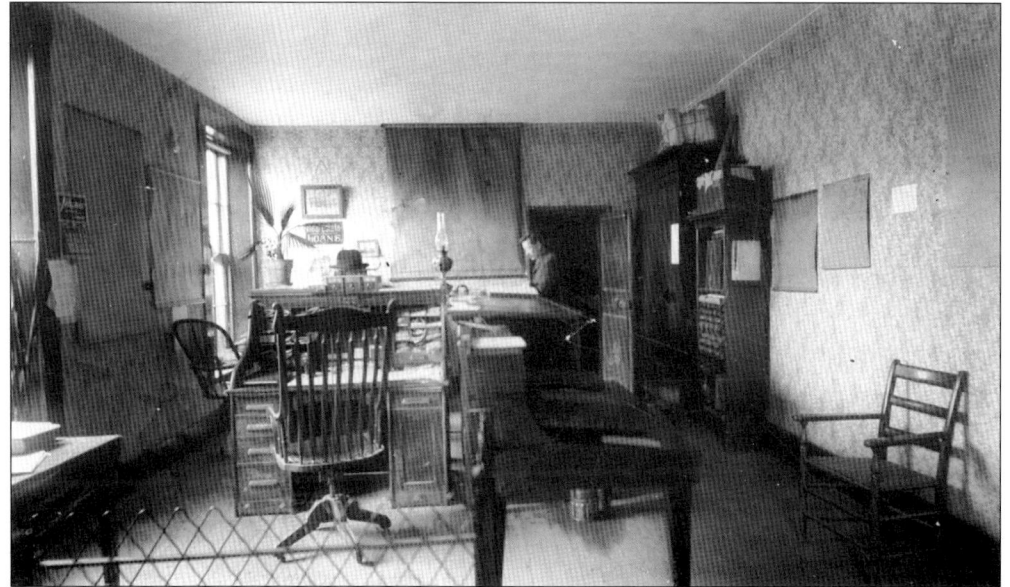

PID was established to provide irrigation water to farmers on the Ridge. Families were not supposed to use the water in their homes but did anyway. Pictured here in May 1916, George Bille, the first secretary of PID, is standing at the back of the original office. (Courtesy Paradise Irrigation District and George Bille.)

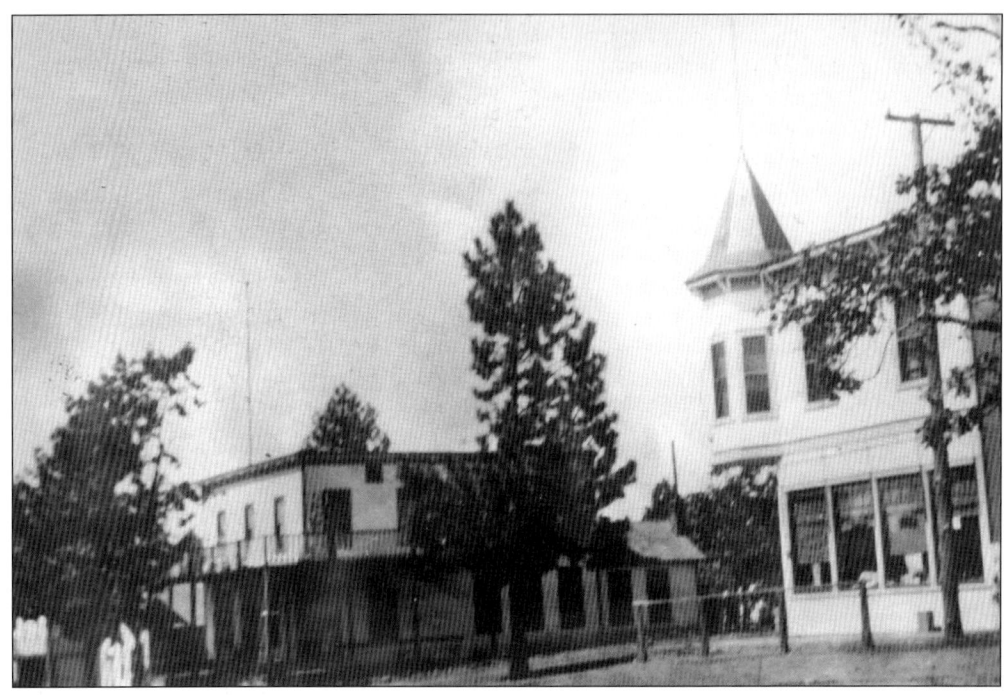

Above, this pre-1919 view of the intersection of Olive and Birch Streets looks from just north of the depot. The Ralston Hotel, left center, was built in 1904 and burned in 1919. By 1934, this is how the intersection looked, and Jack Post's gas station and service garage stood on the old site of the hotel. The corner is now a vacant lot. The Thramer/Gulick/Lovett Building is in both pictures on the right. For 99 years, it housed numerous businesses and a church. In 2005, it was found to be structurally unsound and was demolished, thereby destroying the last building of Orloff. (Courtesy Lois McDonald.)

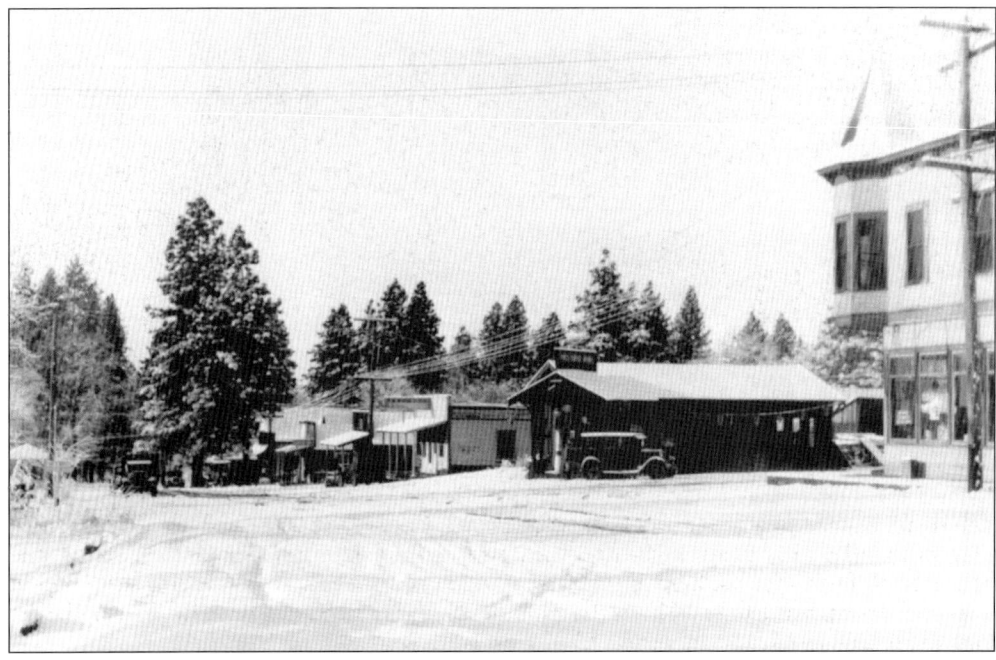

Pictured here in 1972, the "Potter" post office, built around 1919, was the first building constructed as a post office in Paradise. It was on Olive Street between College Avenue and Foster Road and was built while Elizabeth Potter was postmaster between 1917 and 1922, The small building still stands today. (Courtesy Lois McDonald.)

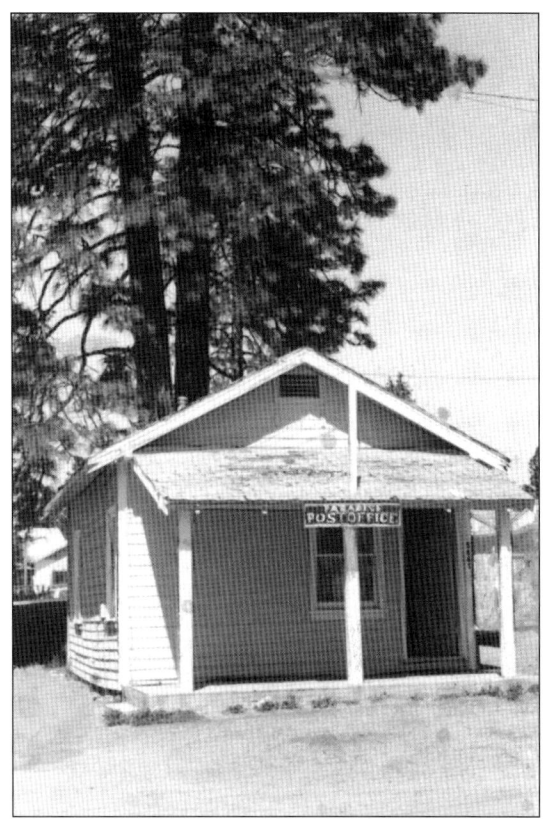

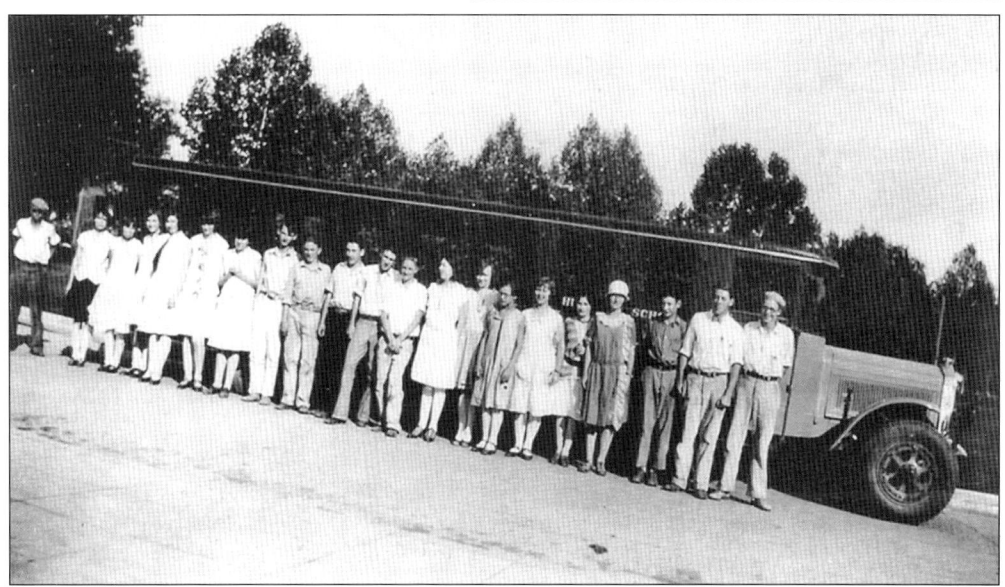

Too small to provide a high school, the three Ridge school districts joined the Chico School District in 1919. This meant high-school students had to board in Chico or be bussed to the high school. Boarding cost hard-found money and bussing over narrow, winding dirt (mud in the winter) roads was tedious. This is the Paradise-Chico bus in September 1920, 35 years before Paradise had a high school. (Courtesy Gold Nugget Museum.)

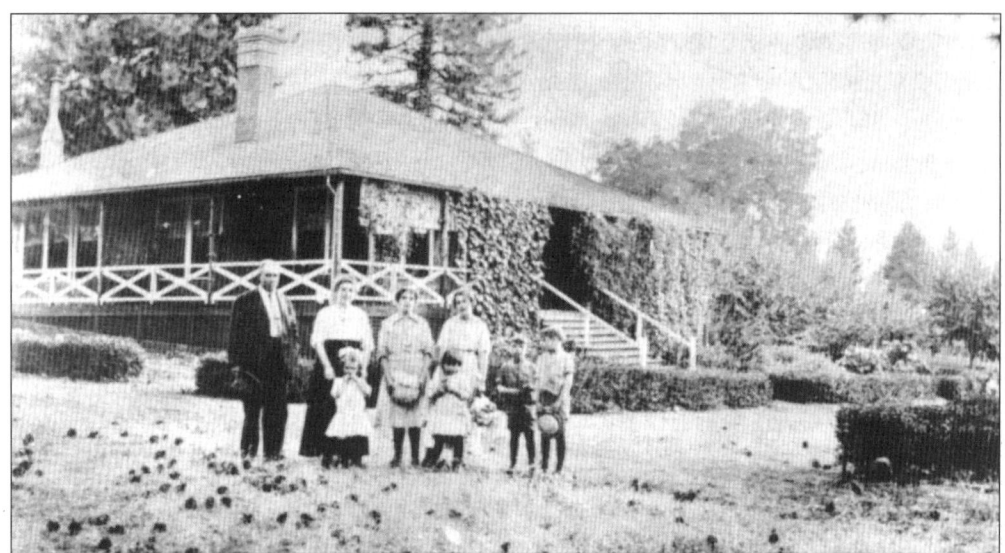

Charles S. Compton built this home, known as Ranchita (little ranch), on Neal Road before 1900. Pictured here, from left to right, are (first row) daughters Edith and Claire and sons Raymond and Donald; and (second row) Compton, wife Joanna, and daughters Ruth and Helen. He was president of the short-lived Sierra Polytechnic Institute and lost the home to foreclosure on a mortgage for money that he lent to the institute. (Courtesy Gold Nugget Museum.)

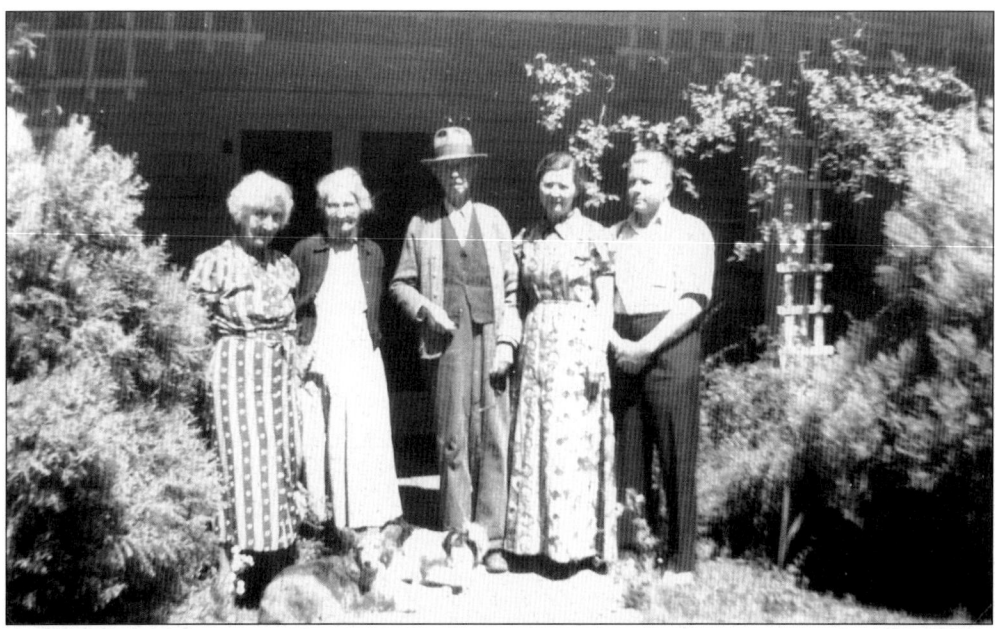

This 1939 photograph was taken 31 years after James "Jim" Pearson and his family settled in Paradise. He and his wife, Katherine, became very active in the community. He had been a cartoonist for the *Denver Post* and was an editor of the *Paradise Progress Review*. Pictured, from left to right, are Aunt Kate (?), Katherine Pearson, James Pearson, Mrs. Warner, and Gene Warner. (Courtesy Paradise Genealogy Society.)

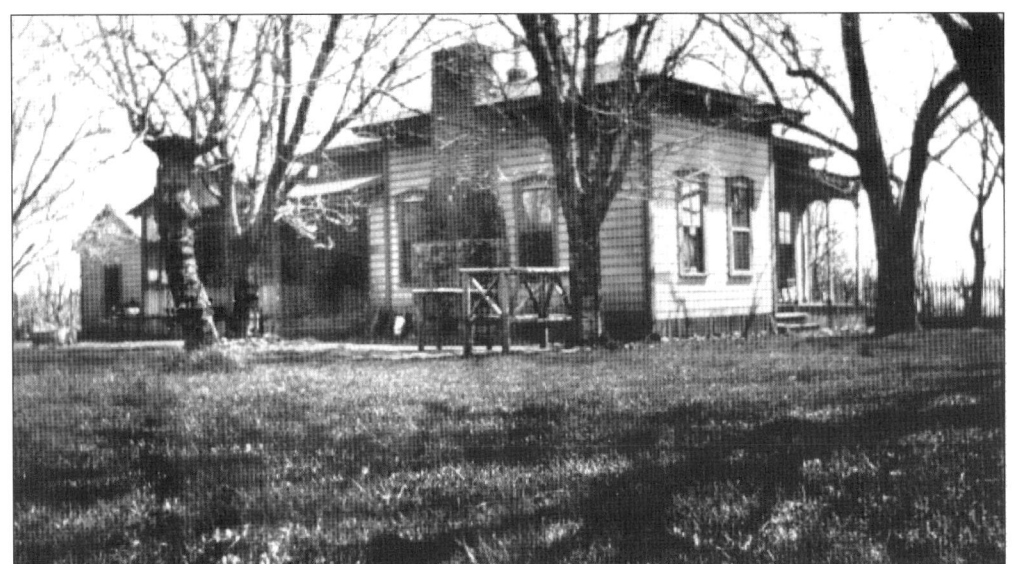

The Pearson home was on the southeast corner of the "Four Corners," now Pearson and Clark Roads. When they bought this property in 1910, there were several acres of apples, olives, prunes, pears, and berries. In 1927, they sold the farm and built a home at Almond and Fir Streets. At age 71, James was not really up to the one-mile walk into town. (Courtesy Gold Nugget Museum.)

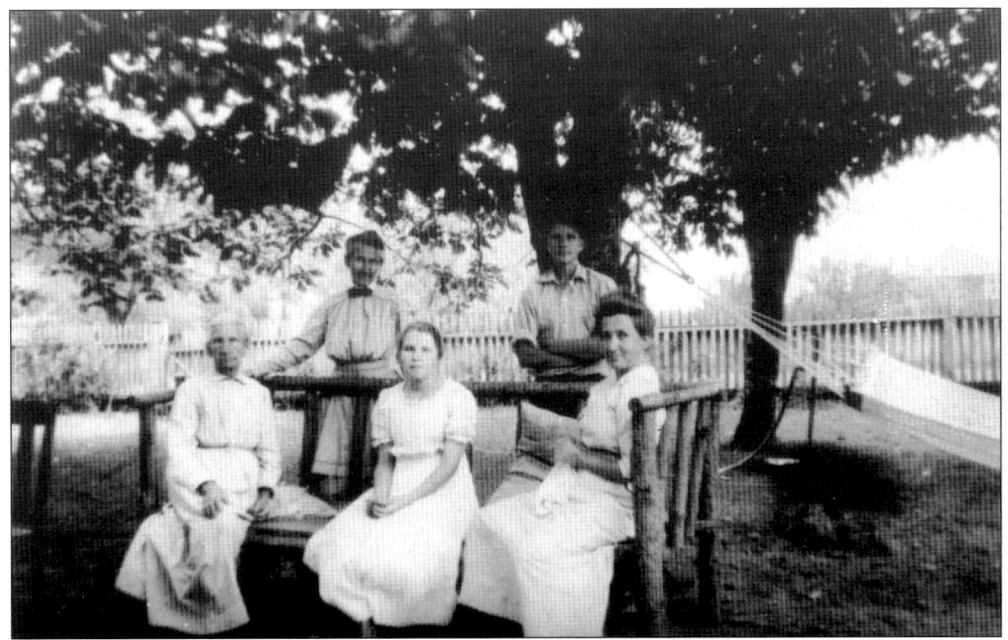

Katherine Pearson (with black tie) entertains in the front yard of her Four Corners home. The young man on the right may be her son George Pearson, who died during the flu epidemic of 1918 while serving in the U.S. Army. The other ladies are not identified. (Courtesy Paradise Genealogy Society.)

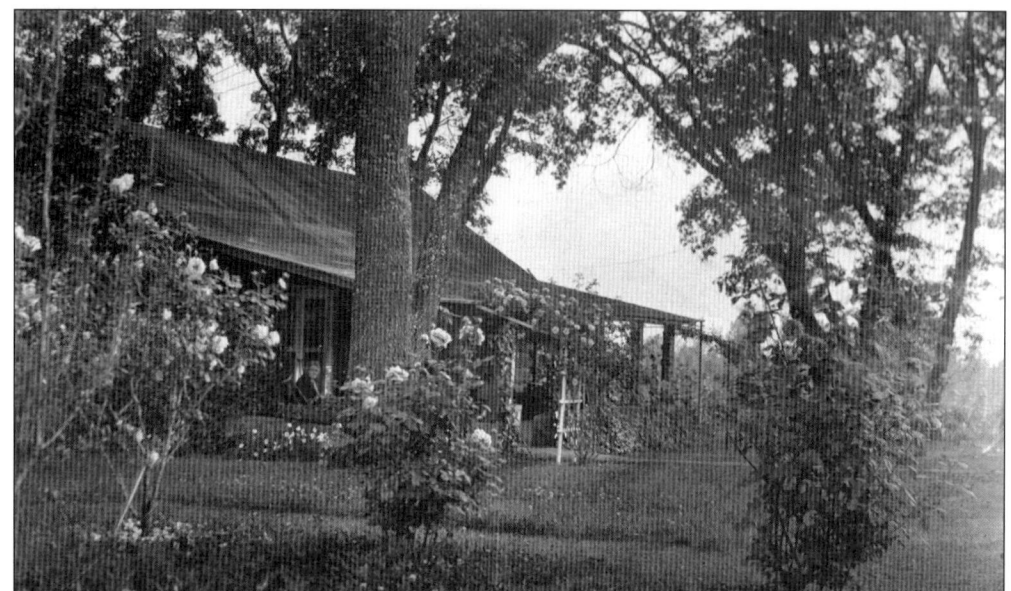

When the Fink family came to Paradise in 1911 they bought this ranch on the east side of Foster Road below Roe Road. This photograph is undated. (Courtesy Paradise Genealogy Society.)

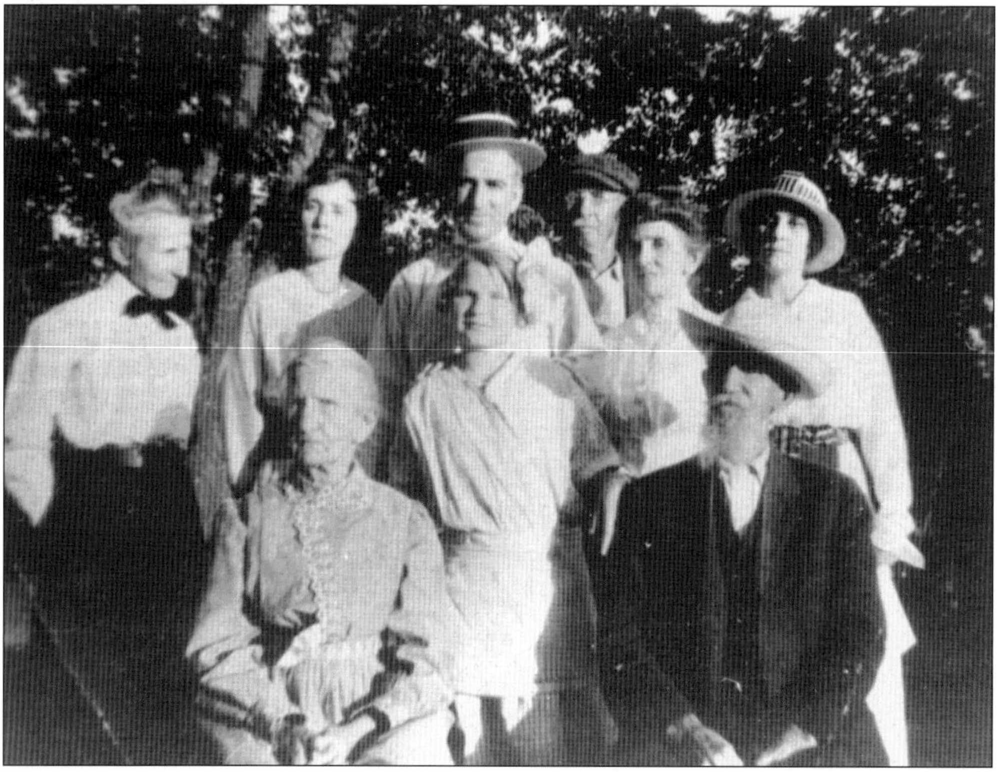

Pictured here, from left to right, are (first row) Grandma Sara, Catherine Warner, and Grandpa Ira Fink; (second row) Katherine Fink Pearson, Eugenia Fink, John Fink, James Pearson (in cap), Lottie Fink, and Mollie Fink Warner. Three years after the Pearsons came to Paradise from Colorado, the Fink family followed in 1911. (Courtesy Paradise Genealogy Society.)

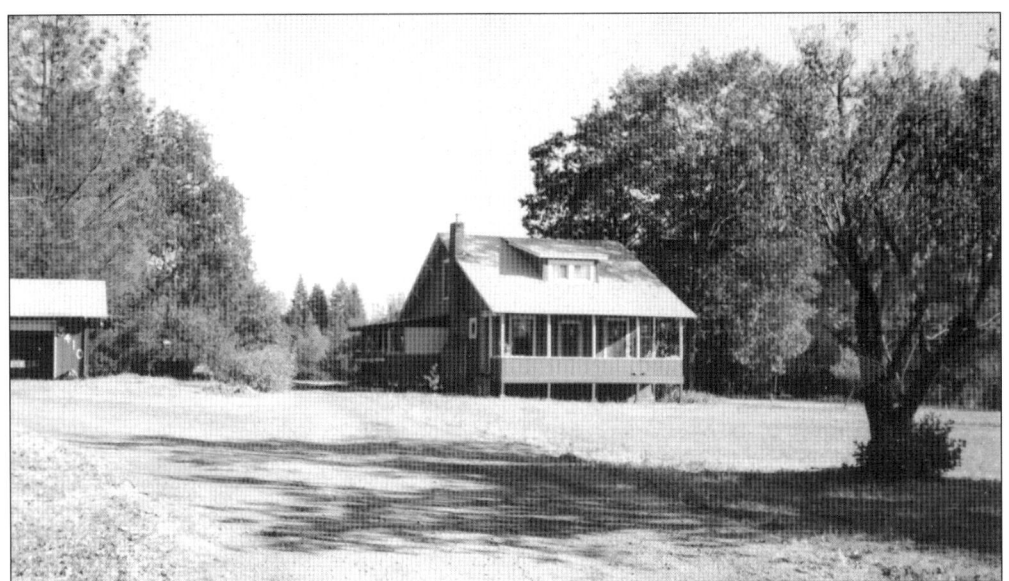

Sam Coleman, an early director at PID, came to Butte County in 1909 to work for the Diamond Match Company. That year, he and his wife, Jessie, built this home on 26 acres along Neal Road. It is supposed to have been the second house in Paradise to have a concrete foundation. They grew peaches, apricots, grapes, and blackberries. (Courtesy Janeece Webb.)

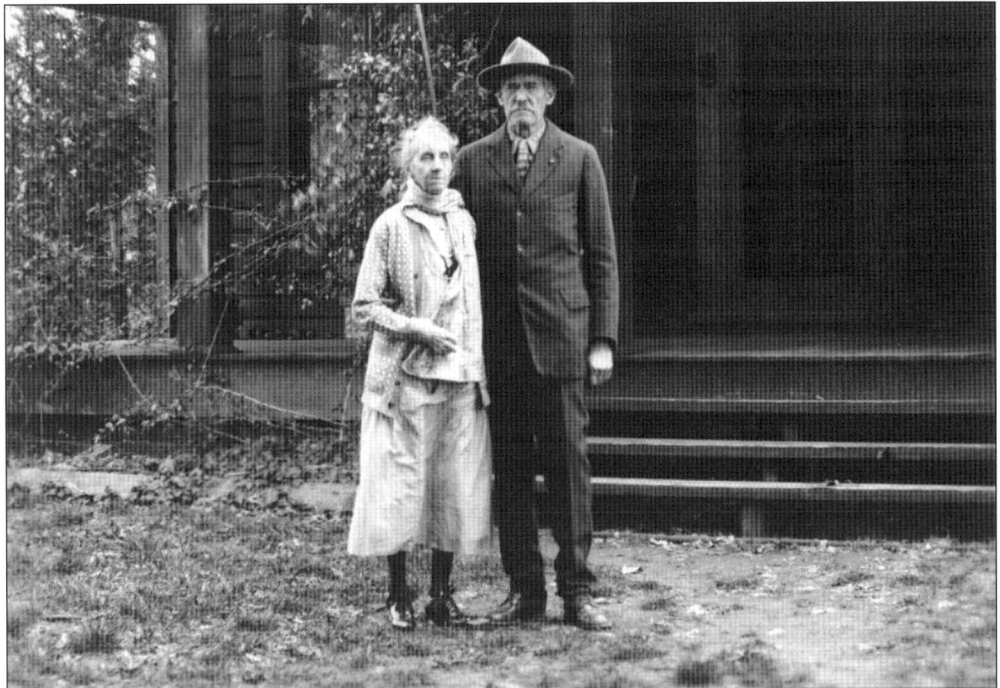

Luther Sage Kelly and his wife of 30 years, Alice, retired to Paradise in 1915. Known on the Ridge as Captain Kelly, he joined the U.S. Army during the Civil War and served in the campaigns against the Plains Indians and in the Philippine Insurrection. He never said much about his military service, but he was the famous "Yellowstone Kelly," soldier, scout, and advisor to Pres. Theodore Roosevelt. (Courtesy George Bille.)

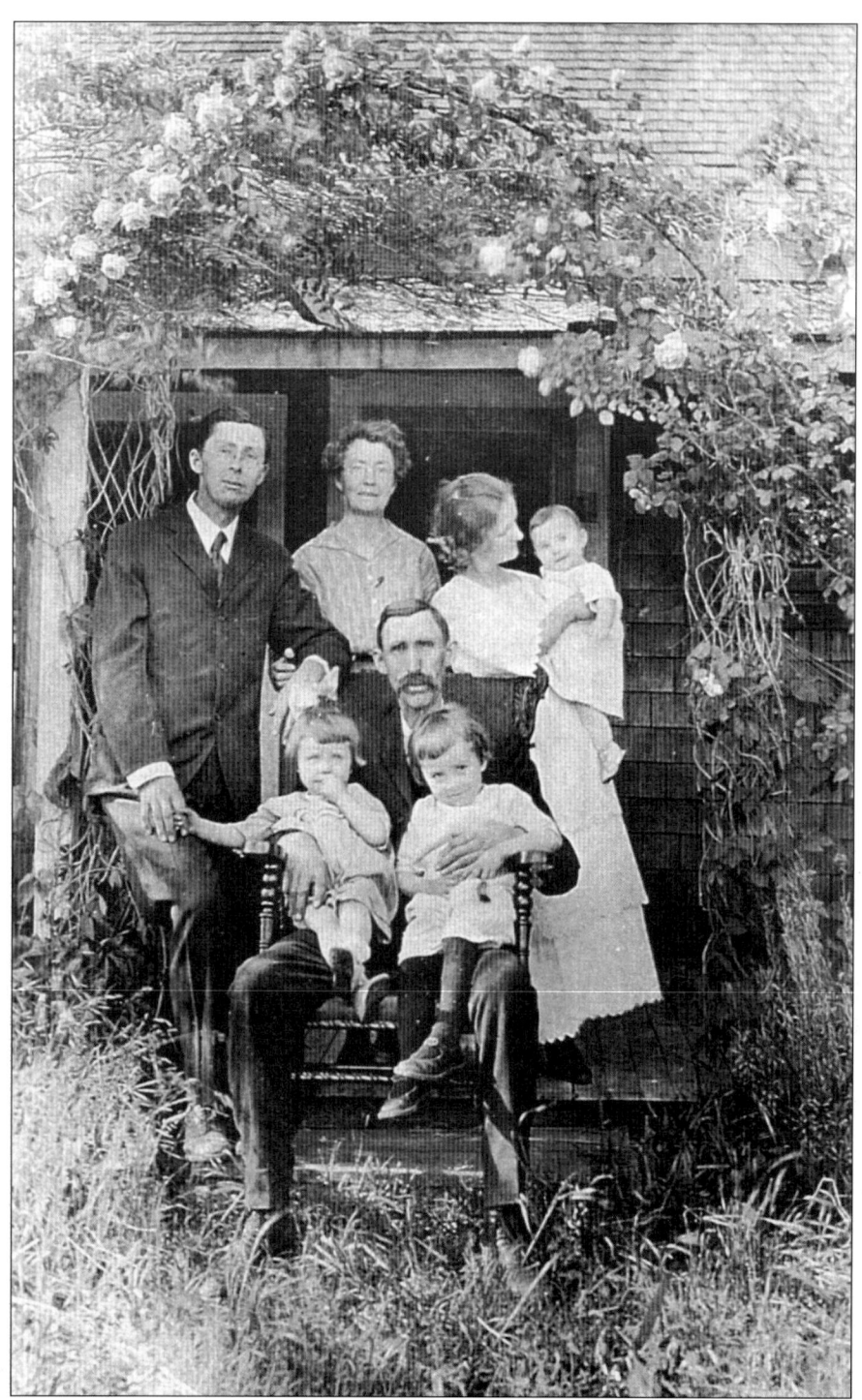

Carl Eckles was the owner and driver for a stage line between Stirling City and Chico from 1915 to 1920. He also ran a taxi service in Paradise. Later he moved to Southern California and started a bus line. Carl is standing on the left next to his mother and wife holding the baby; seated is his father holding two of his grandchildren. (Courtesy Paradise Genealogy Society.)

Four

APPLES, TIMBER, AND MORE

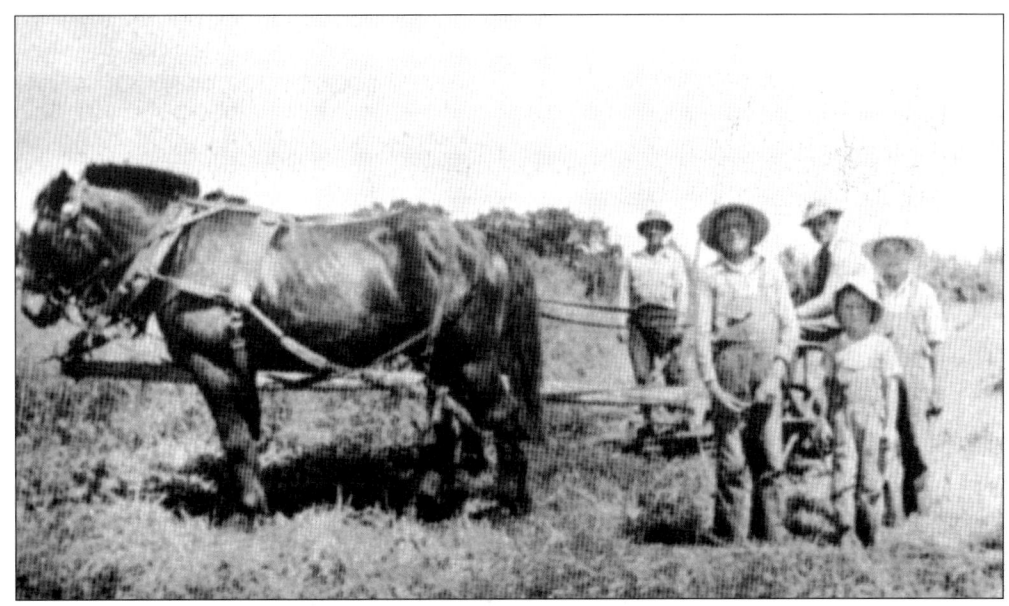

Around 1915, Herman Heinke and his family bought land in Paradise. They raised pears, peaches, apples, and grapes and starting in 1960, kiwis as well. Taken in the mid-1940s, this photograph shows, from left to right, John, James, and David. On the left in the rear is Julius Seliger and sitting on the mower behind the boys is their father, Carl Heinke. (Courtesy John and Jean Heinke.)

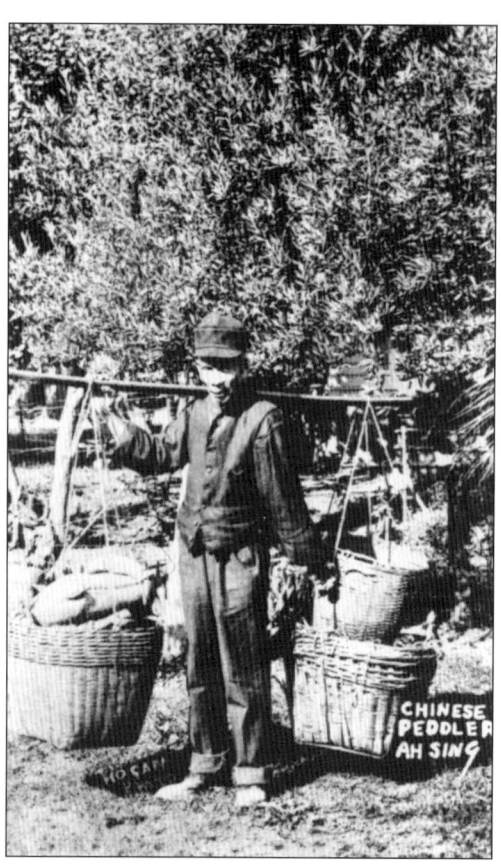

The Chinese were known as industrious miners throughout California and as diligent laborers on the Central Pacific Railroad. In Butte County, they were miners too, but some cultivated gardens along Little Butte Creek. They sold vegetables and fruit to the miners and also peddled their produce to residents of the Ridge. Ah Sing was one of the Chinese gardeners who frequented the Ridge in the 1880s. (Courtesy Gold Nugget Museum.)

Pictured here in 1964, the Curtis olive orchard was planted in 1888. According to Dr. William Mack, who is credited as recognizing that the Ridge was suited for commercial agriculture, Joe Curtis was one of the first to plant olives on the Ridge. (Courtesy Ruby Swartzlow and Lois McDonald.)

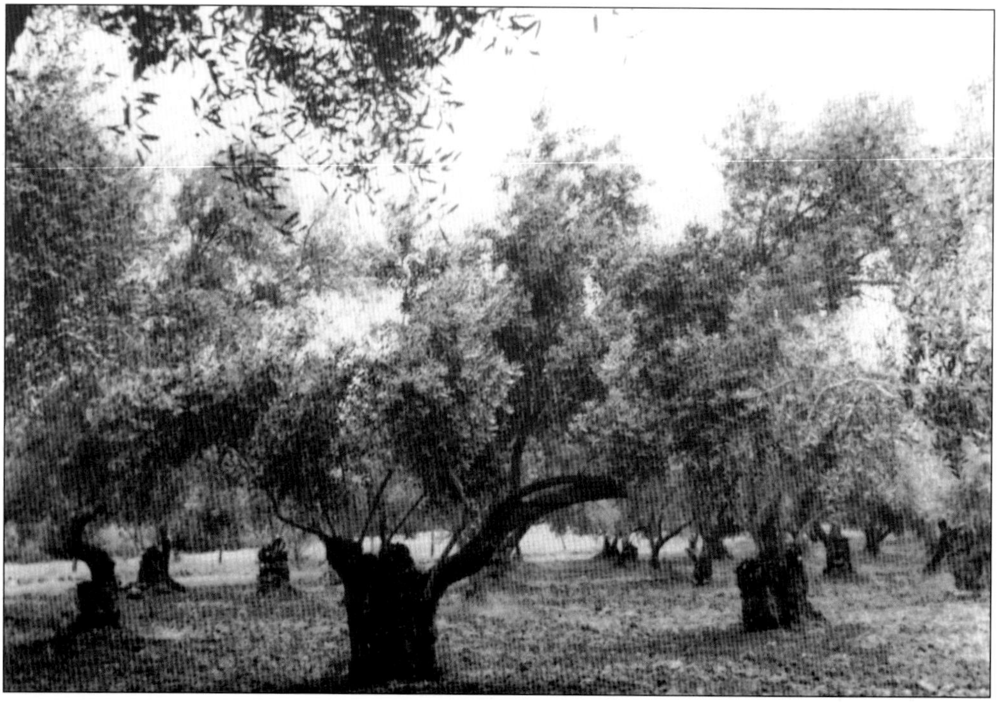

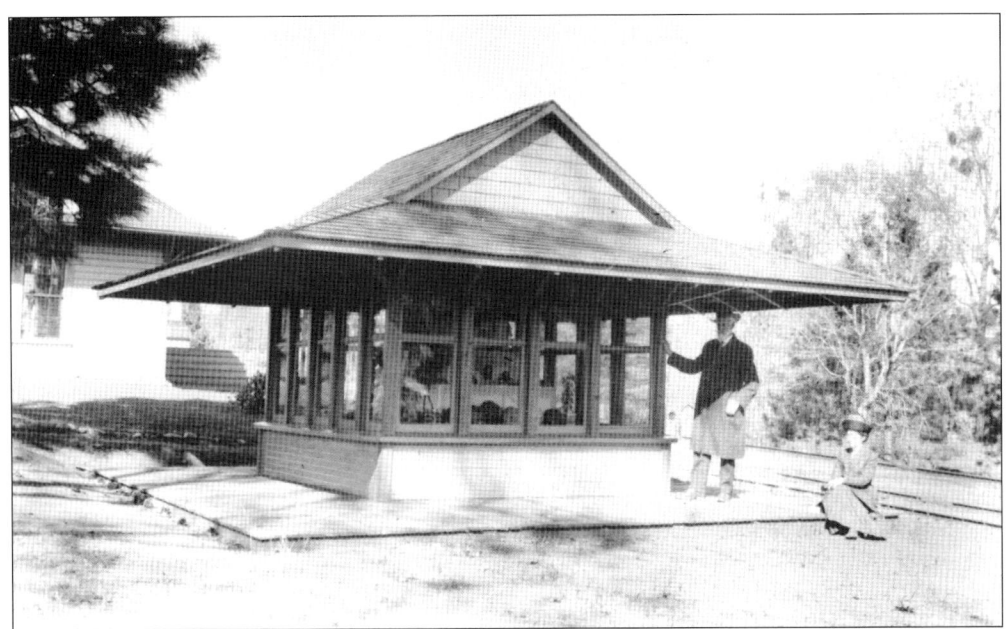

Designed to showcase Paradise Ridge produce, the Agricultural Exhibit building was constructed by the Fruit Grower's Union just south of the depot (in left background). In 1918, Butte County purchased it and remodeled it into the town library. The justice of the peace court also met there. Damaged in a 1930 snowstorm, the building collapsed on the books. (Courtesy Satterlee Photo.)

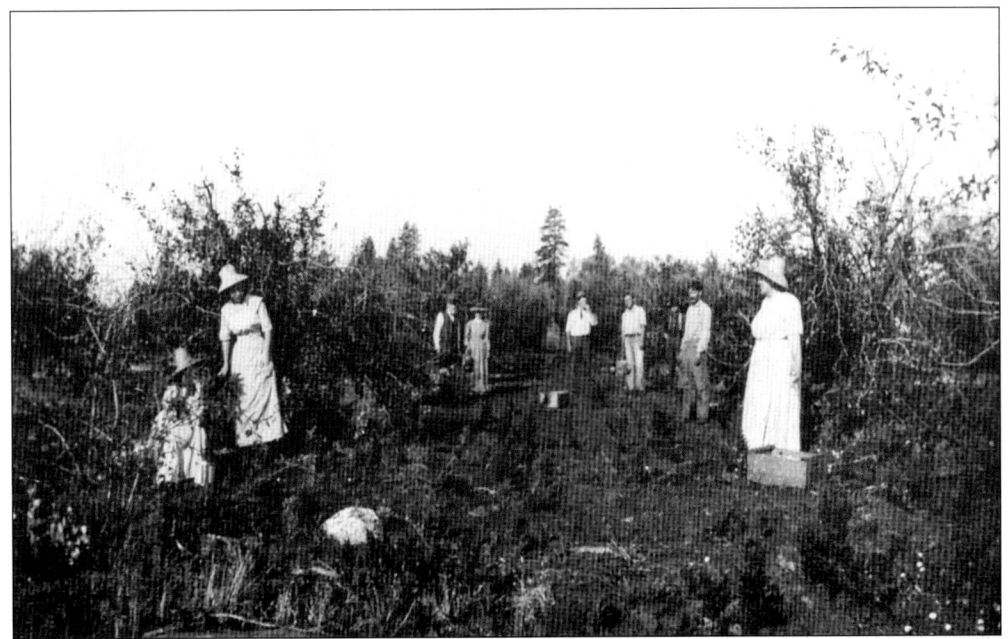

These people are picking prunes in 1912, possibly on James Pearson's place at the southeast corner of Clark Road (later Pearson Road), where Ace Hardware stands today. In 1890, John Hedge owned the property, grew prunes and pears, and had a prune-packing plant. (Courtesy Iva Collett.)

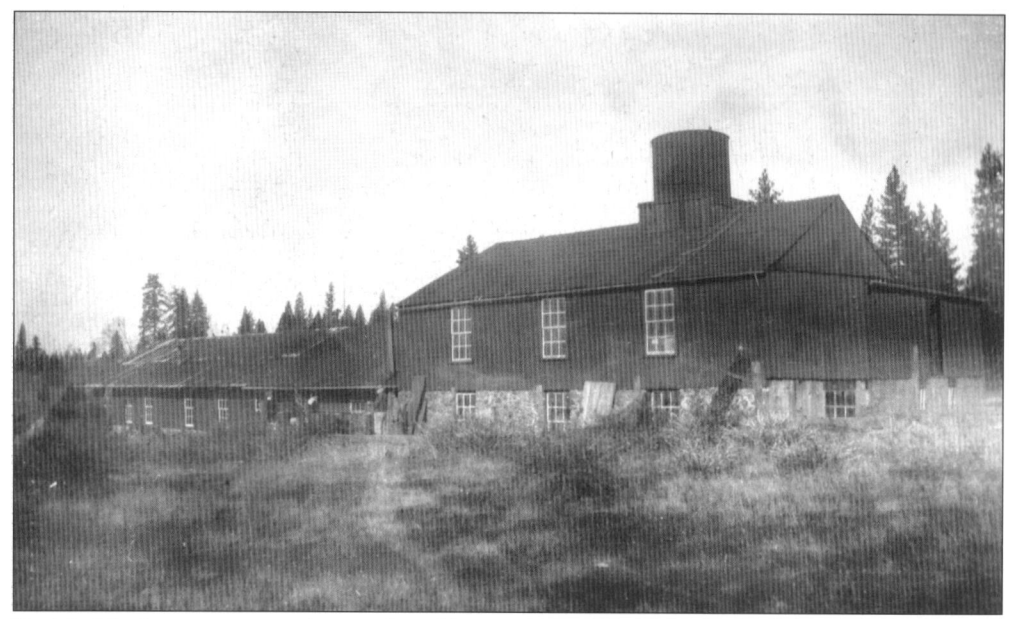

Dr. Mack's olive processing plant and cookhouse, pictured here in 1915, operated into the 1940s. Joseph Curtis was the first to plant and pack olives on the Ridge, off Pentz Road. However, it was Dr. Mack who turned olive growing into a successful commercial venture. (Courtesy Paradise Genealogy Society.)

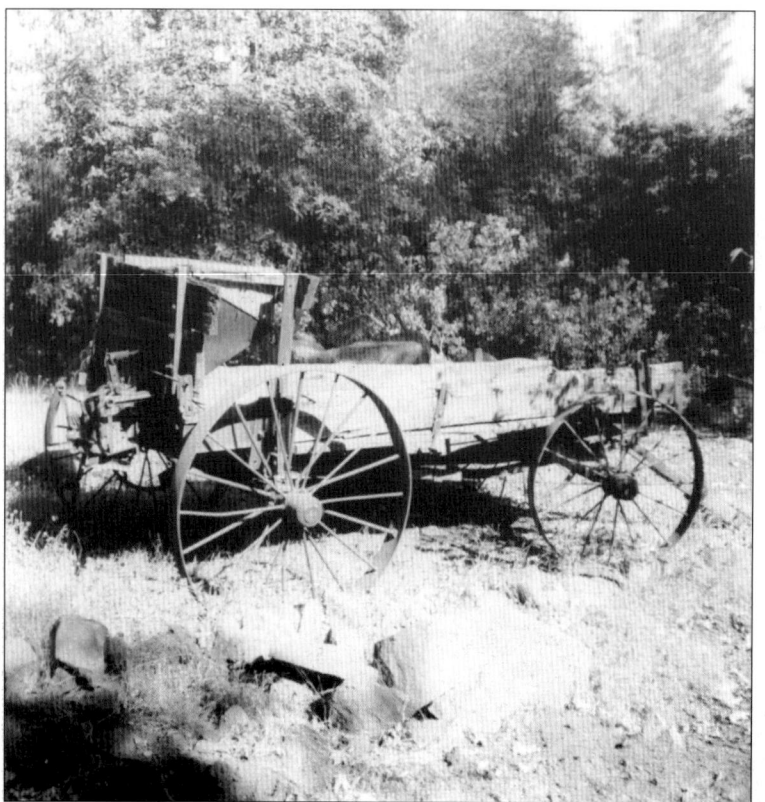

This old wagon was photographed years ago down the Ridge at the Bourgeois Ranch on Wayland Road in lower Paradise. The valves, plumbing, and tank on the back probably were used for agricultural spraying. Grapes and fruit trees were susceptible to fungus and natural, organic chemicals were sprayed to kill it. (Courtesy Janeece Webb.)

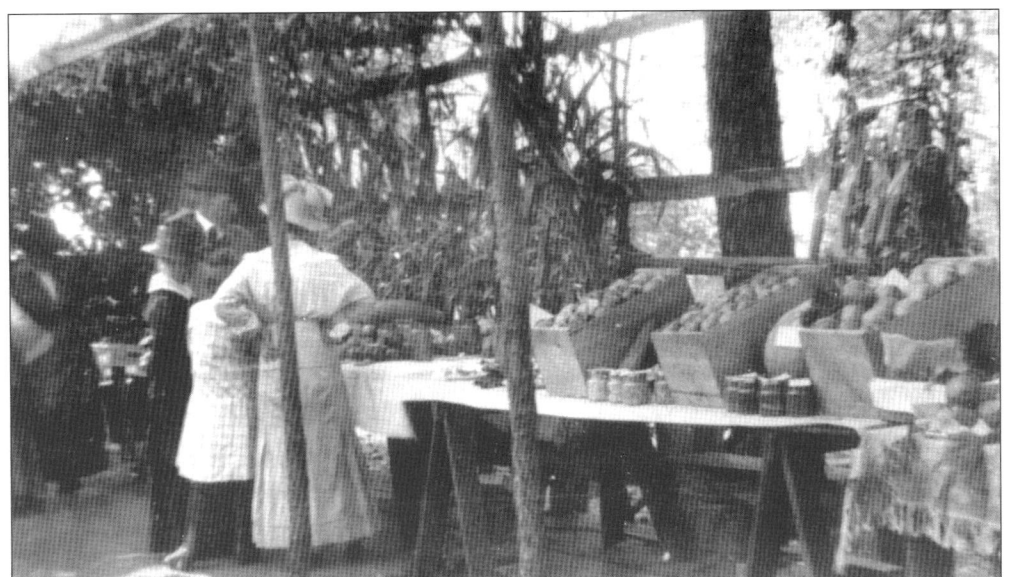

The Paradise Harvest Festivals were held at the Woodman Dance Platform in 1912 and 1913. Above, visitors are inspecting both fresh produce and canned preserves. In those days, "goin' to town" was a special occasion so people got dressed up in their best clothes. Below, people are inspecting apples. Harvest festivals started on the Ridge as early as 1888, in that year to celebrate A. A. Nickerson bringing water via his ditch to the farmers around Clark Road. Nineteen hundred and five saw the first Fruit and Flower Festival, complete with a dinner cooked by local ladies and evening music. Livestock and poultry were added by 1923, and in 1927, the Women's Improvement Club in Paradise made the more-or-less annual fairs their project. Soon the 4-H Club and the Boy Scouts were participating. (Above courtesy Paradise Genealogy Society; below courtesy Lois McDonald.)

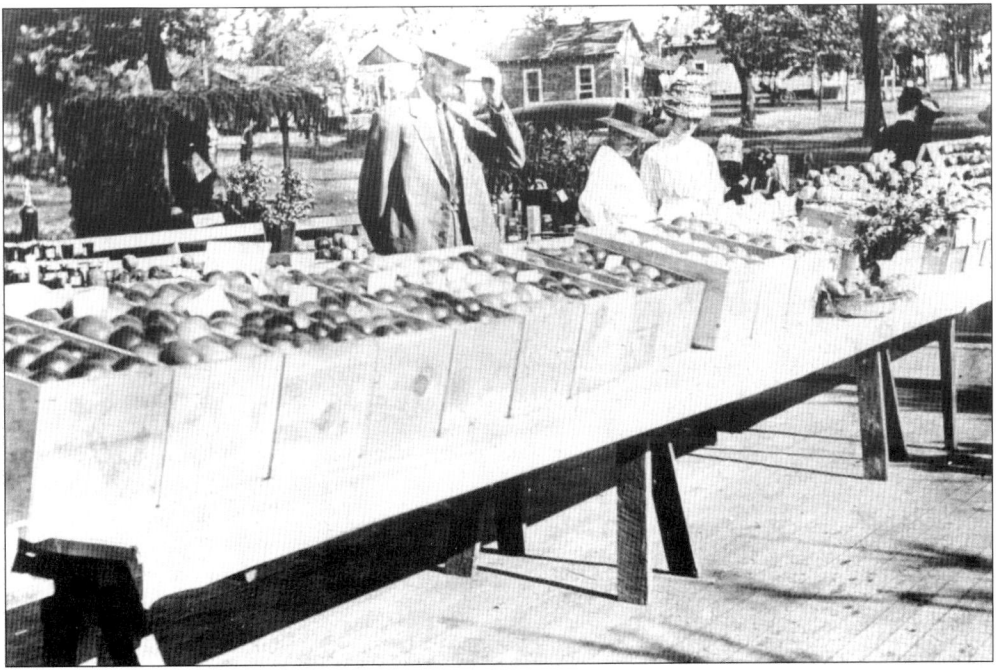

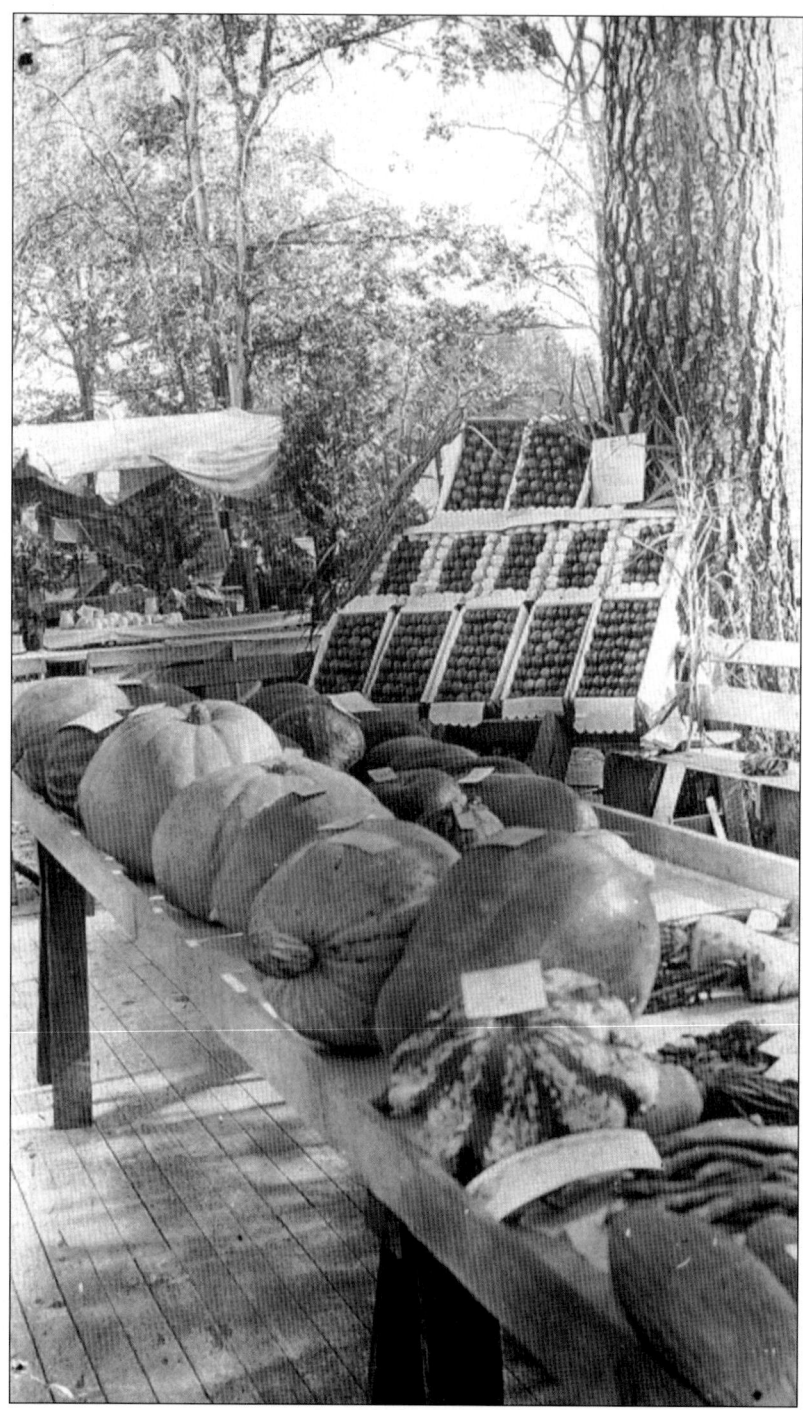

These pumpkins, melons, squash, and crates of apples are displayed at the 1910 or 1912 Harvest Festival. These festivals were precursors of the Johnny Appleseed Days event, which Paradise holds each year. This latter-day festival features home-baked apple pies that remind visitors of bygone years. The apples are grown by the Noble Orchards, the last orchardist on the Ridge. (Courtesy Gold Nugget Museum.)

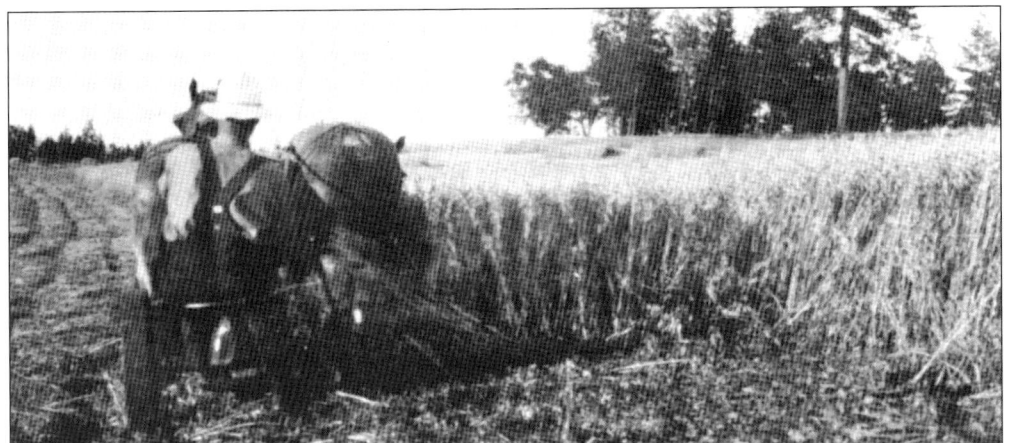

Most of the people who came to Leonard's Mill/Paradise in the late 1800s and early 1900s had been farmers back East. They were impressed by the mild climate and stands of huge trees on the Ridge. Once they cleared their land, vegetables, fruits, and grains grew in abundance. Here a farmer cuts grain on a farm along Neal Road in lower Paradise around 1918. (Courtesy Carl Peterson and Ruby Swartzlow.)

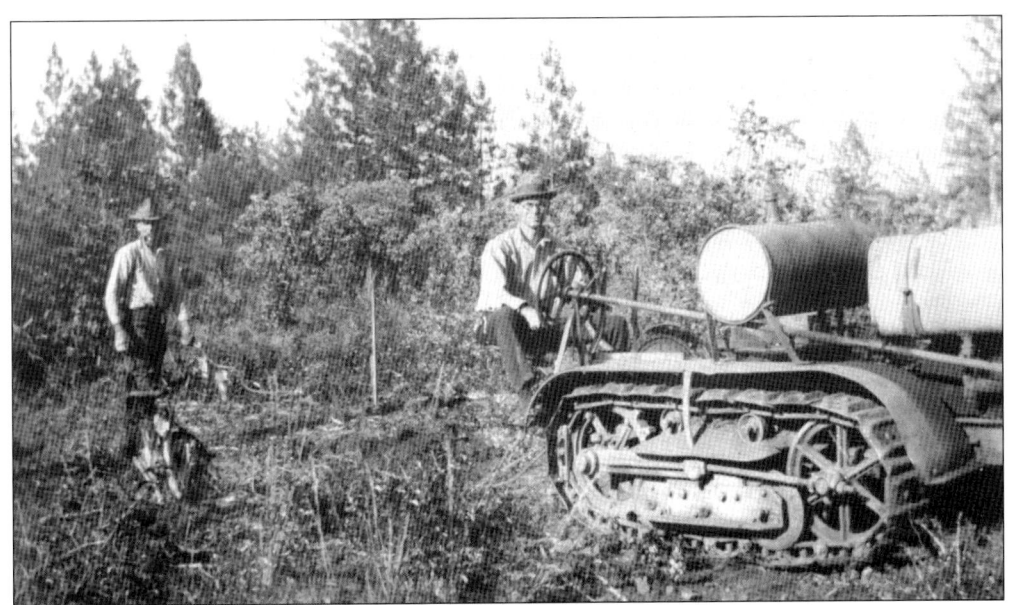

Brothers William and Edward Haffner owned land between Rocky Lane and the railroad tracks up the Ridge from the center of Paradise. In the early 1920s, clearing the land, even with their newly acquired Holt Midget Tractor, was hard, time-consuming work. In this photograph, Edward is on the tractor, and it looks like William is getting ready to loop a cable around a stump. (Courtesy Lois McDonald.)

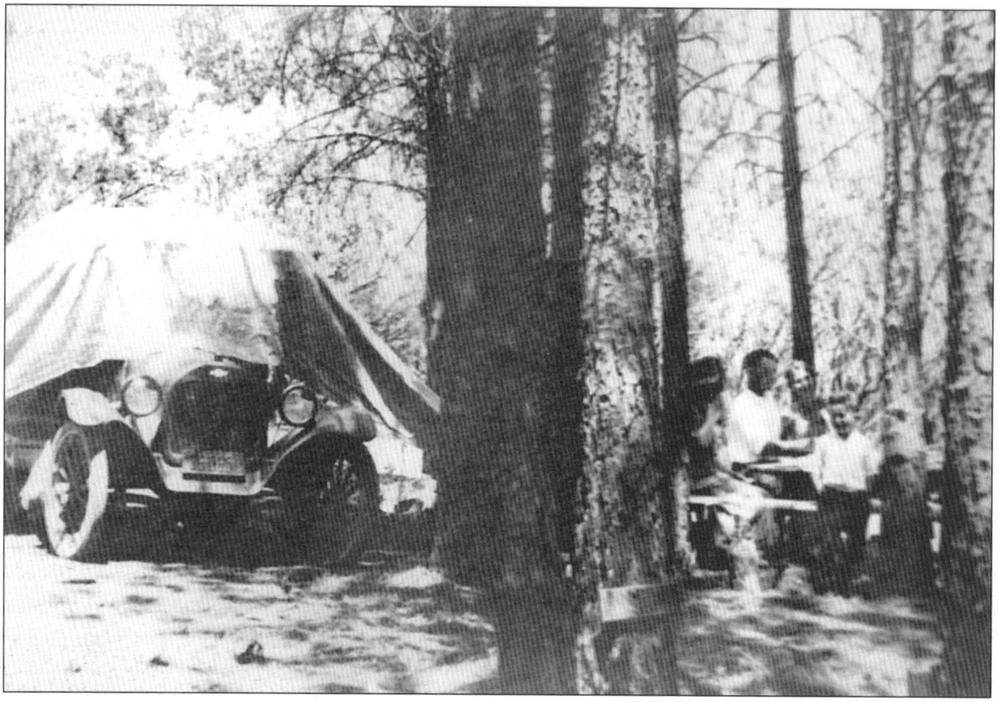

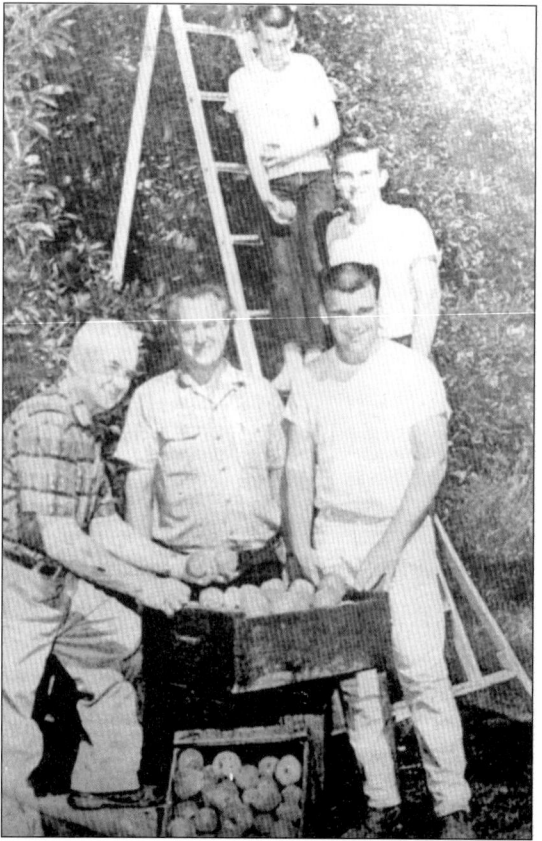

After selling their farm in Turlock, Perry and Ethel Noble and their son Vincent moved to Paradise in 1921. Here the family camps at the Pearson place before buying their 43 acres on Pentz Road. After a hard winter in 1921–1922 killed the apple trees in their orchard, Perry cleared the land by hand and planted new apple and walnut trees and row crops. (Courtesy Gold Nugget Museum.)

Pictured here are three generations of Nobles: Perry Noble (left), his son Vincent (center), and grandsons Jerry (right), James (behind Jerry), and John (on the ladder holding the apple). James "Jim" still operates the family business on Pentz Road, the last of over 50 apple growers on the Ridge. This photograph was used on the farm section cover of the *Sacramento Bee* October 6, 1963, issue. (Courtesy Gold Nugget Museum.)

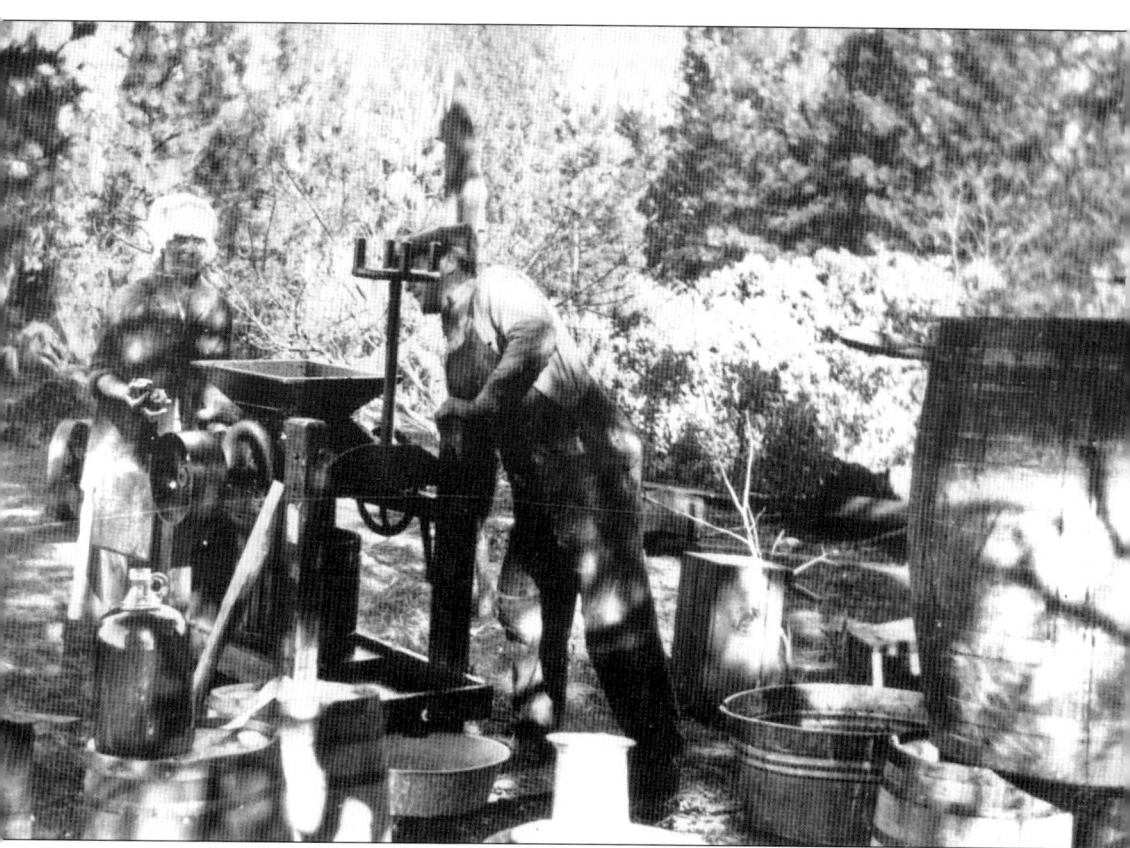

If one was in the apple-growing business on the Ridge, one probably had a press to squeeze apples for cider and juice. In this photograph, Ethel Noble loads apples into the press while Perry Noble squeezes them. They may be making cider for sale at the county fair. After 85 years of growing apples, the Noble Orchard is the last on the Ridge. (Courtesy Gold Nugget Museum.)

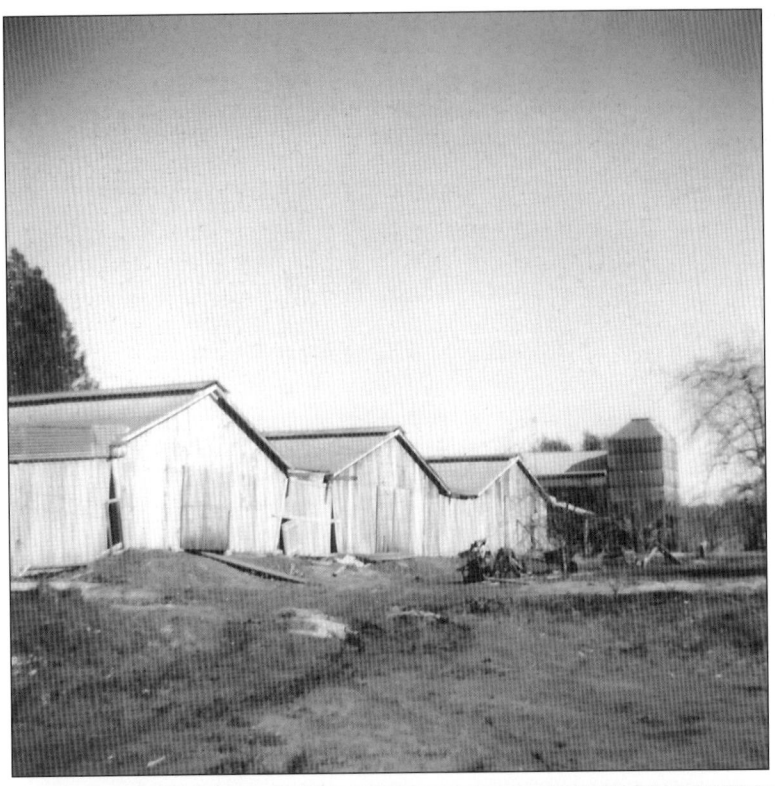

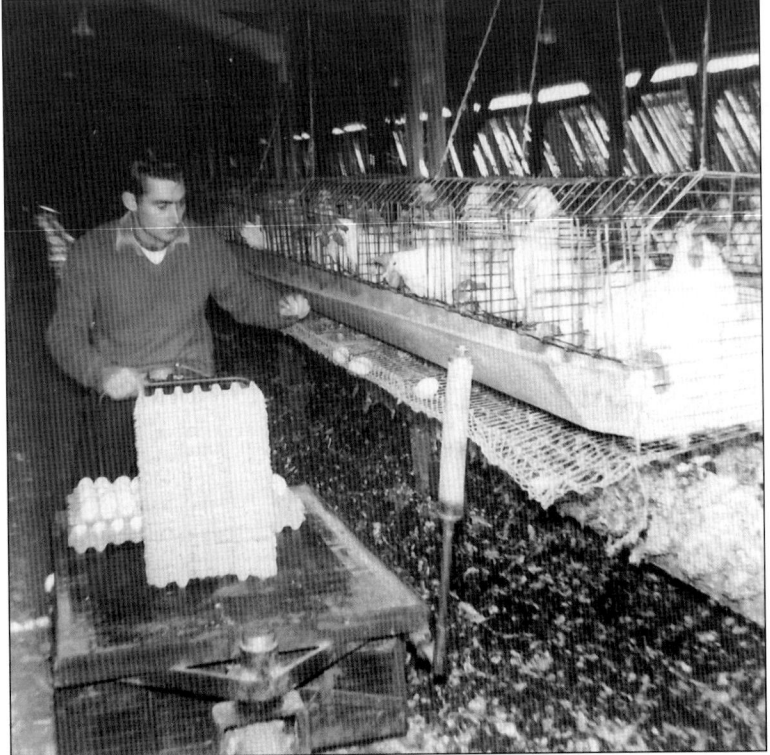

Around 1929, as a sideline to the orchard, Ethel Noble started a commercial poultry business with 500 laying hens. The Depression "killed" the business so Ethel opened a shop in Chico selling chicken pies, which finished off the 500 hens. By 1935, she was back selling chicken meat, and by 1947, she was selling eggs as well. By 1957, she was out of the business, this time for good. In 1948, there were 70 large poultry raisers on the Ridge. The Henry Becker family bought five acres on Sawmill Road and started raising poultry in 1950. The Becker Egg Ranch had 8,000 to 12,000 laying hens that produced 5,000 to 8,000 eggs a day. It closed around 1970 and was the last major poultry-raising business on the Ridge. Above, is the Becker Egg Ranch, and below, Dean Hales gathers eggs. (Courtesy Velma Butler.)

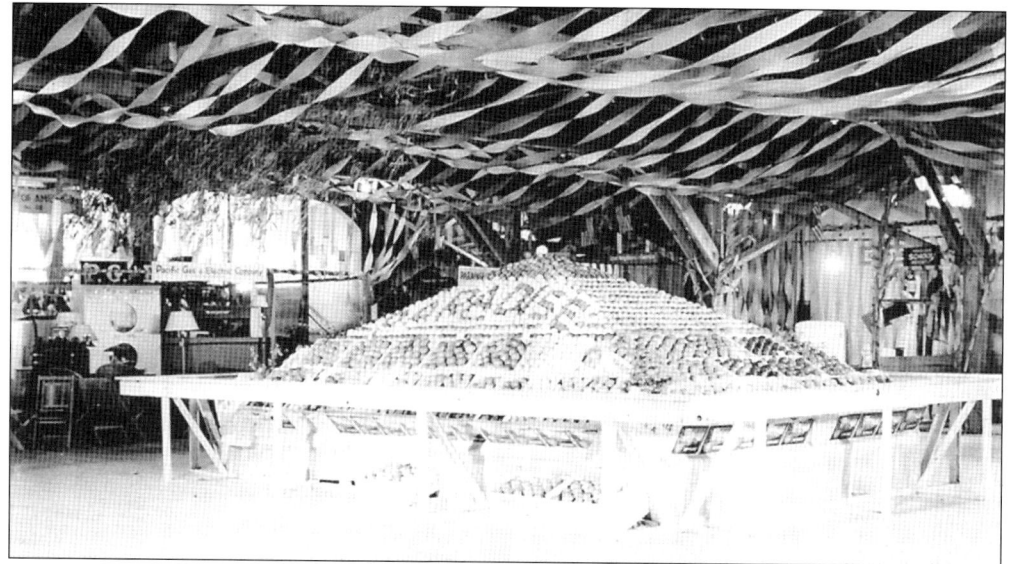

In response to the doldrums of the Great Depression, the first Paradise Fair and Apple Show was held at the Veteran's Memorial Building in October 1937. Many other communities participated, and the fair was a great success. Actor Errol Flynn, star of *The Adventures of Robin Hood*, which was being filmed in Chico's Bidwell Park, made a surprise visit. Above is the Paradise display. In early 1938, the site of the Butte County Fair was undecided, so Paradise bid and won. Farmers and businesses from the entire county participated, and the fair attracted over 8,000 people, including California governor Merriam. The photograph below shows a part of the Paradise exhibit. The Paradise Festival and Apple Show continued until 1956 and were precursors to today's Johnny Appleseed Days festival. (Above courtesy Gold Nugget Museum; below courtesy Lois McDonald.)

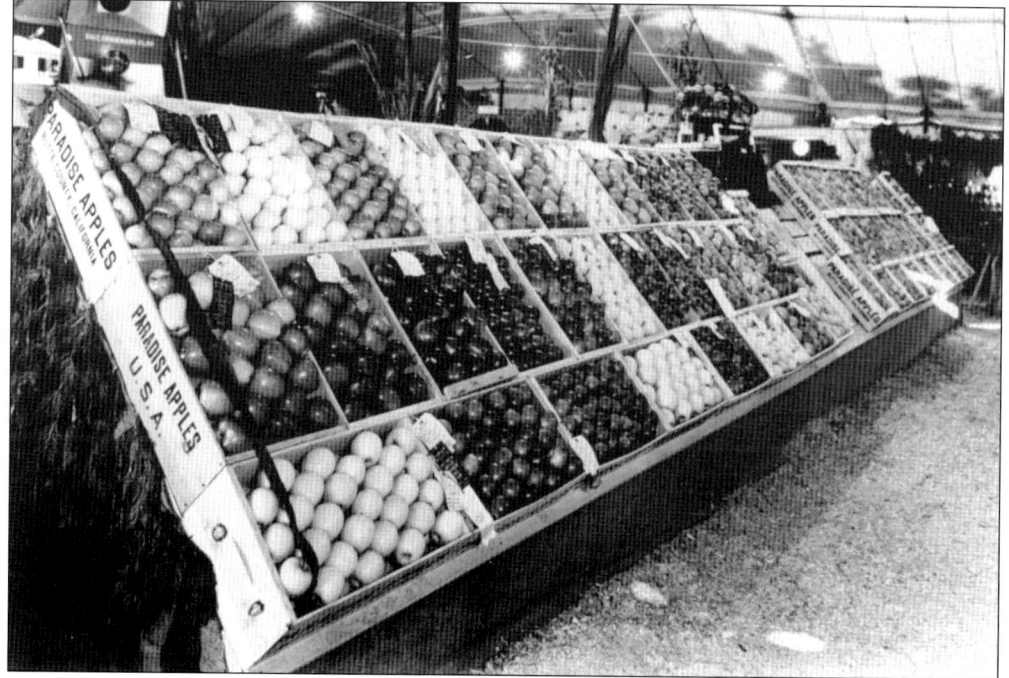

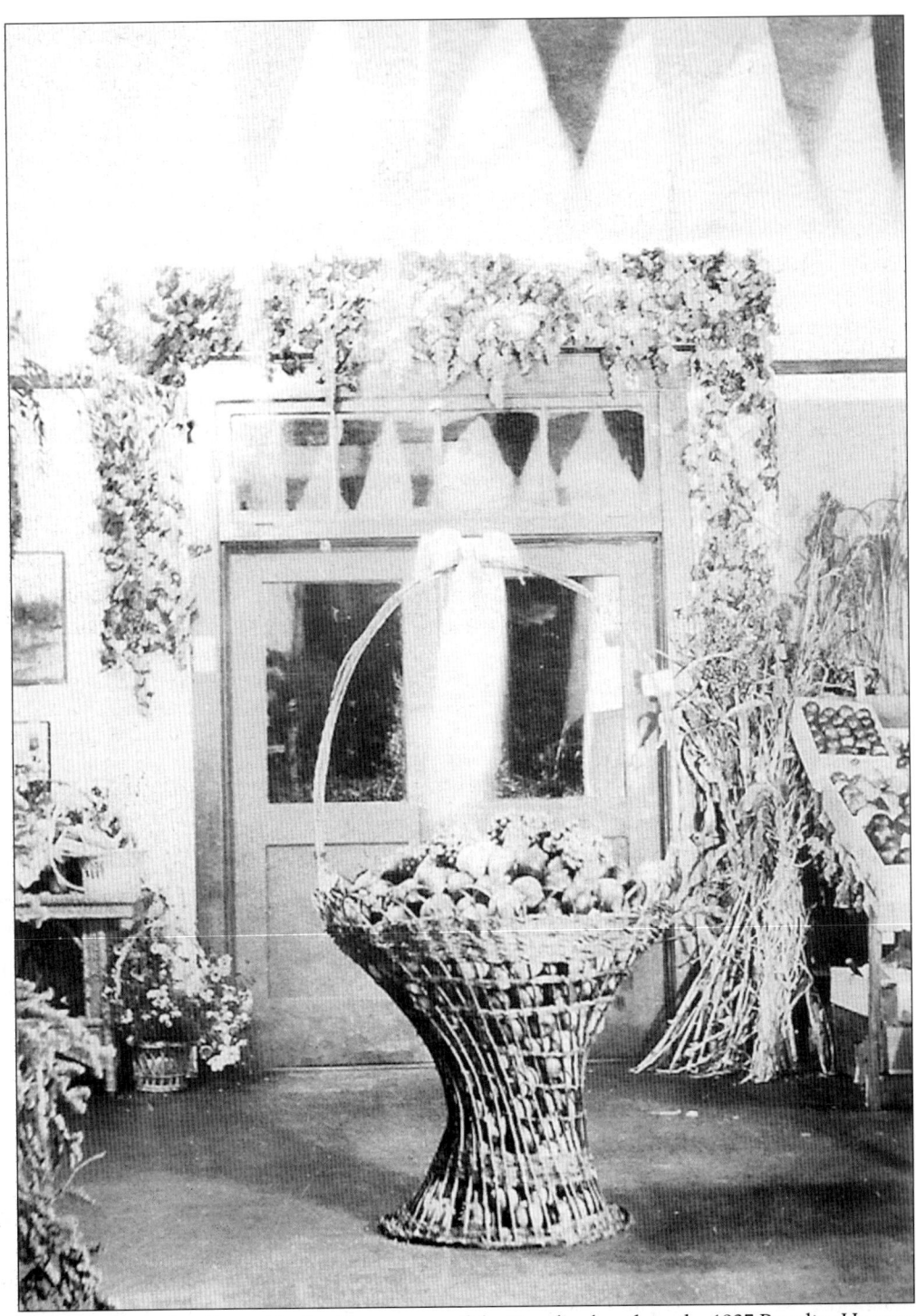

Elsie Hamburger's willow withe basket was part of the Paradise booth in the 1927 Paradise Harvest Festival, the first one sponsored by the Paradise Women's Improvement Club. At the end of the festival, the tall basket, for which she had collected the willow twigs and paid $10 to James Michelson to make, disappeared. She never saw it again. (Courtesy Gold Nugget Museum.)

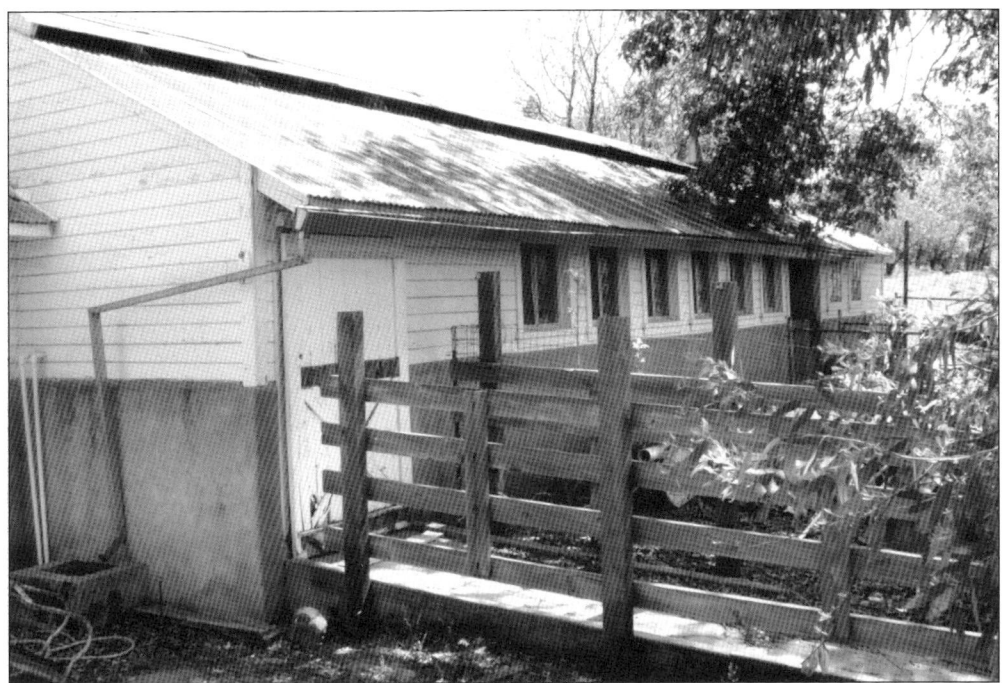

Paradise farms had a cow or two for milk, cream, and butter, and what was not consumed was sold or bartered. The first two real dairies on the Ridge were opened in 1926 by Alderson and in 1929 by Davis. They sold dairy products to grocery stores, restaurants, schools, bars, and retail customers. In 1938, Clyde Griffin bought the Alderson Dairy, seen in this 2005 photograph, and operated it until 1948. (Courtesy author.)

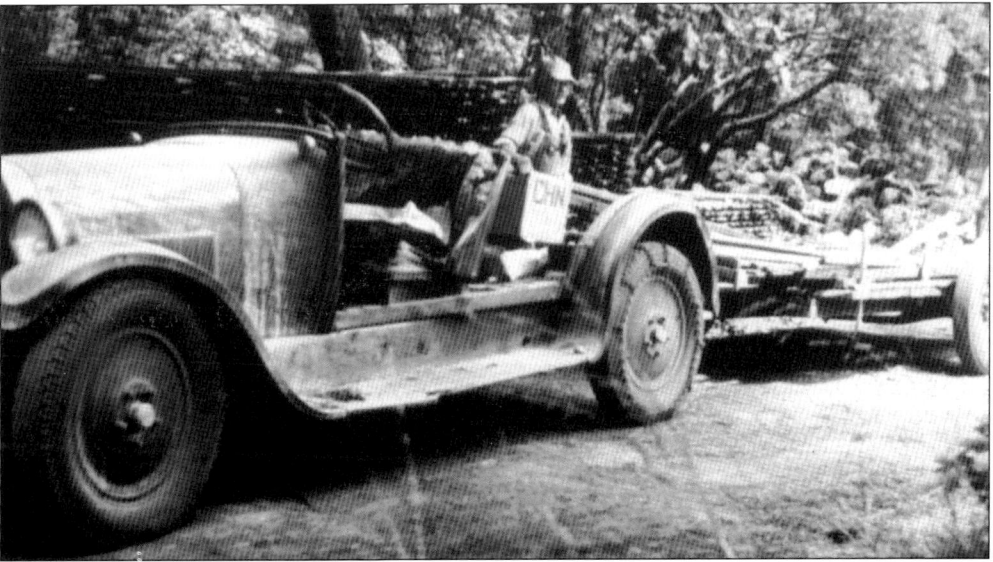

This man is moving irrigation pipe on the Nielsen farm in the 1930s–1940s. In the 1930s, Skinner Lines, lengths of pipe that had spray nozzles 3 feet apart and would spray about 25 feet, were introduced to Paradise farmers. With 50-foot spacing, the farmer created "natural" rain on his crops. Note the chains on the rear tires to help traverse muddy fields. (Courtesy Gold Nugget Museum.)

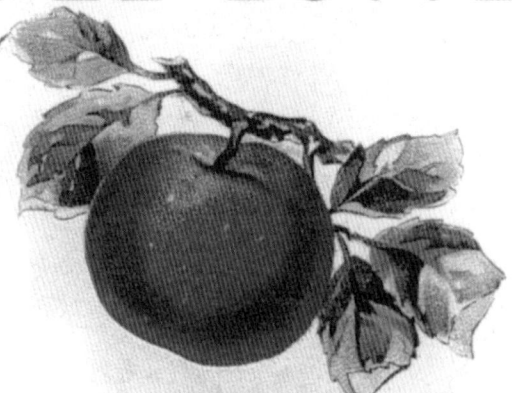

This very colorful label was on apple butter bottles until the late 1930s when the apple-processing partnership of Carl Heinke and W. I. Weast broke up. In 1927, Weast sold his grocery store and gas station at Clark and Elliott Roads to Jim Thomas. Weast also owned Pine Rest Cabins on Bille Road just to the west of Pentz Road. (Courtesy John and Jean Heinke.)

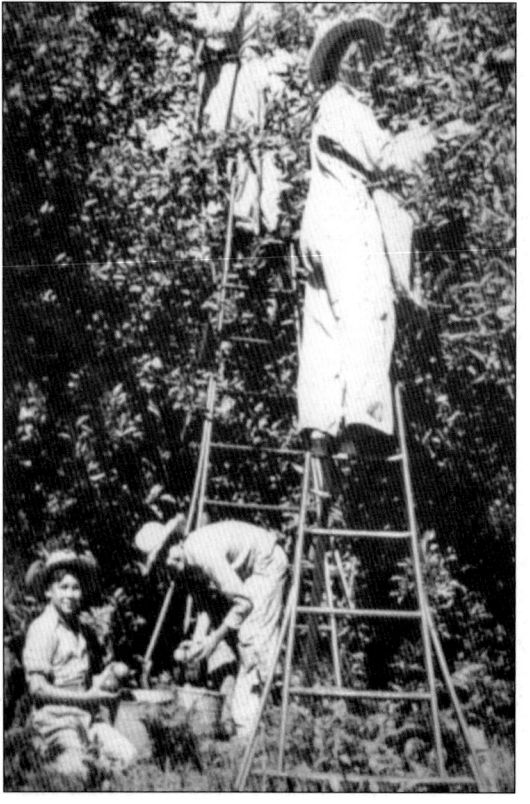

These women are picking Paradise apples in 1945. Ultimately there were over 50 orchards on the Ridge. (Courtesy Gold Nugget Museum.)

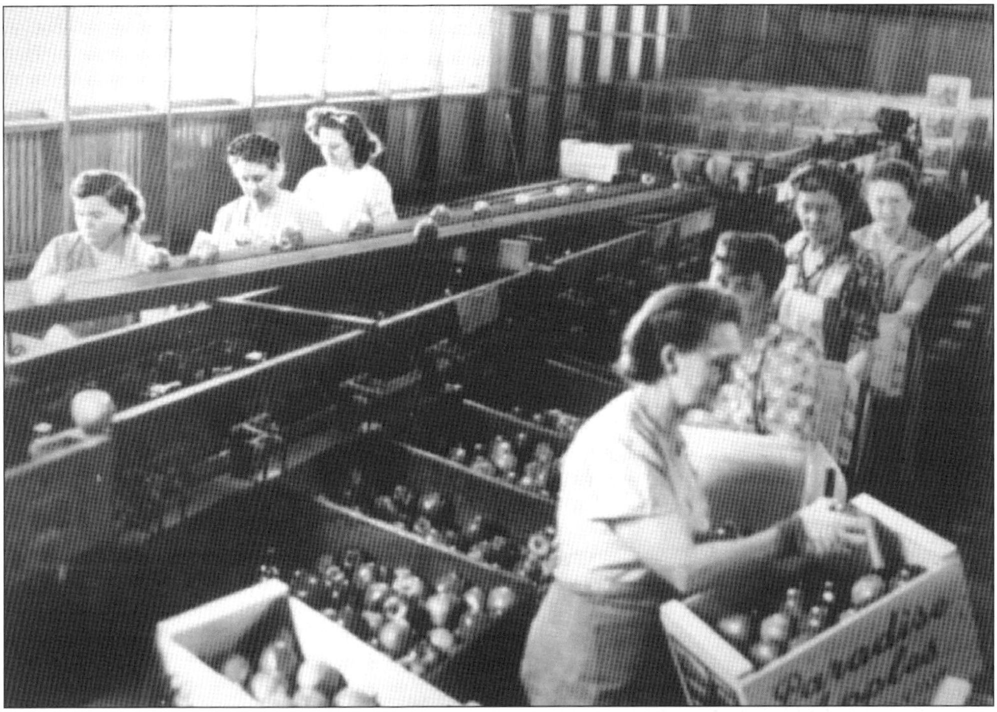

These women are separating apples at the sorting table in the Nielsen Packing Shed, located at Elliott and Sawmill Roads. The woman in the right foreground is packing a box, which appears to have a Sawmill Peak Brand label. (Courtesy Gold Nugget Museum.)

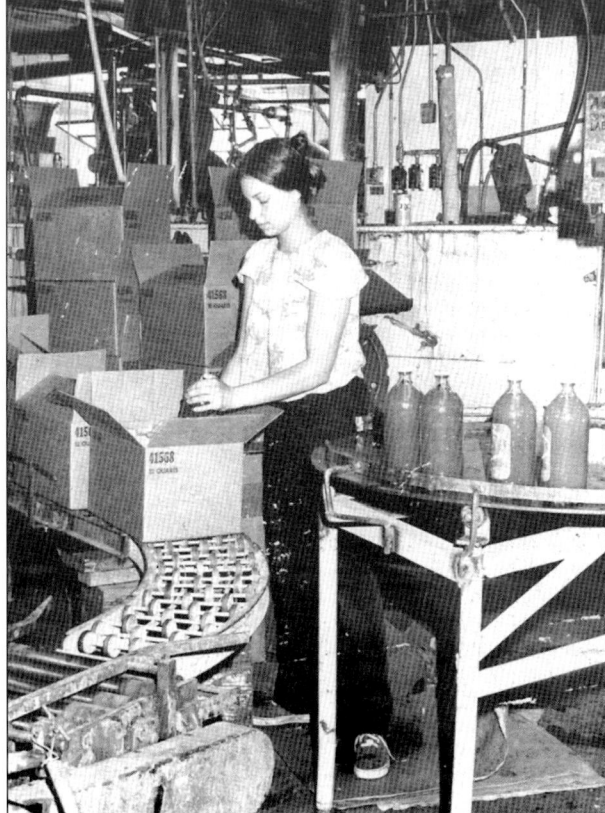

This young woman is packing cartons with bottles of apple juice in the Heinke Bottling Plant on Lower Clark Road in the 1970s. By this time, the Heinkes did not raise apples anymore, instead buying them from other orchards on the Ridge. (Courtesy Gold Nugget Museum.)

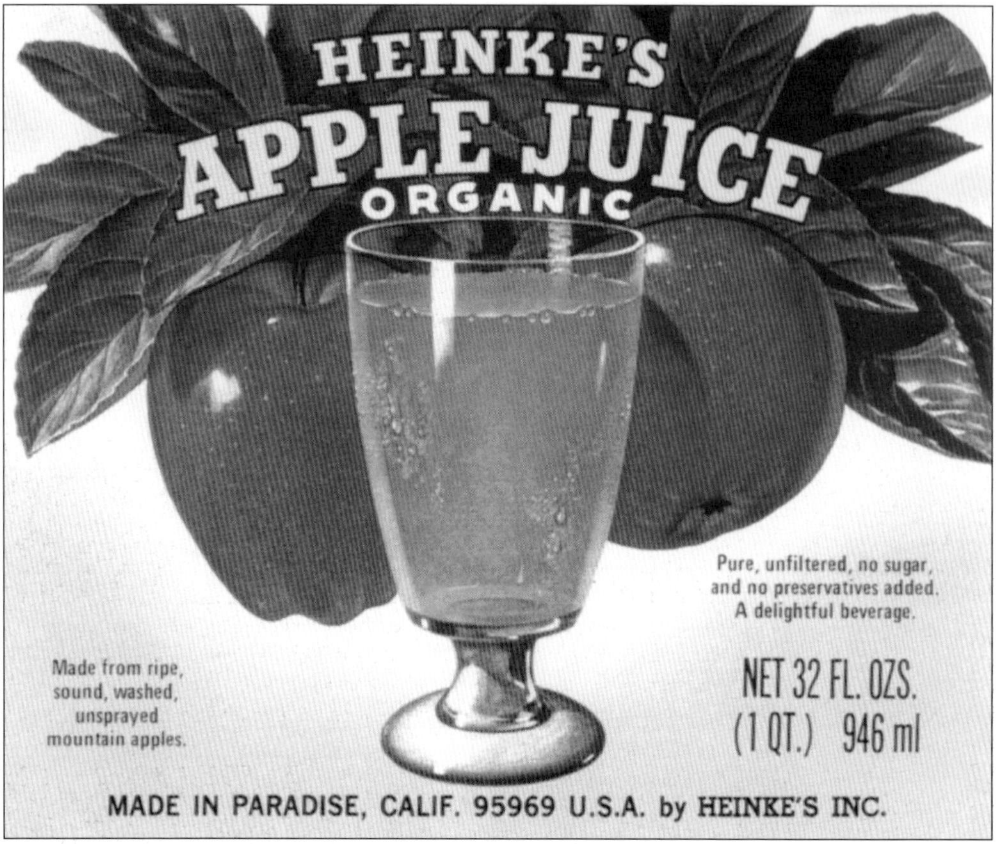

HEINKE'S APPLE JUICE ORGANIC

Pure, unfiltered, no sugar, and no preservatives added. A delightful beverage.

Made from ripe, sound, washed, unsprayed mountain apples.

NET 32 FL. OZS. (1 QT.) 946 ml

MADE IN PARADISE, CALIF. 95969 U.S.A. by HEINKE'S INC.

Although this black-and-white photograph does not do it justice, this very colorful label was used on Heinke apple juice that was bottled and marketed until 1988. Their apple orchard was small, so the majority of the apples that they pressed into juice were bought from other orchards. (Courtesy John and Jean Heinke.)

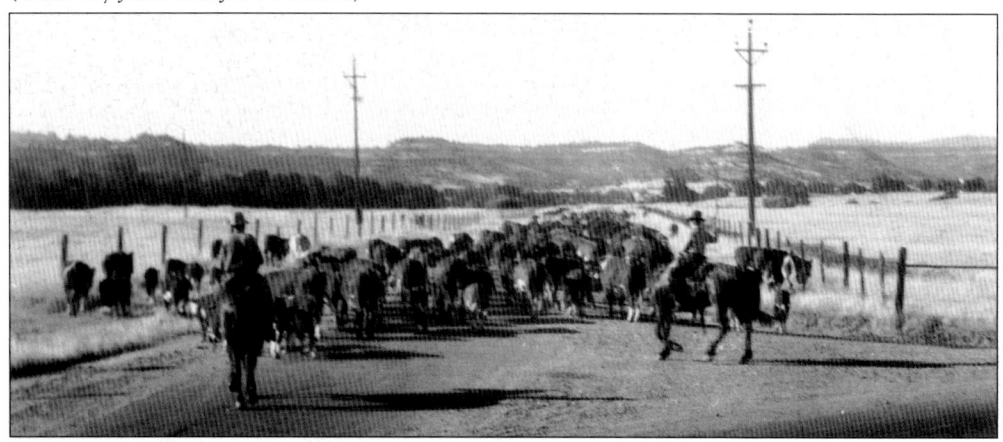

Since Sam Neal's day, valley cattlemen drove their cattle into the mountains to summer pasture and back for the winter. By the 1930s, Victor Van Gooden was driving his herd to Secret Creek. They went up Clark Road through Paradise, Magalia, and Powellton to Inskip. Here, at Clark and Durham-Pentz Roads, Victor is on the left and his son Ed is "cracking a whip" on the right. (Courtesy June Van Gooden.)

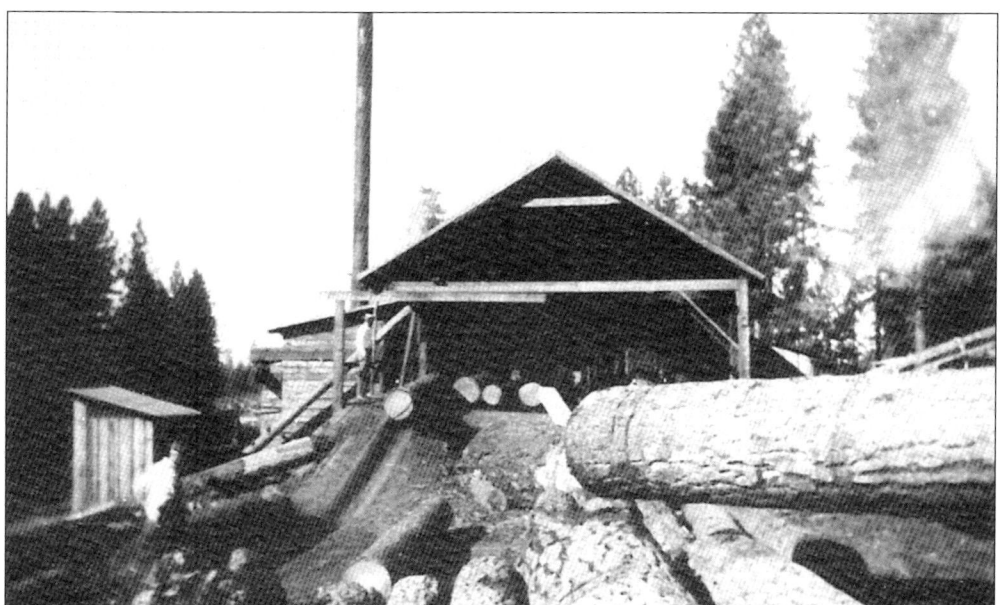

Timber was the first agricultural product harvested on the Ridge. Durville Bequette, a storekeeper at Nelson Bar, apparently erected the first sawmill in Tait Ravine, east of today's Pentz Road. Of the numerous sawmills since then, William Leonard's is best known. This is the Crego Sawmill log deck (where logs waiting to be sawed are stored). On the left, a log has moved up the slipway into the mill. (Courtesy Gold Nugget Museum.)

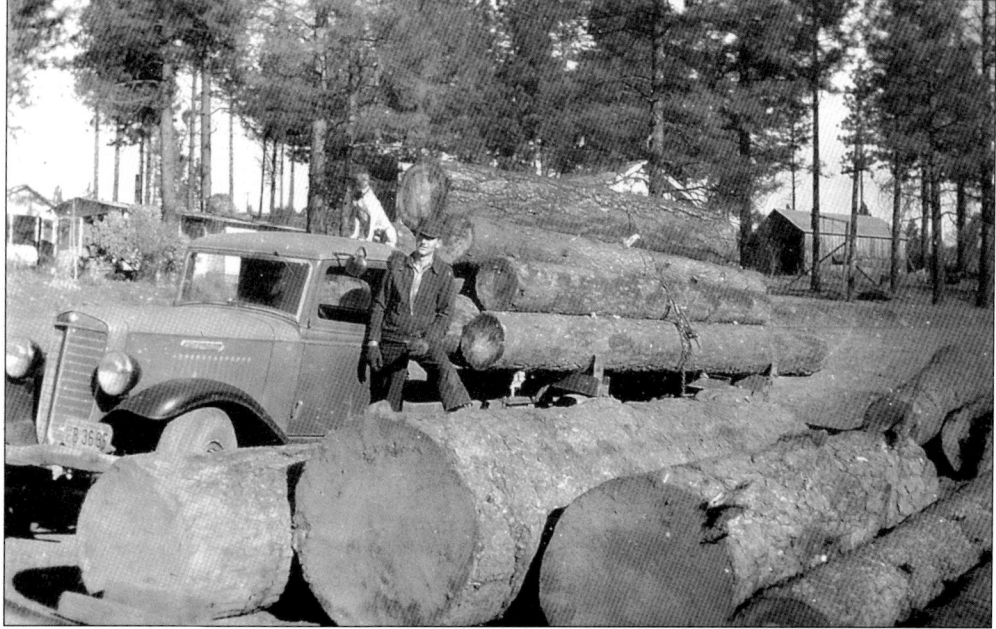

The Crego sawmill was on the Southern Pacific spur track between Neal and Pentz Roads at the north end of Paradise. Originally the Crowfoot Sawmill, it was bought by William J. Crego and Amos J. Lown in 1933. It burned in 1942. This photograph of Dan Hartley and his dog waiting for his truck to be unloaded was taken from the log deck of the Crego Sawmill. (Courtesy Pat Brice.)

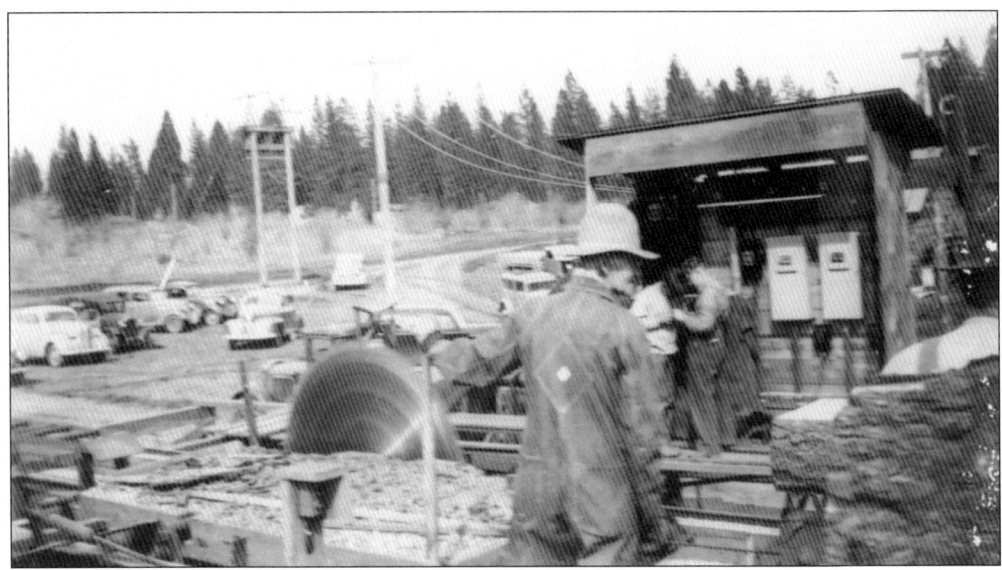

In 1946, I. T. "Pat" Becker built a sawmill on Pentz Road where Ponderosa School is today. Ahead of its time, his sawmill was electrically powered. Here George Smith, the sawyer, watches the log being carried into the saw. Becker sold the sawmill to the Richter brothers, who operated it until 1955 when it closed, a victim of too many houses being built around it. (Courtesy Pat Berry.)

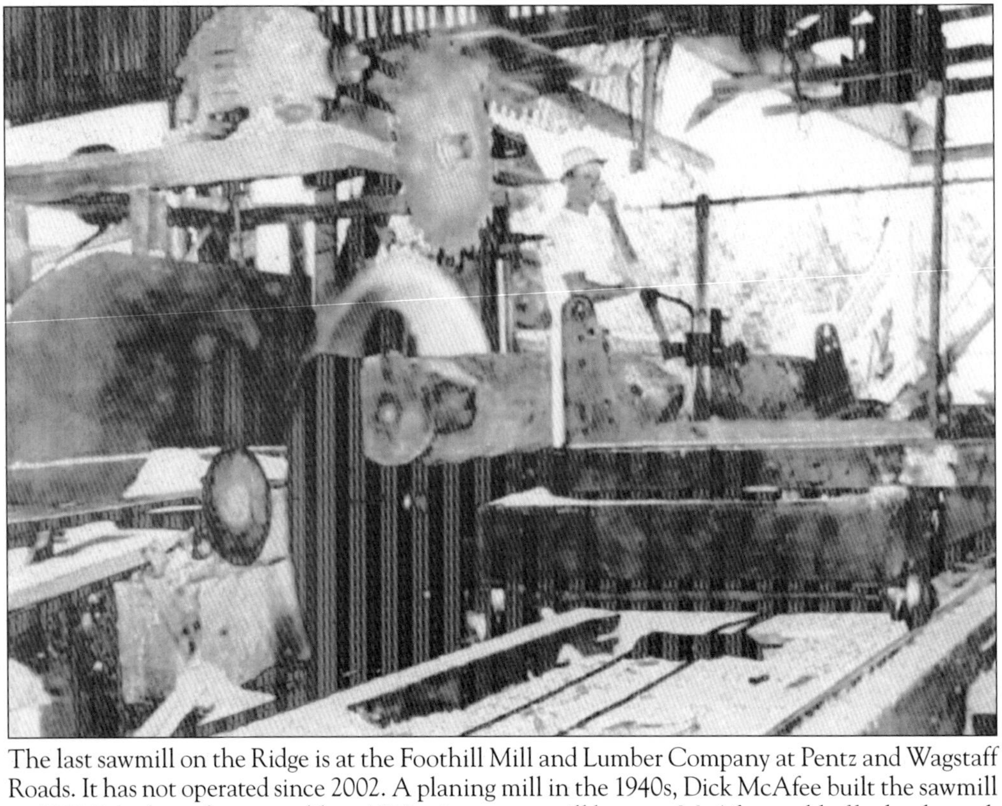

The last sawmill on the Ridge is at the Foothill Mill and Lumber Company at Pentz and Wagstaff Roads. It has not operated since 2002. A planing mill in the 1940s, Dick McAfee built the sawmill in 1963. It looks and operates like a 1930s vintage sawmill because McAfee could afford only used, obsolete parts. McAfee is the sawyer pictured here as the log is cut. (Courtesy *Paradise Post*.)

Five
WATER AND POWER

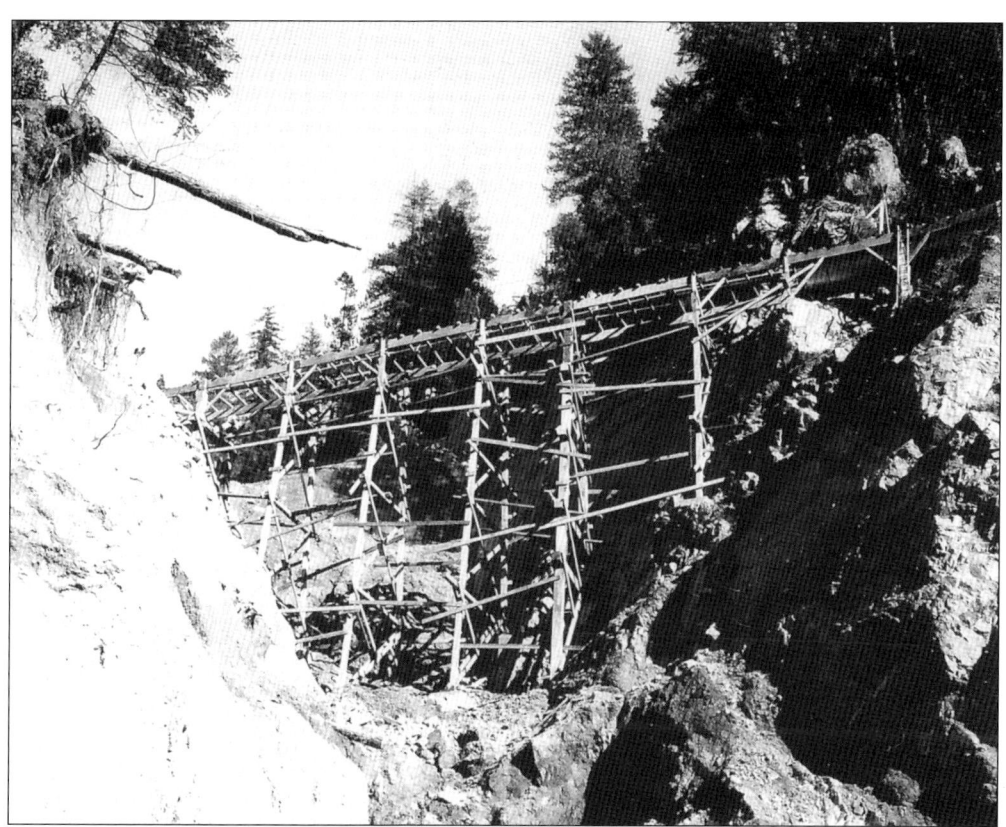

This 1964 view of the Butte Canal illustrates the difficulty of building a ditch and flume system through mountain country. This canal brought water from Butte Creek, first for mining and later for irrigation and hydroelectric power generation. Ditches and flumes took ingenuity to build and required constant maintenance by ditch tenders who watched for leaks. (Courtesy Ruby Swartzlow and Lois McDonald.)

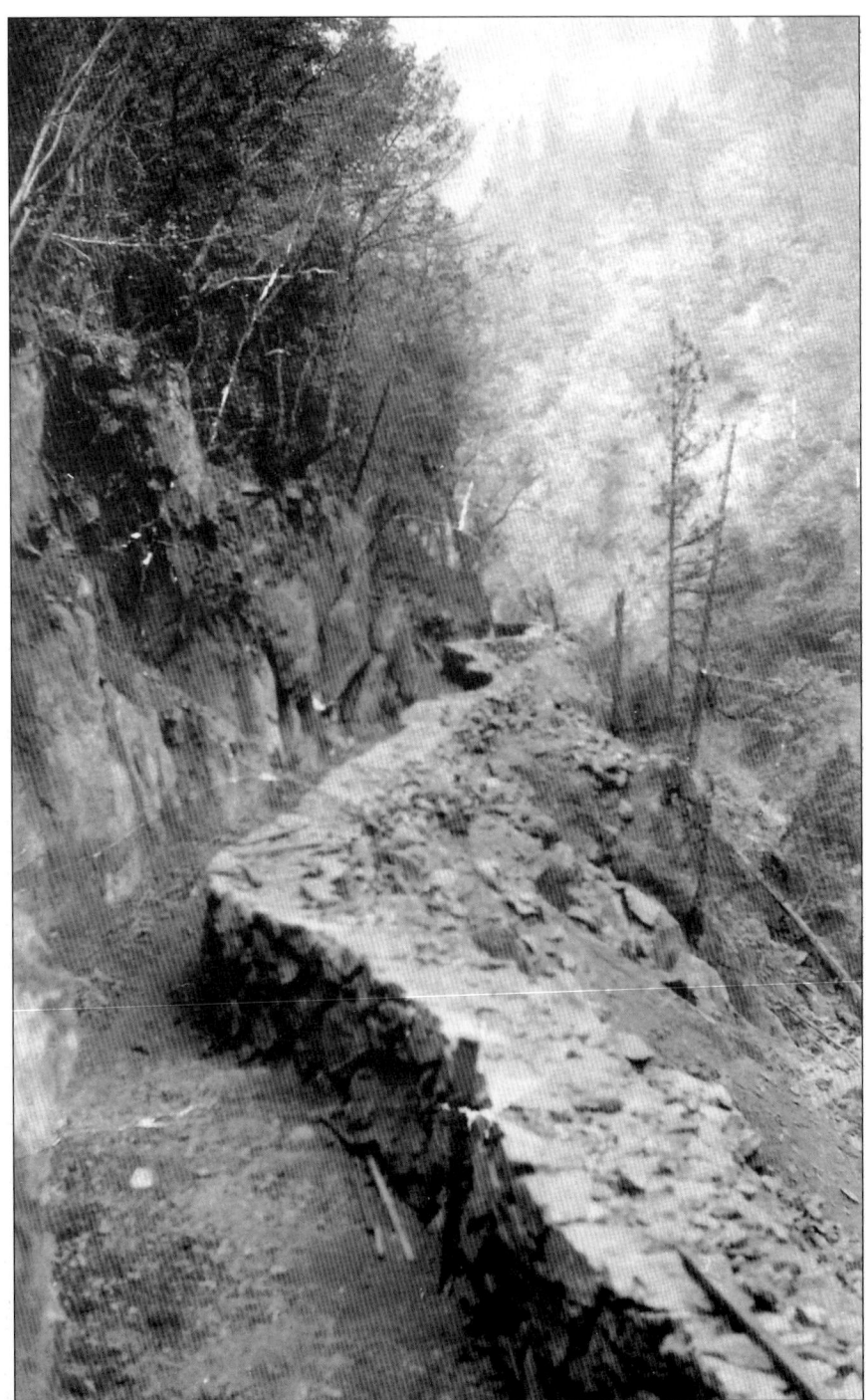
Ditch making was an art, as is indicated in this photograph. Initially ditches brought water to mines and later to foothill and valley communities and hydroelectric powerhouses for electricity. This is the 1873 Hendricks Ditch, which conveyed water from the West Branch down the east side of the Ridge to Table Mountain. Ridge farmers certainly "hi-graded" water from the ditch for their crops. (Courtesy Lois McDonald.)

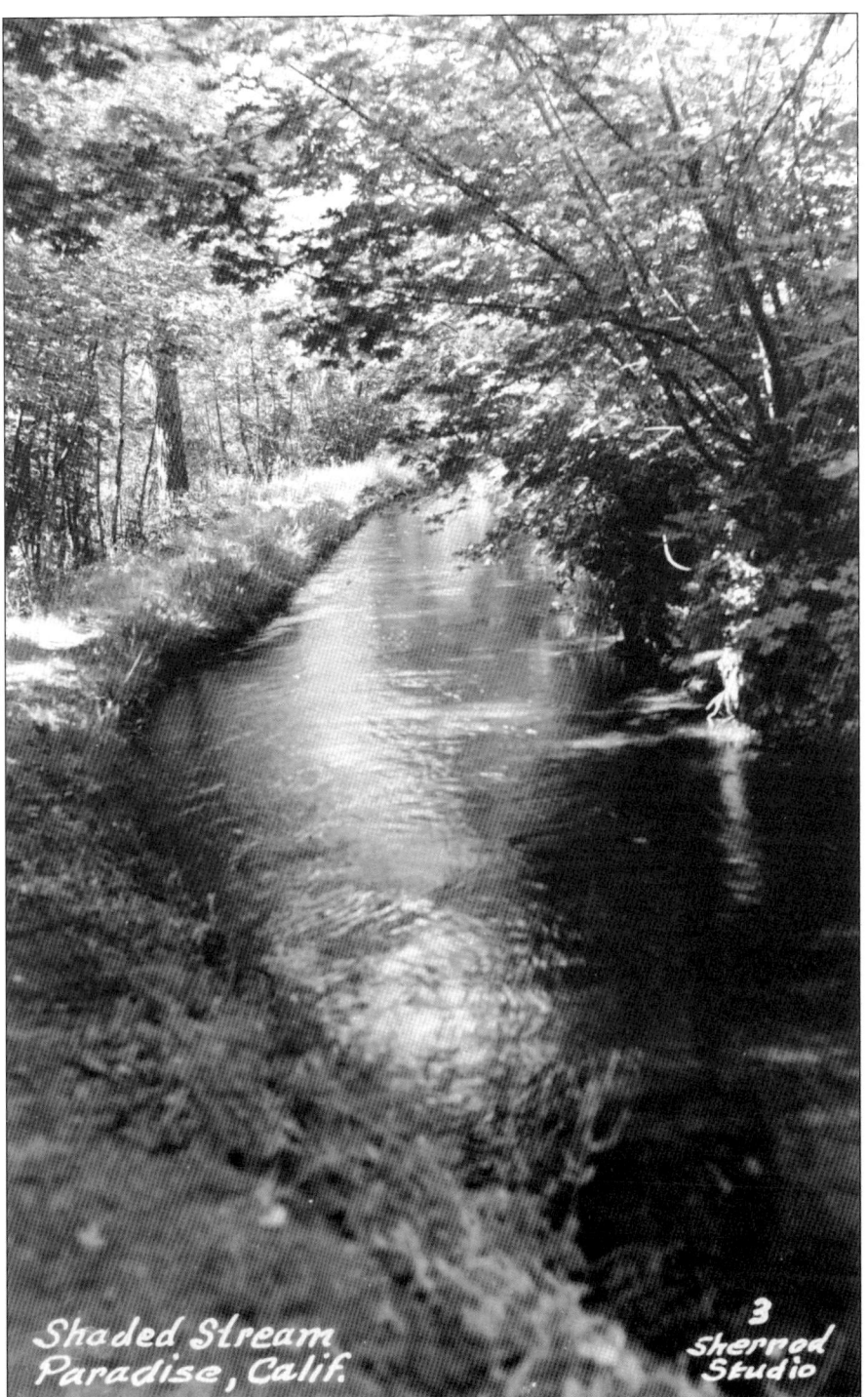

Shaded it may be, but stream it is not. This is a PID ditch carrying water from the Magalia Reservoir. It may have been part of the old Nickerson Ditch that PID used before installing a pipe to bring water from the reservoir to the Ridge for irrigation use. The back of the photograph is marked 1934. (Courtesy Audrey Youngs and Lois McDonald.)

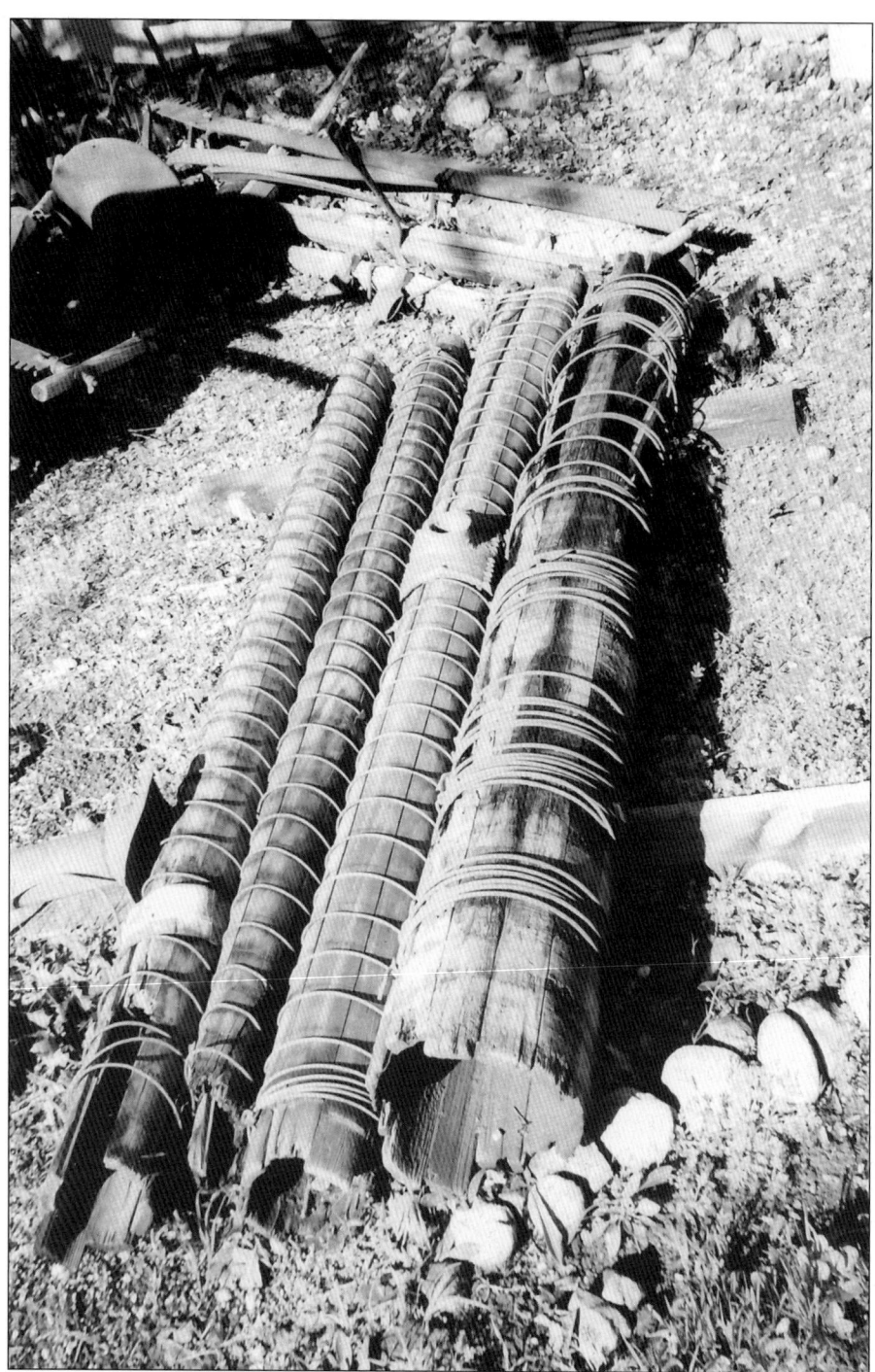

From the beginning, leaks in the PID water system were a problem. Because of steel shortages in World War I, pipes made of redwood staves bound with steel wire were used. With 2,966 leaks in 1944, PID started replacing the pipes, but quality steel pipe was unavailable because of World War II. Even today, much of PID's budget goes to replacing the inferior World War II steel pipe. (Courtesy author.)

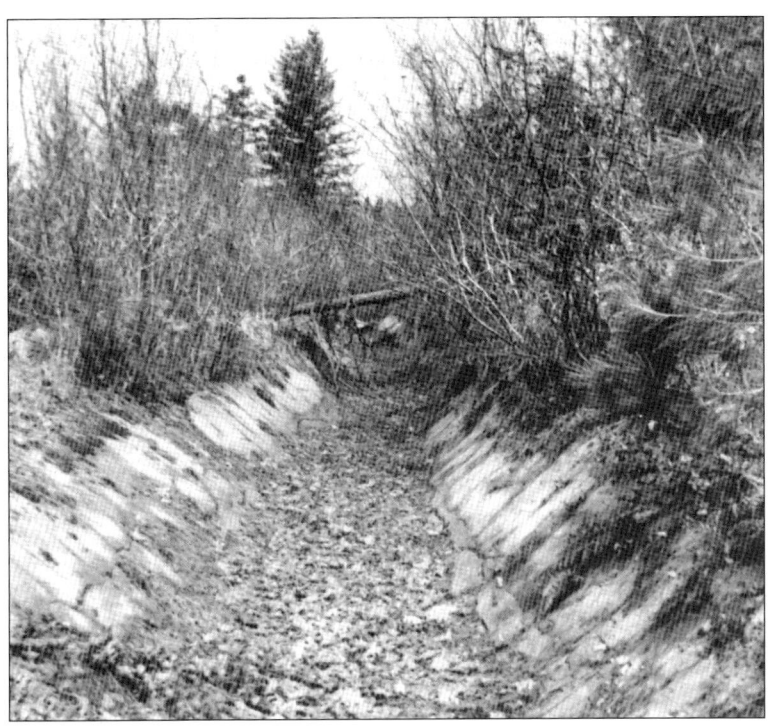

This is the old Nickerson Ditch above Optimo, not used since 1964. Dug in 1864 by Charles Delaplain, it brought Little Butte Creek water to Old Paradise for irrigation. A. A. Nickerson purchased it in 1888, refurbished it, and sold water to farmers along Clark Road. In 1939–1940, PID used the part of the ditch west of Neal Road to bring water from Magalia Reservoir to farmers in Paradise. (Courtesy Lois McDonald.)

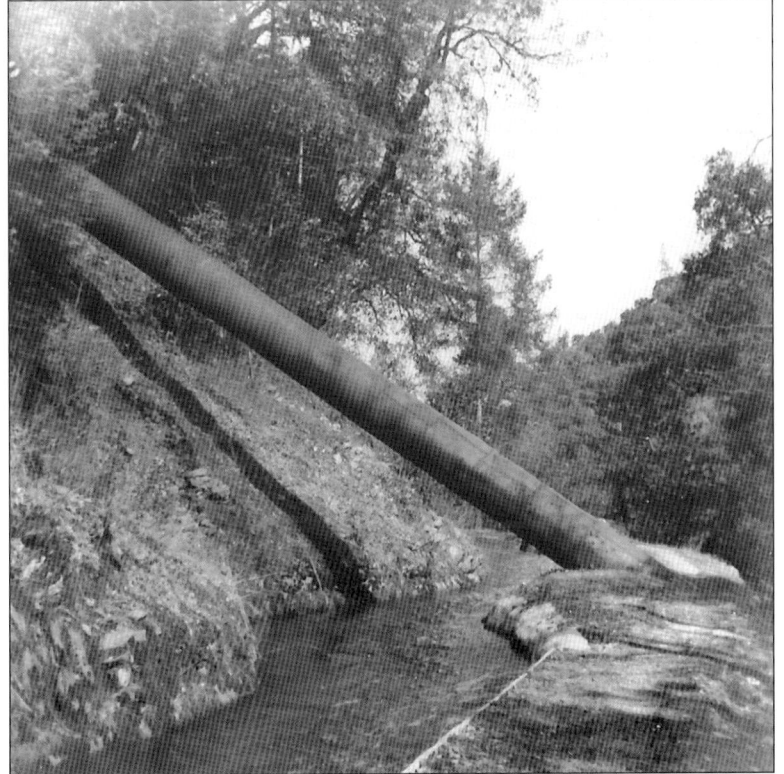

The Cherokee Siphon was part of a system that carried water from the High Sierra, across the Ridge to the Spring Valley Reservoir, and on to the Cherokee hydraulic mine. It spanned the 900-foot-deep West Branch canyon below Paradise with an inverted siphon. Made of riveted iron pipe three feet in diameter, this section, now 131 years old, is still in position crossing the Miocene Canal. (Courtesy Velma Butler.)

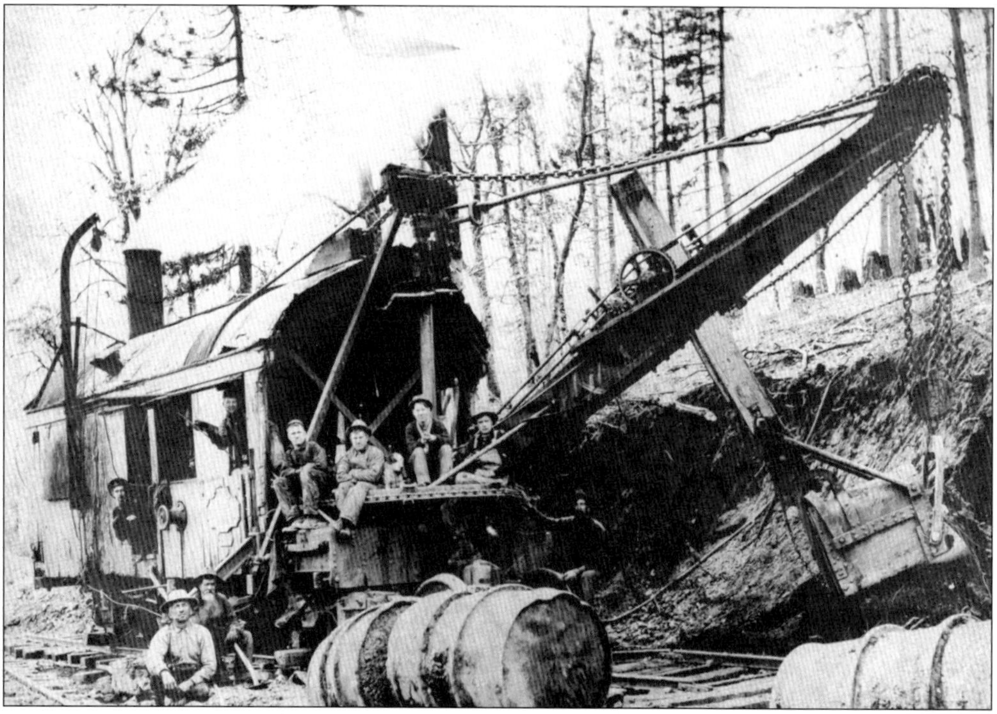

This steam shovel, pictured here in the summer of 1904, is digging a trench in which to install an inverted siphon under the Butte County Railroad tracks above Wagstaff Road and Rocky Lane. The siphon was needed to be able to carry water in the Nickerson Ditch to farms and ranches on the Ridge. George Bille's uncle Lee Smyth is sitting to the left of the four men. (Courtesy George Bille.)

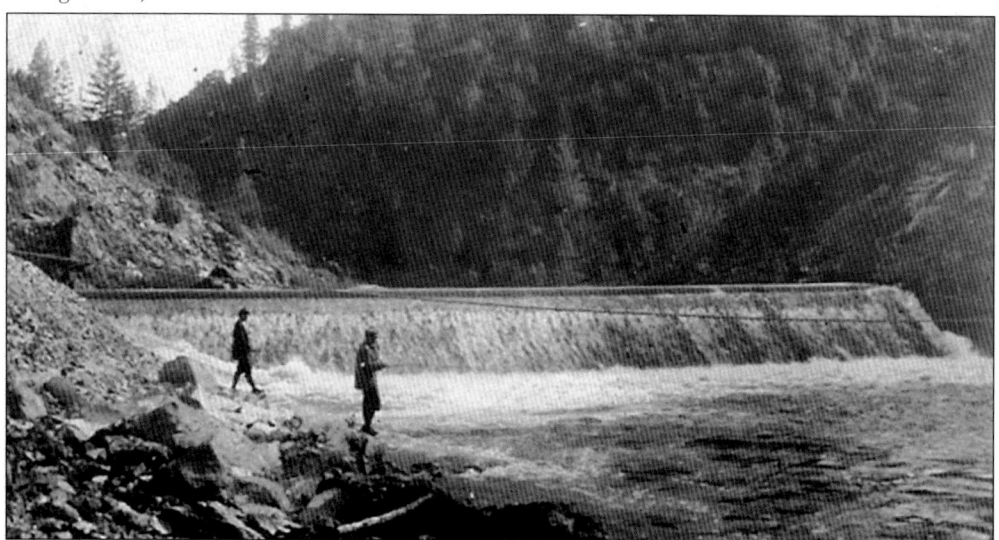

A favorite pastime of Paradisians, Chas and Owen fish below the Oroville Water Light and Power Company Dam on the West Branch below Magalia. Built in 1875, it diverted water for hydraulic mining into the Miocene Canal, which ran along the canyon wall below Paradise to Thompson Flat near Oroville. When hydraulic mining was outlawed, the water was used for irrigation and later for hydroelctric power generation. (Courtesy Gold Nugget Museum.)

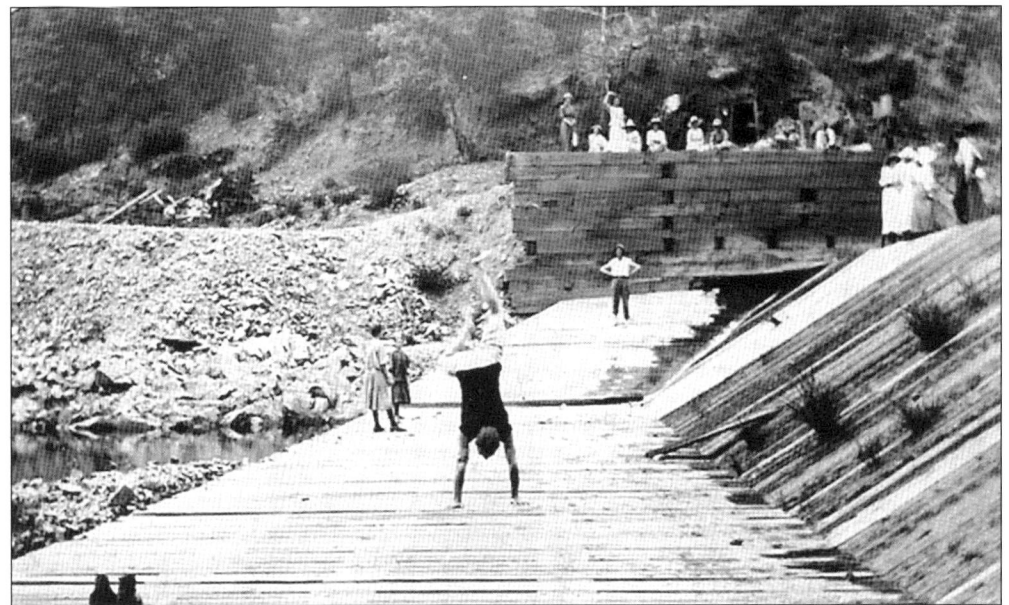

At any age, boys will be boys, showing off for the ladies on the Miocene Canal Diversion Dam in an unusually dry year before 1909. The dam was a favorite weekend spot, only a short, strenuous walk down from the Ridge. In 1909, every dam and bridge on the West Branch, including this one, was swept away when the original Philbrook dam failed. It was later replaced. (Courtesy Gold Nugget Museum.)

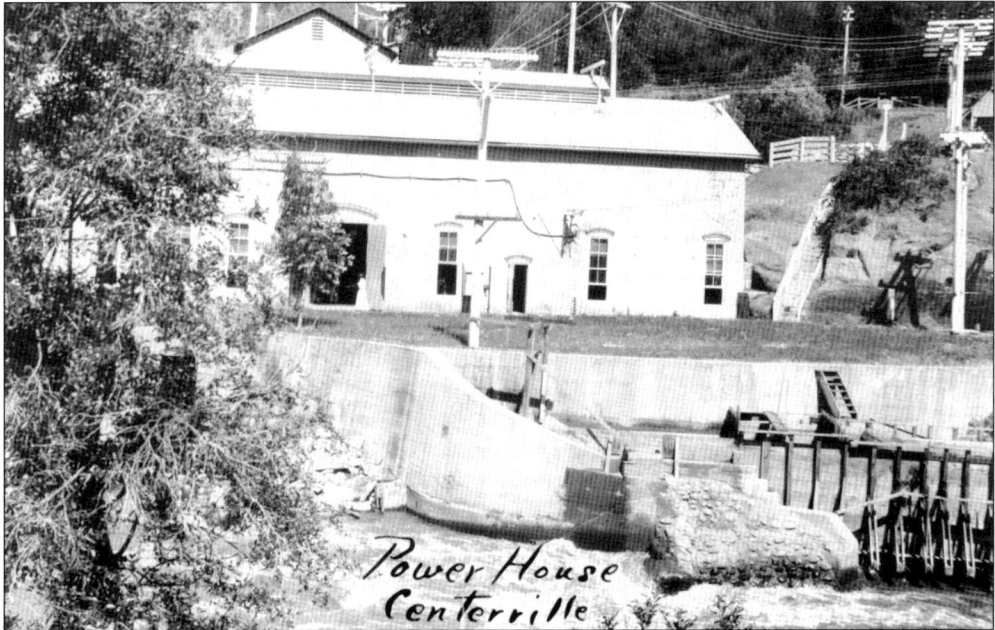

In 1900, the Butte County Electric Power and Light Company built the Centerville hydroelectric powerhouse on Butte Creek to supply electricity to local towns. However, power lines were not extended to Paradise until 1916. This early 1900s photograph shows the powerhouse with Butte Creek in the foreground. Today Centerville, operated by PG&E since 1905, is the oldest operating powerhouse in California. (Courtesy Paradise Genealogy Society.)

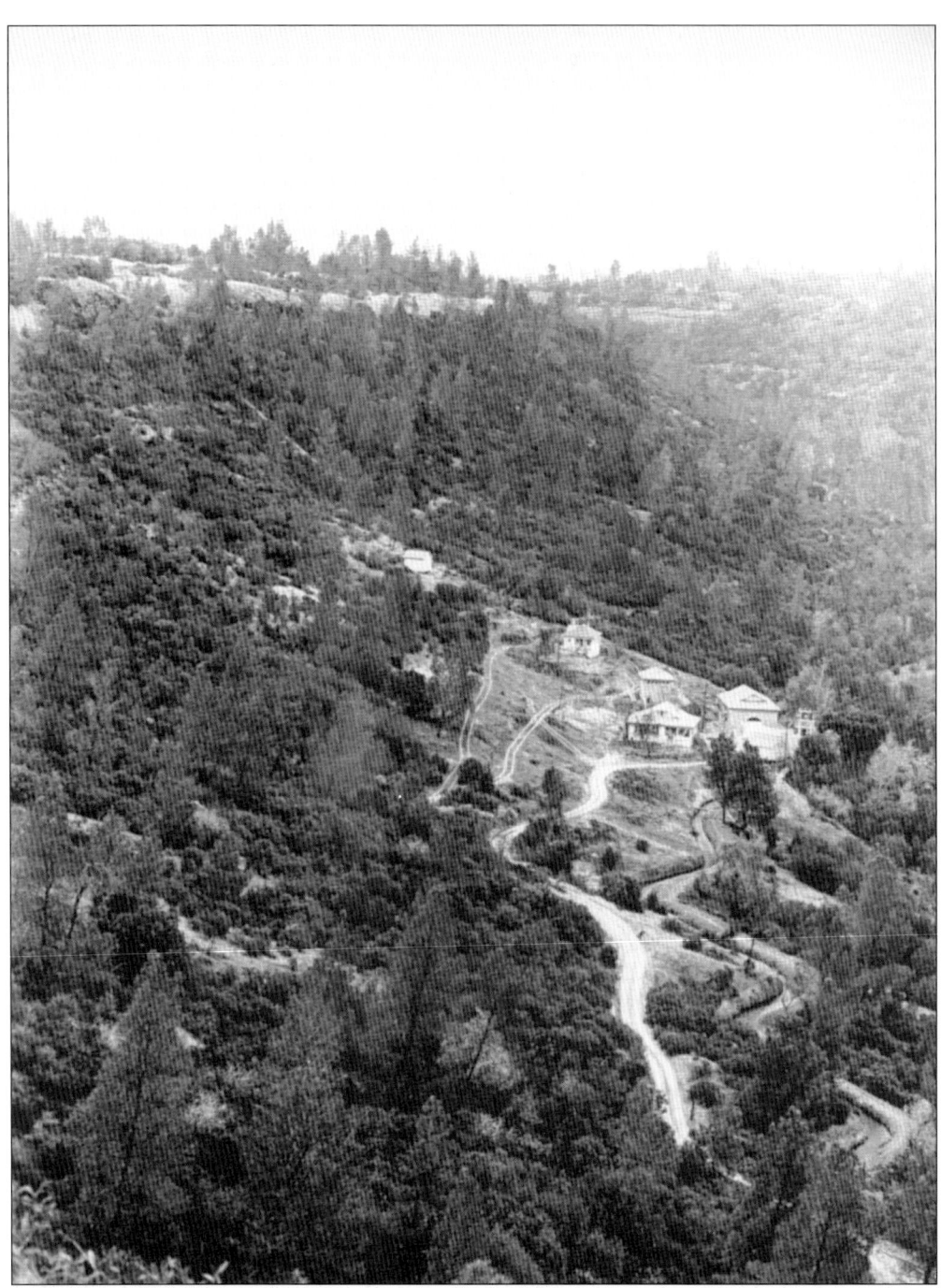
In 1905, the Lime Saddle hydroelectric powerhouse was built in a canyon off the West Branch below the lower Paradise Ridge. Water came by a former miner's ditch, the Miocene Canal, visibly zigzagging from the powerhouse on the right. Part of the PG&E system since 1917, only the powerhouse and Miocene Canal remain. The powerhouse is still generating electricity using much of the original equipment. (Courtesy PG&E Archives.)

Six

ROADS, RAILS, AND AEROPLANES

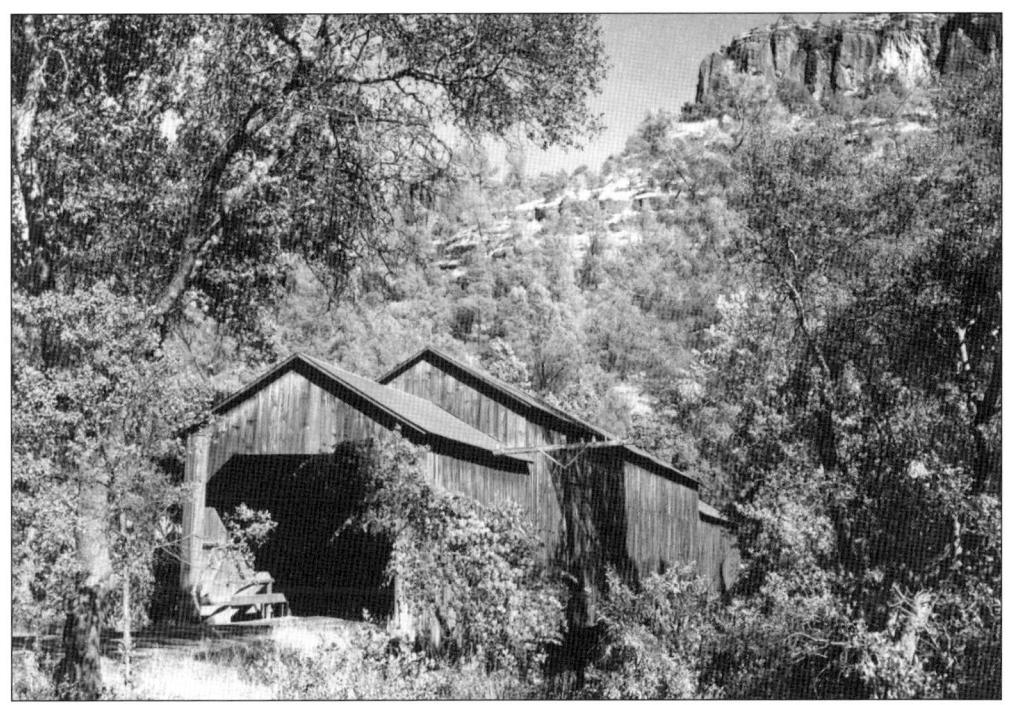

In 1886, the Honey Run Covered Bridge was built across Butte Creek, connecting Centerville Road from Chico to the 1884 Carr Hill Road to Paradise. Renamed Honey Run Road, its name may have come from a young man's picnic with his sweetheart along Little Butte Creek. Spying a bear that apparently smelled the food, the young man jumped up and ran, shouting to his sweetheart, "Run honey, run!" (Courtesy Fred Baldinger.)

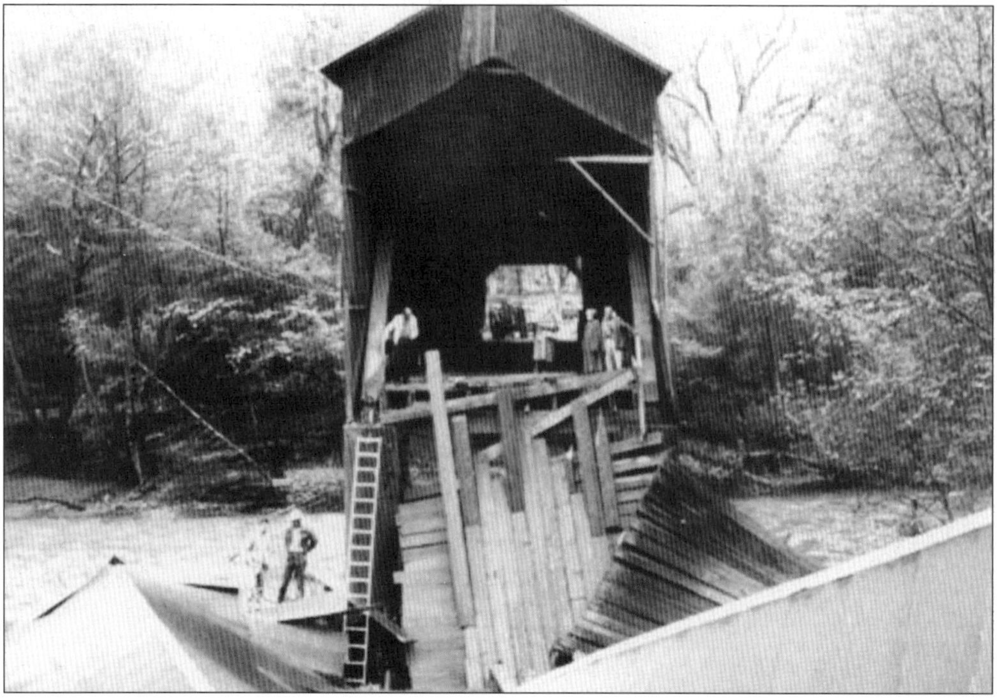

Honey Run Covered Bridge withstood traffic and weather until 1965 when a truck crashed into the east end, collapsing 80 feet into Butte Creek. The old bridge was already scheduled for replacement, so the county decided not to repair it. However, a citizens group, recognizing this covered bridge was one of a few remaining, raised funds to repair the structure. It opened to foot traffic in 1972. (Courtesy Butte County Public Works Department.)

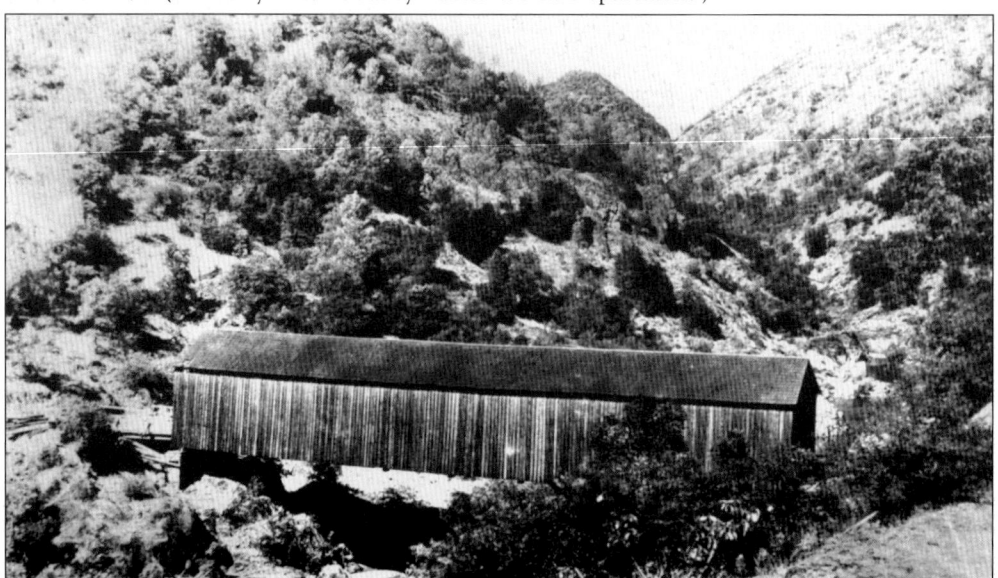

In 1855, Charles Curtis came to the gold camp at Nelson's Bar on the West Branch. He built the first road down to the river from Pentz Road and operated a ferry. In 1858, he constructed a toll bridge across the river. It was washed out in 1862–1863 and again in 1865. In 1885, the covered bridge seen in this photograph was built and lasted until 1909. (Courtesy William Lesson.)

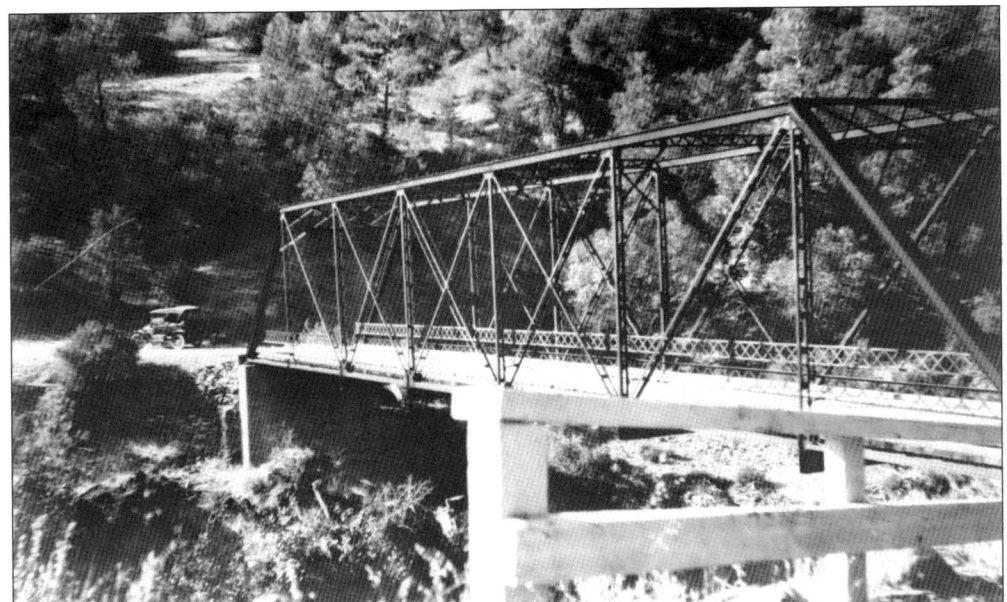

This steel bridge replaced the Nelson Bar covered bridge that washed away in 1909 when the Oro Water Light and Power dam at Philbrook failed. The deluge washed out every bridge and diversion dam on the West Branch. In 1967, the steel bridge was dismantled before being submerged by the rising water of Lake Oroville. In this photograph, A. A. Richardson's 1913 Ford has just crossed the bridge. (Courtesy Velma Butler.)

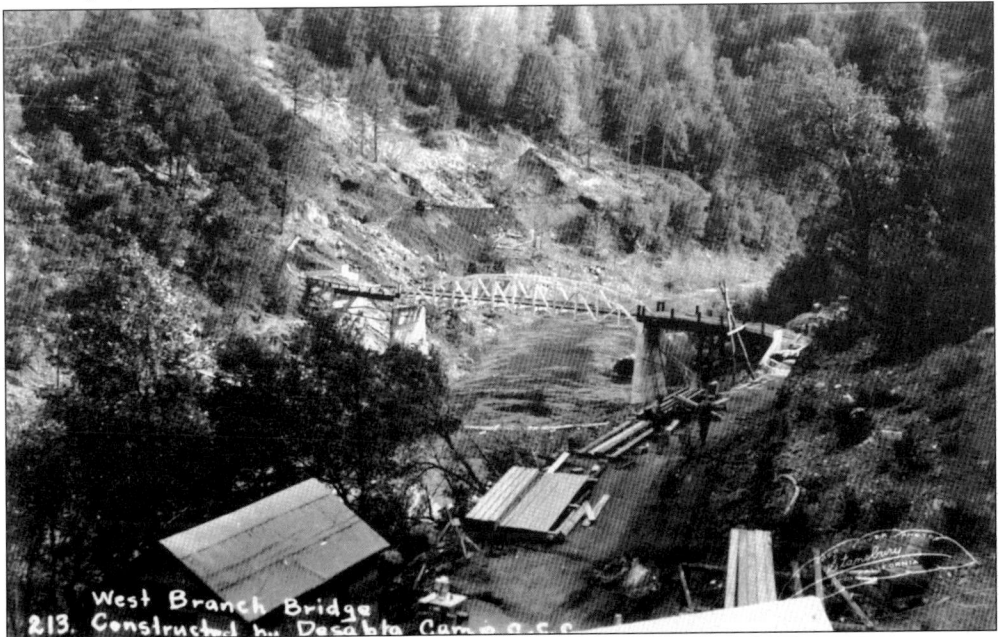

The West Branch Bridge, seen here during construction, crosses the river below Magalia. It was built by the Civilian Conservation Corps for the U.S. Forest Service's Ponderosa Way firebreak, which ran 760 miles up the Sierra foothills. In this 1934 photograph, the road has not yet been completed up the east canyon wall, but once finished, it connected the Ridge with Sawmill Peak and Concow and is used today. (Courtesy Lois McDonald.)

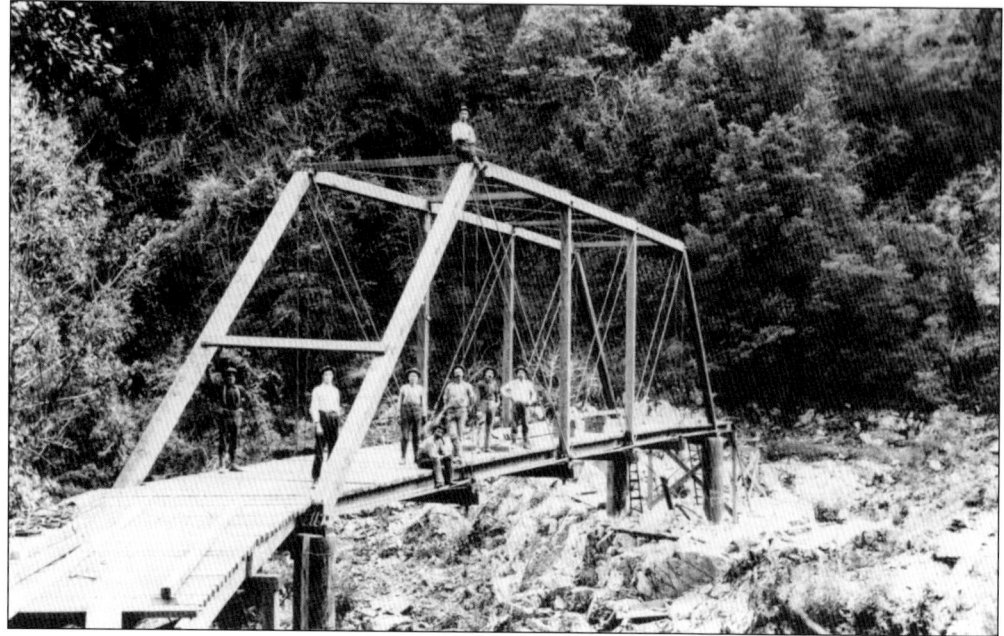

In 1859, the 54-pound Dogtown Nugget, found on the east side of the West Branch, was taken to Dogtown on the west side across a bridge at Whiskey Flat, which washed away in the 1909 Philbrook dam failure. This wooden bridge replaced the one that was destroyed. It was dismantled in 1934 after the West Branch Bridge, about a mile upstream, was completed. (Courtesy Gold Nugget Museum.)

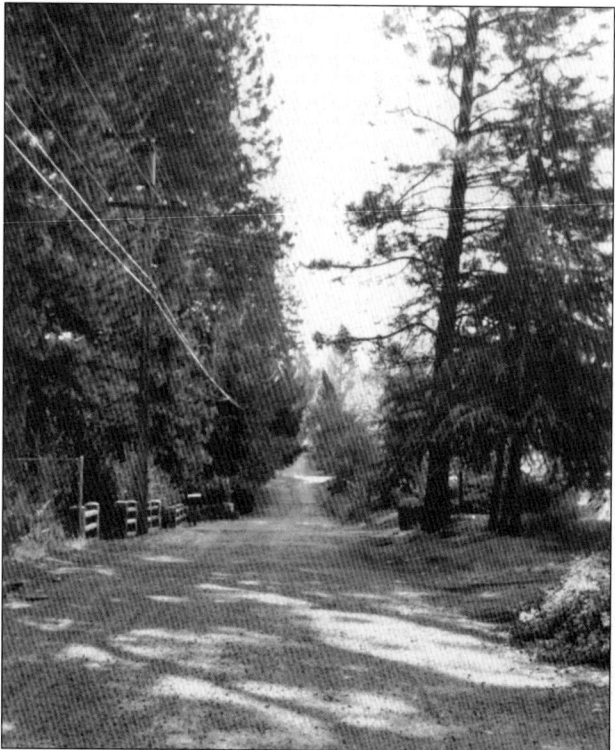

Forest Lane runs between Wagstaff and Bille Roads and predates 1920. It was just a trail until about 1971 and is an example of what early roads were like—dusty in the summer, muddy in the winter, and potholes in any season. Today the north end is still rough due to a partial paving job apparently done by a resident who dumped leftover asphalt in the potholes. (Courtesy Lois McDonald.)

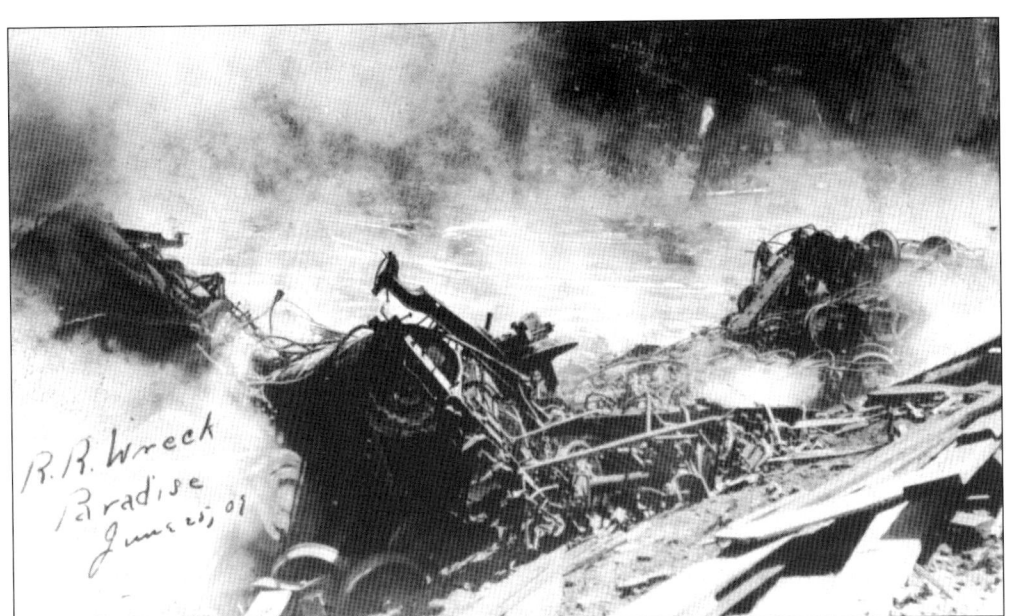

On June 25, 1909, a 27-car lumber train left Stirling City for Chico. Leaving the Magalia Depot, the train "ran away" on the down slope, passing the Paradise Depot at 70 miles per hour, and three quarters of a mile below the depot at Neal Road, it derailed. Engineer John Nisbet and brakeman Earl Amos were killed, while two other brakemen and fireman John Myers survived. Conductor Albert Johnson, who was in the caboose with passengers, realized what was happening, and he decoupled the caboose and applied the hand brake, finally bringing it to a stop as it reached the Paradise Depot. Smoking lumber and twisted railroad equipment is evident above. Engine No. 1, on the right, usually hauled lumber to Chico and was probably the one involved in the wreck. (Above courtesy Gold Nugget Museum; right courtesy Lois McDonald.)

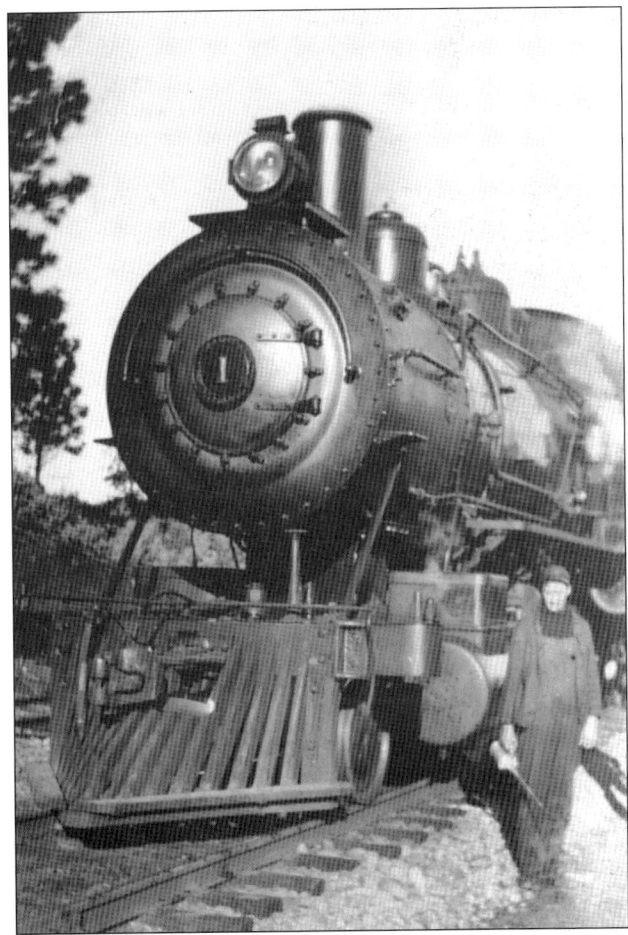

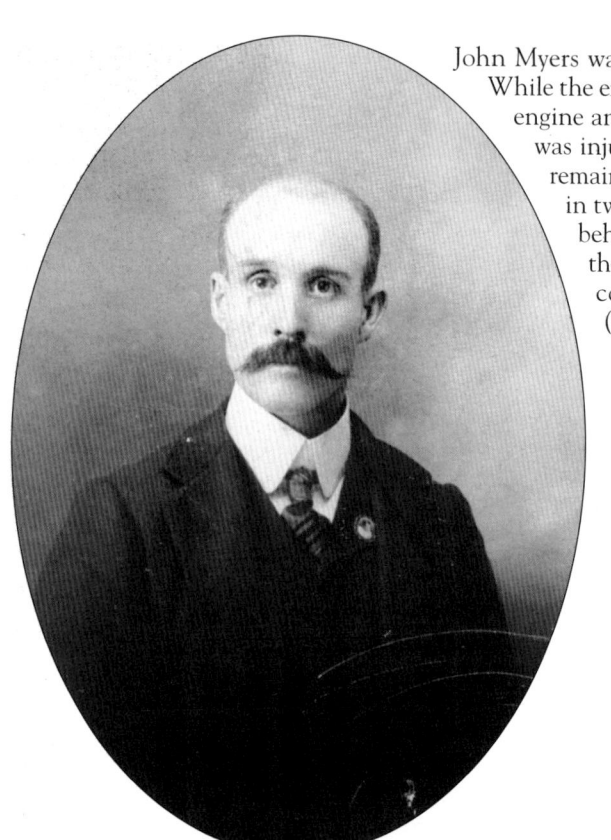

John Myers was the fireman on the ill-fated train. While the engineer, John Nisbet, jumped from the engine and was killed, Myers stayed with it but was injured and disabled for life. The engine remained upright although it was nearly torn in two. Fortunately an up-bound train was behind schedule and several miles down the track. If it had been on schedule, there could have been a head-on collision. (Courtesy Lois McDonald.)

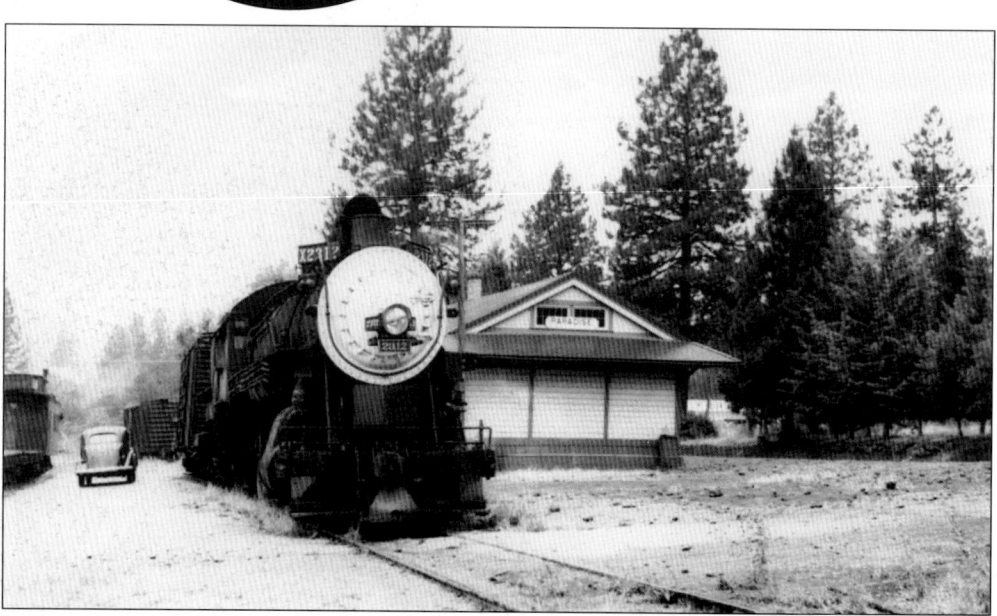

Pulling the up-bound freight for Stirling City, this Southern Pacific engine is stopped at the Paradise Depot to perhaps pick up additional freight cars. The photograph was taken in the late 1930s or early 1940s and sometime late in the year, as smoke can be seen coming from the stovepipe on the caboose to the left. (Courtesy W. C. Whittaker and Kent Stephen.)

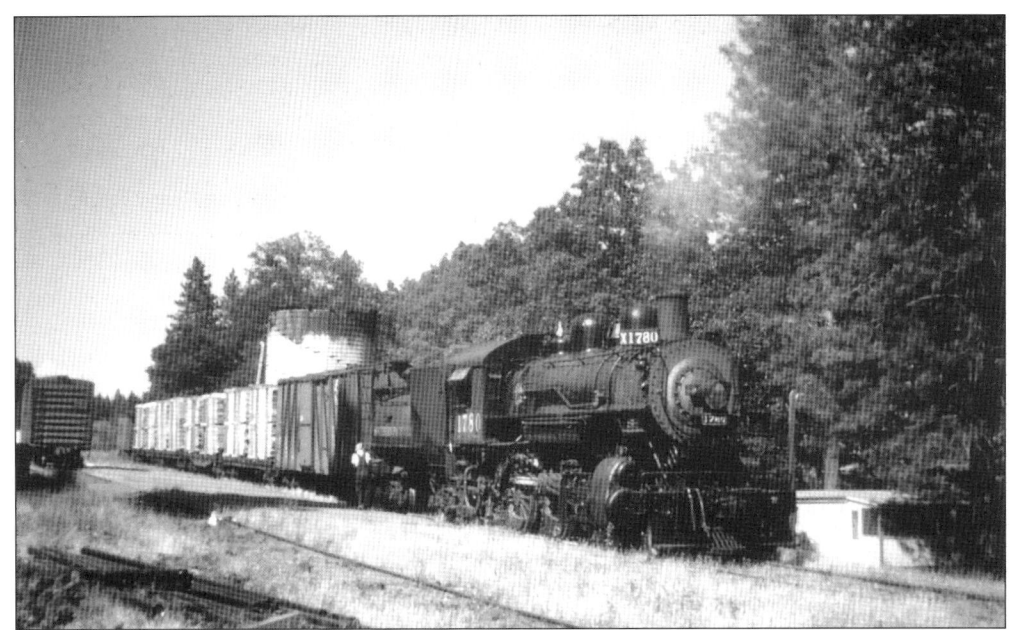

This Southern Pacific engine, bound for Chico, is pulling several flatcars loaded with lumber from the Stirling City sawmill to the Diamond Match plant. The engineer appears to be inspecting the tender on the siding at Paradise Depot, perhaps while waiting for an up-bound train to pass. The depot is out of sight to the left. (Courtesy Ruby Swartzlow and Lois McDonald.)

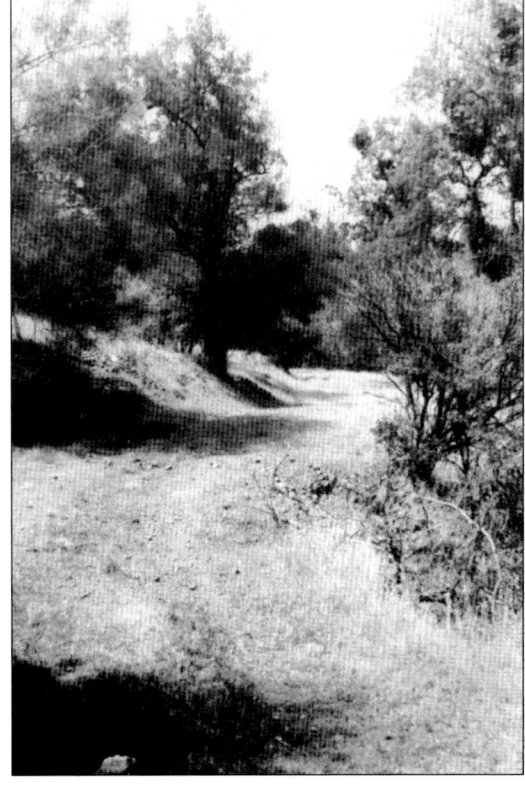

In this 1964 photograph, the old Pentz Grade winds up onto the Ridge from Pence's Ranch in the Mesilla Valley. It is not known whether the spelling of the grade and ranch are different because of Manoah Pence's desire or just a mistake when the post office at the ranch was named. Pentz Road, part of the Oroville-Honey Lake Stage Road, was locally called the Oroville-Dogtown Road. (Courtesy Ruby Swartzlow and Lois McDonald.)

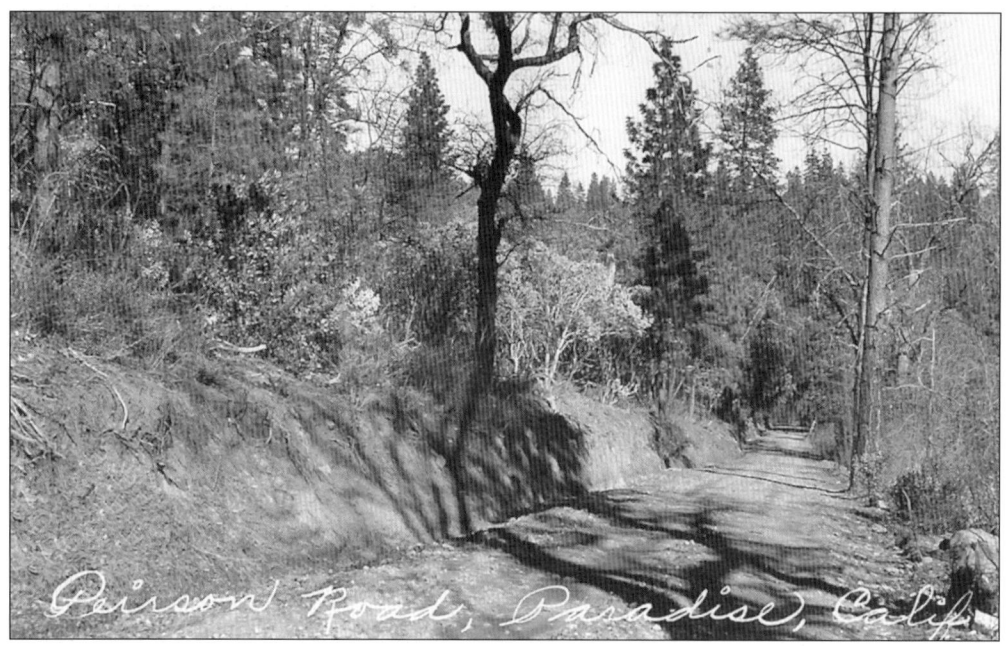

The above photograph shows a narrow, dirt portion of what would become the east section of Pearson Road between the Four Corners at Clark and Pearson Roads. The road also went west from the Four Corners to connect with Neal Road (Skyway). In 1944, the sections were pulled together and named for the Pearson family, who came to Paradise in 1908 and owned the southwest corner, where Ace Hardware is today. Below, this 1930s photograph shows the paved, western part of the road where it crosses the railroad tracks and then Olive Street. In this area, it first was known as College Avenue and sometimes called Manzanita Road, a name that dates back to a 1904 subdivision map. (Both courtesy Gold Nugget Museum.)

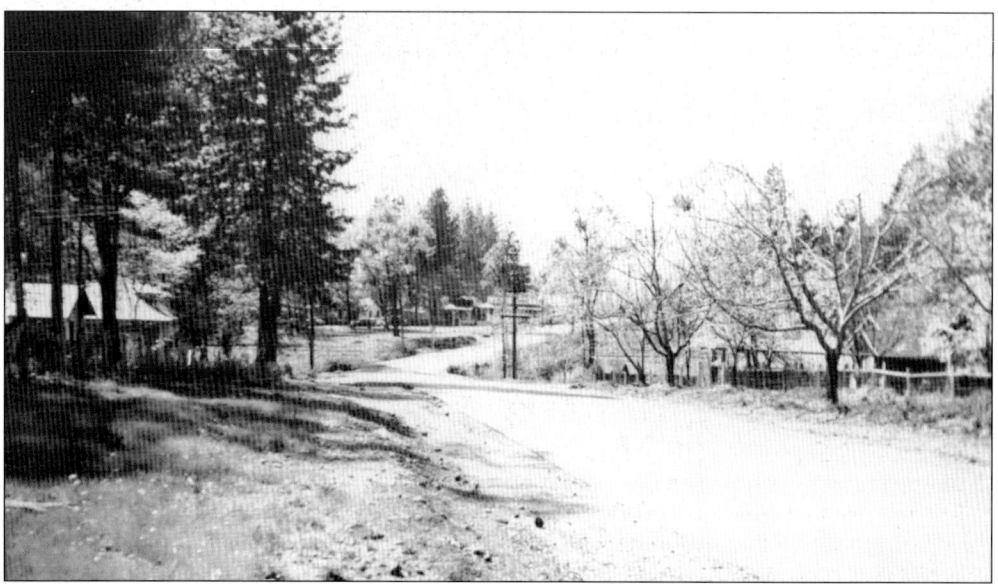

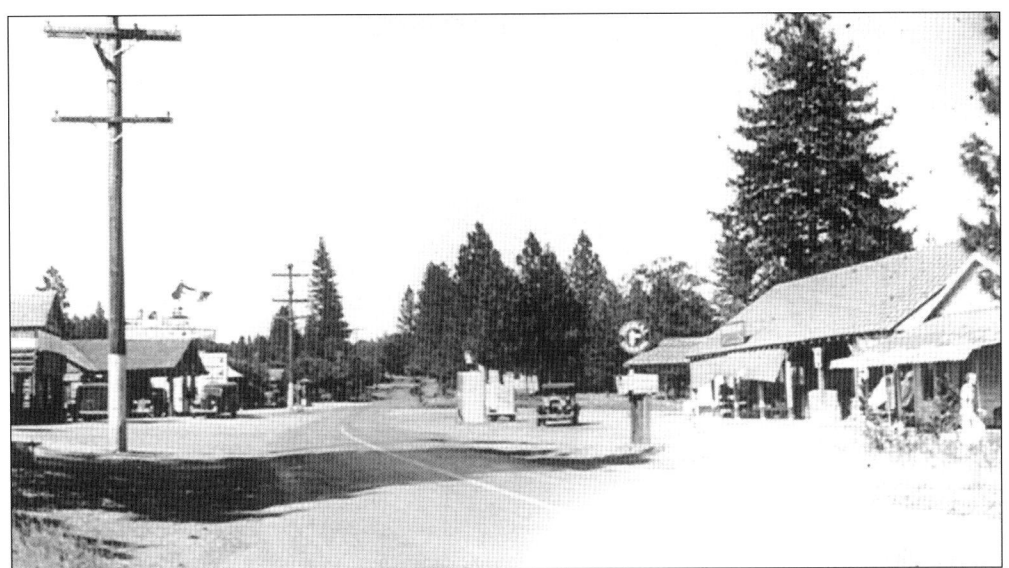

In 1935, Sam Neal's cattle trail through Paradise had a center white line. Blazed in 1845 to get his cattle from Rancho Esquon to summer pasture in the Sierra, it was the first route up the Ridge. In 1952, when the Skyway opened between Chico and Paradise, Neal Road, from Paradise to Butte Meadows, was renamed Skyway. This photograph looks north from Pearson Road. (Courtesy Paradise Genealogy Society.)

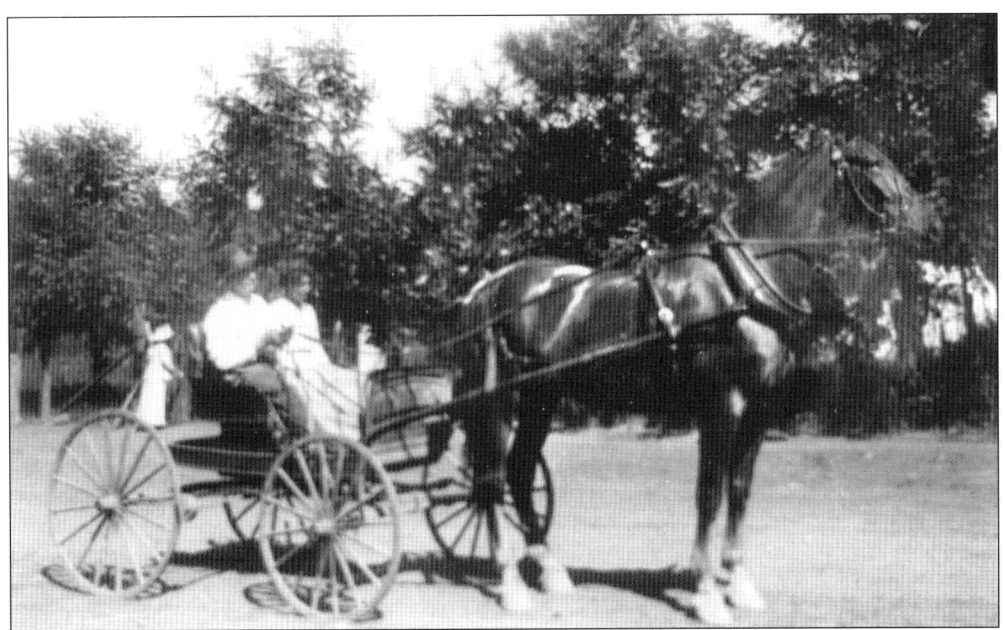

A typical means of transportation on the Ridge was a buggy, as illustrated by Mary Jane Wagstaff and an unidentified driver. In 1897, one could get a buggy through the Sears and Roebuck catalog for as little as $21; a full leather top cost an extra $5. A stage, wagon, horse, mule, or "shanks mare" were the only other ways to get around in those days. (Courtesy Paradise Genealogy Society.)

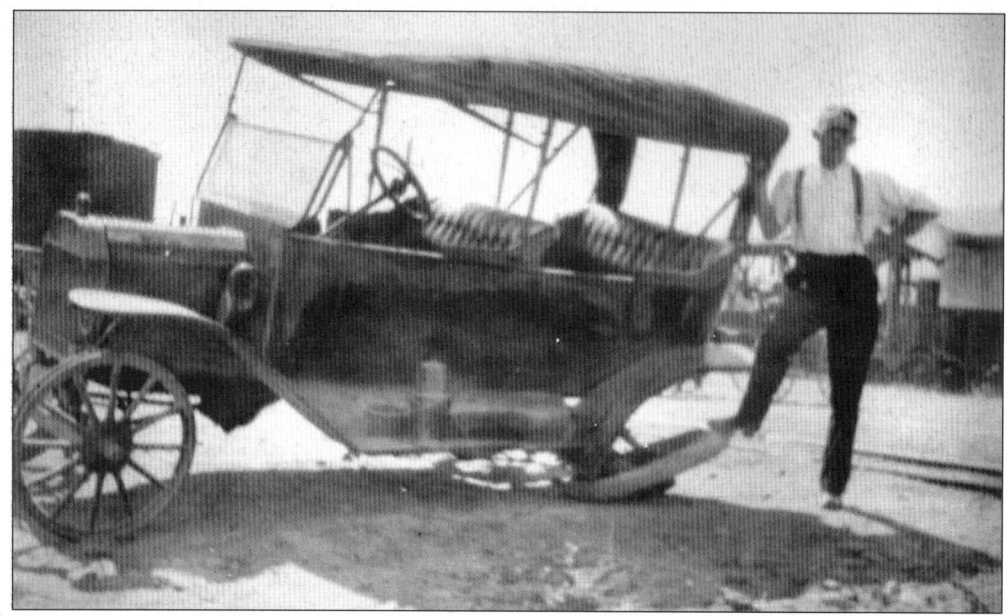

George Strong, Fannie Breese's younger brother, had the first auto accident in Paradise. In 1915, George apparently tried to beat the train in his Motel T Ford as it crossed College Avenue just south of the depot. He was lucky as only a rear wheel was damaged and the left front tire came off the rim. George does not seem too concerned. (Courtesy Gold Nugget Museum.)

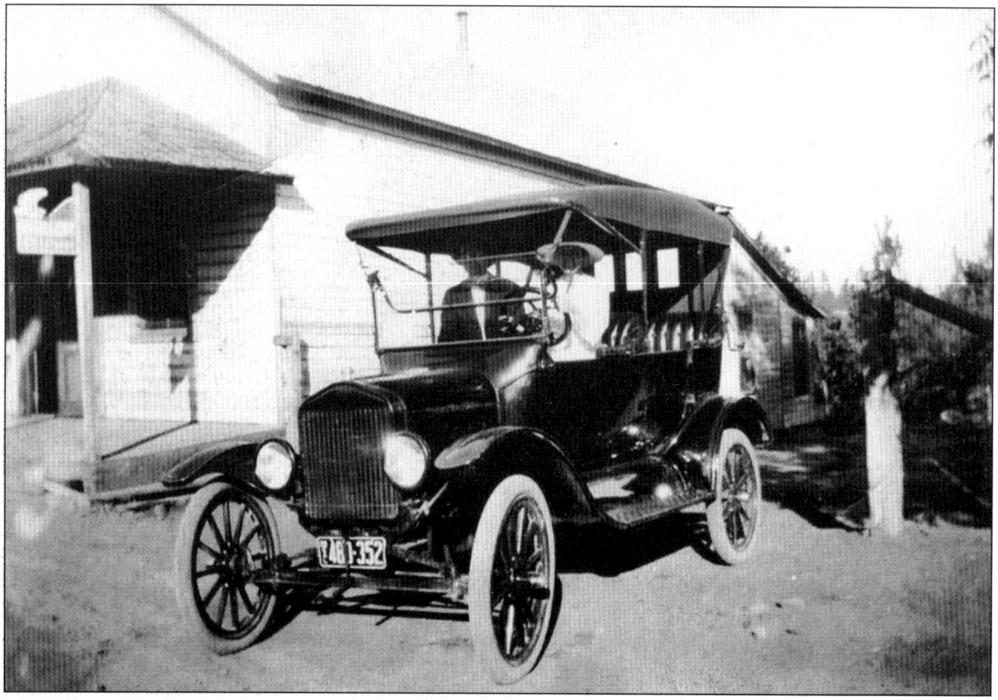

In 1918 or 1919, Iva Carlton, in front of Galbraith's store on Clark Road in Old Paradise, is in her first Model T Ford, which she did not have to crank because it had an electric starter. After receiving her teaching credentials in 1910, she taught grades one through four at Paradise School in 1911. She was a teacher in Paradise schools for 45 years. (Courtesy Ruby Swartzlow.)

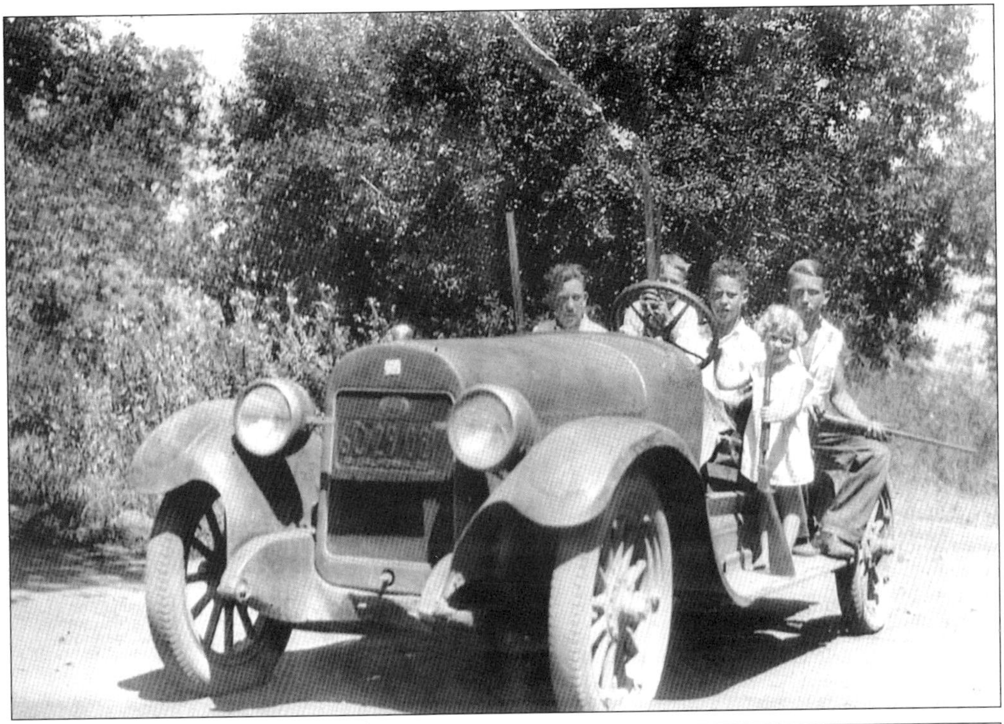

Around 1935, one did not need a license to drive an automobile; a person just got in and drove. So it was with George Bille's 1923 Buick. George is behind the wheel, his cousin Jimmy Wiley in the passenger seat, his sister Bernice on the running board, and cousins Hank (left) and Don (right) are in the back seat. In those days, kids knew how to handle guns too. (Courtesy George Bille.)

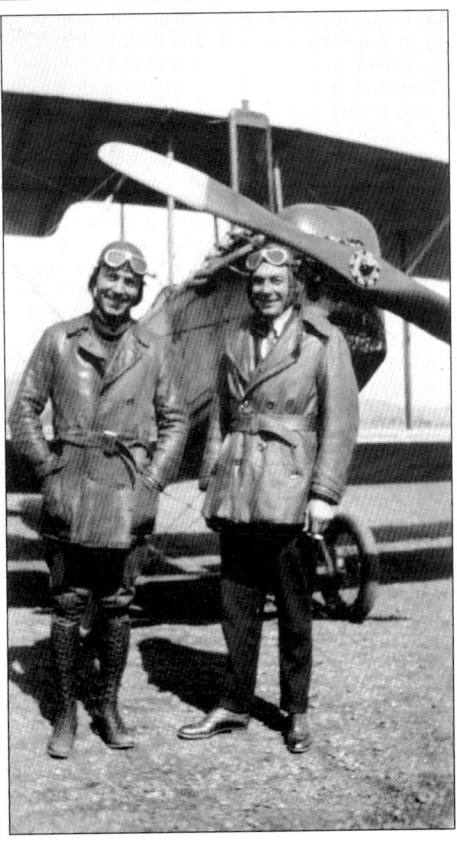

The Penfield twins, Tom and John, were daredevils by Paradise standards—they actually flew flying machines they built. In October 1926, the brothers completed a Curtis airplane and took it for a spin. On the second flight, Tom crashed on landing but walked away unhurt. This c. 1927 photograph of the brothers apparently was taken at their Paradise airstrip. They later flew in early motion pictures. (Courtesy Ruth Haffner Warner.)

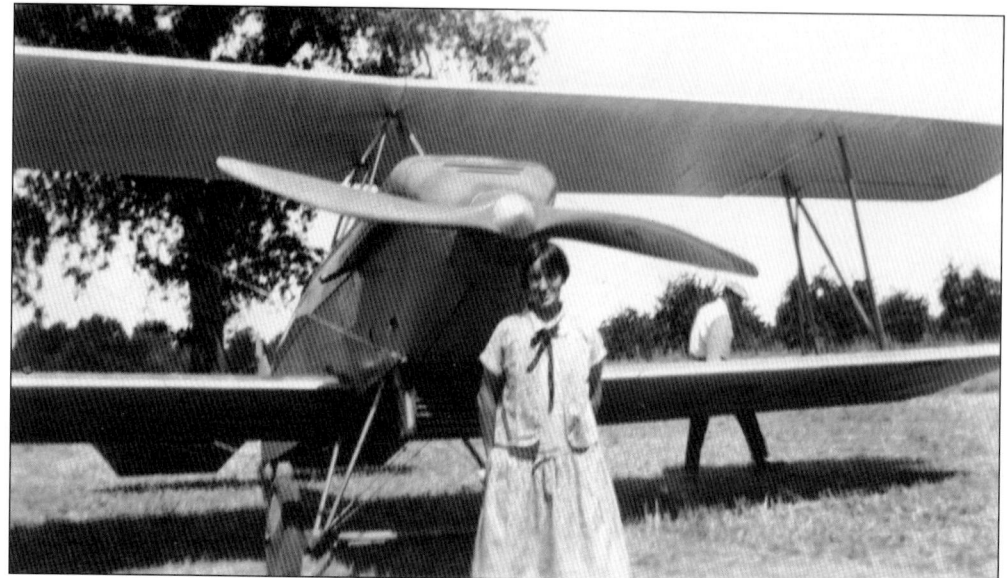

Eleanor Haffner stands in front of a Penfield airplane in this July 1927 photograph. Shortly after it was taken, Eleanor took an aerial photograph of the Penfield airstrip from this airplane. The brothers bought a two-and-a-half-acre parcel for their airstrip from the Haffner family. In the best "barnstorming" tradition, they offered rides to people in Paradise for $5 to $10. (Courtesy Eleanor Haffner Warner.)

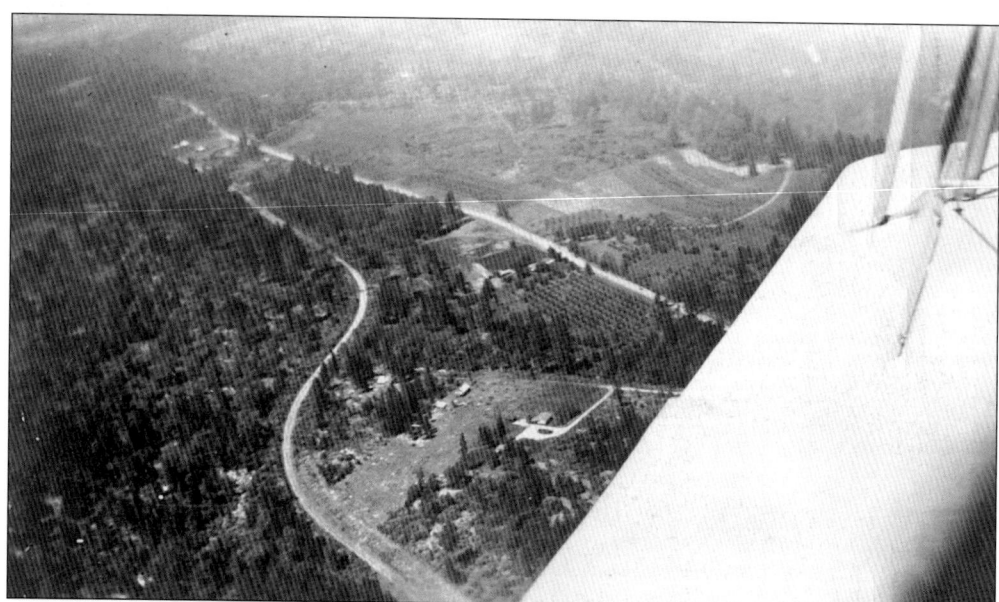

This aerial view of the Penfields' airstrip, taken by Eleanor Haffner, looks south. The narrow piece of land along the curving railroad track just behind the wing was the airstrip. Neal Road is the straight road above the railroad. The Haffner home is on the short road off Rocky Lane in the middle of the photograph. (Courtesy Eleanor Haffner Warner.)

Seven

"MODERN TIMES"

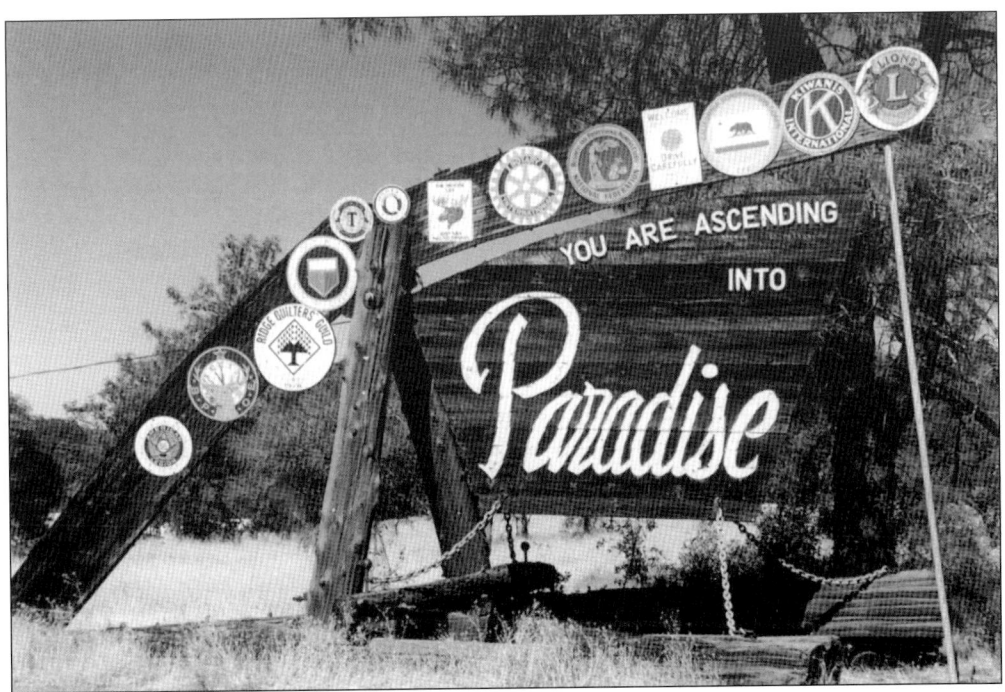

Erected in 1963 along Clark Road below Paradise, this sign greets newcomers; the second one constructed after the original was brought down by wind and weather. The land on which the original sign was built was Doug and Barbara Flesher's bull pasture. When the idea for the sign was proposed to Doug, he replied, "O.K., I don't think that the bulls will mind." (Courtesy Takao Wakida.)

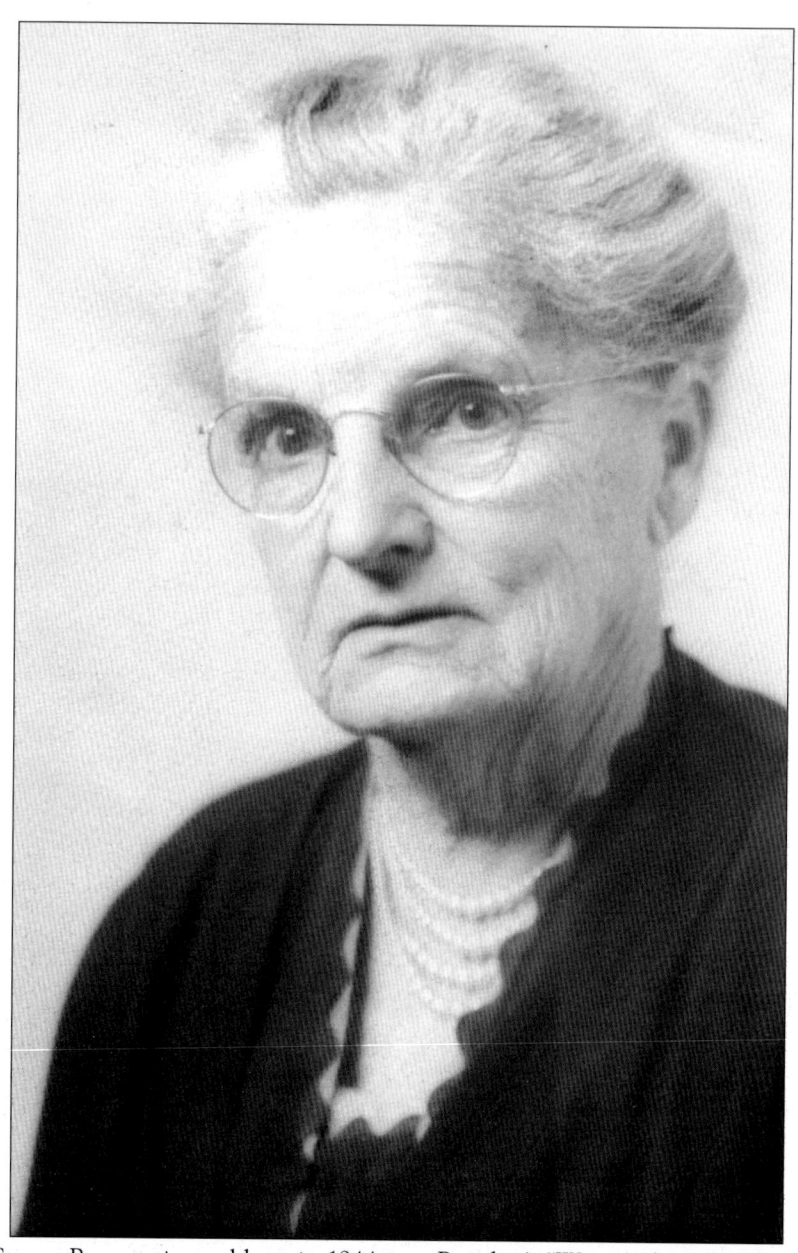

Frances Strong Breese, pictured here in 1944, was Paradise's "Woman for All Seasons." Nine-year-old Frances, Fannie to all who knew her, came with her family by train to Chico in 1876 and then to Leonard's Mill by stage. Her two uncles had preceded her family by about a year. For their first dinner in what later would be called Old Paradise, her aunt served strawberries, sliced tomatoes, string beans, butter, and milk. Coming from snowy Illinois, Fannie said, "We thought we had struck paradise." A typical farm girl, she had more "gumption" than most, and her role in acquiring the cemetery land proved this. And that was just the beginning; she was active in the community of Paradise all her life. She was a keen observer of her times and in 1946, described 70 years of life on the Ridge to a reporter for the *Chico Record*. Her "I Live for Paradise" interview later was republished in *Tales of the Paradise Ridge*. She lived here for 74 years and is buried in the cemetery she helped build. (Courtesy Norma McKillop.)

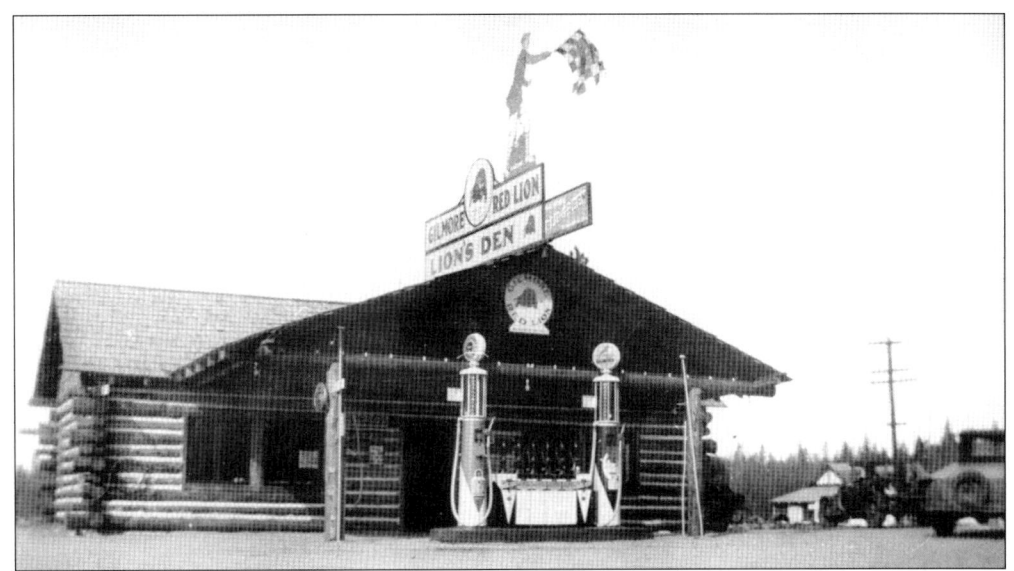

The Lyon's Den, pictured here in the 1920s, was the place to stop for gas and food on Neal Road between Honey Run and Pearson Roads. Today the La Cantina bar sits on this site. (Courtesy CSU, Chico, Meriam Library, Special Collections and Plumas County Museum.)

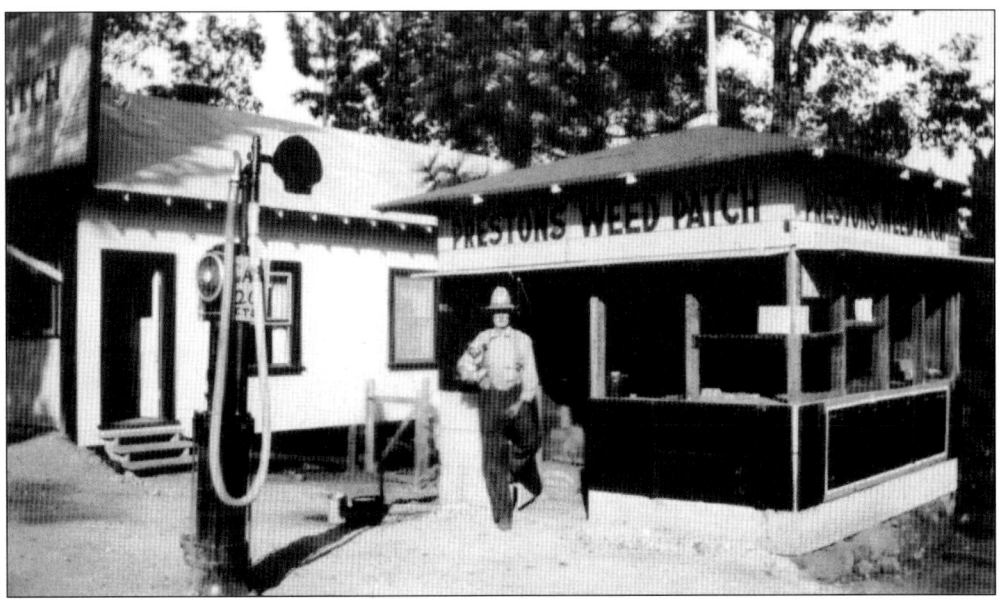

Around 1920, Elijah Preston, a veteran of the Alaskan gold rush, bought a piece of property on the east side of Neal Road just south of Manzanita (Pearson) Road. "Dad" Preston named his place Preston's Weed Patch and sold strawberries and apple cider, adding a gas pump as autos became popular. His cider was delicious. Everything went into the old-fashioned press: apples, cores, worms, and all. (Courtesy Gold Nugget Museum.)

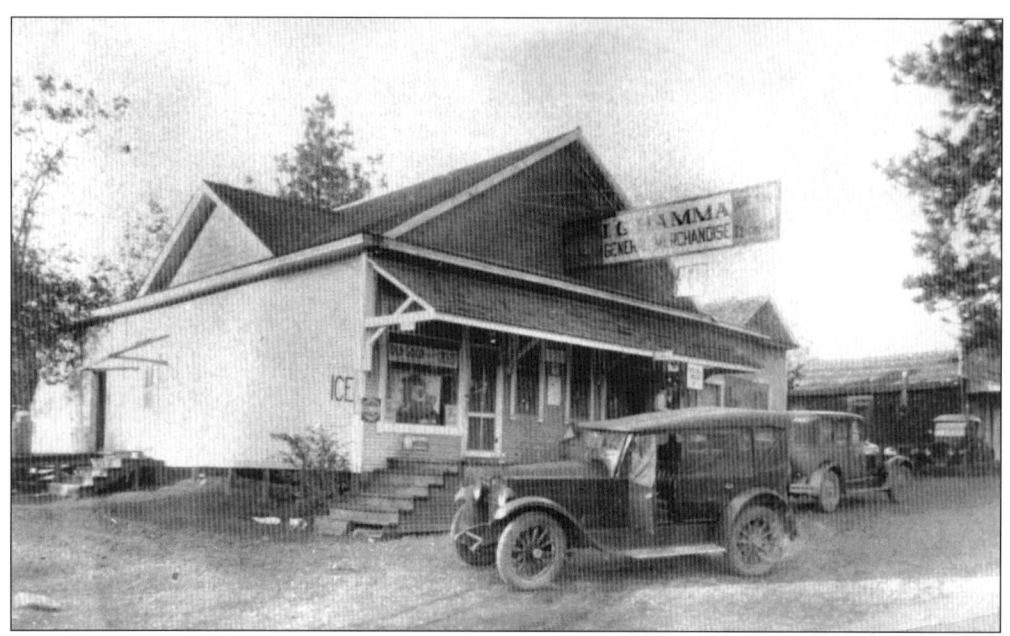

On the corner of Olive Street and College Avenue (Pearson), this building has housed many different businesses, including the Paradise Irrigation District office and post office in 1916. The top photograph was taken around 1923, when Irwin and Gertrude Hamma had their Hamma's General Merchandise store there. It looks as if the driver of the touring car was in a hurry and just jumped out and ran in to make a quick purchase. The same store is below, but the Hammas were now operating it as part of the Red & White chain, probably around 1934. The Hamma family was one of several who were enticed to move to Paradise around 1916 by "The Pied Piper of Paradise," entrepreneur and insurance salesman extraordinaire Isaiah Cook. (Above courtesy Paradise Genealogy Society; below courtesy Lois McDonald.)

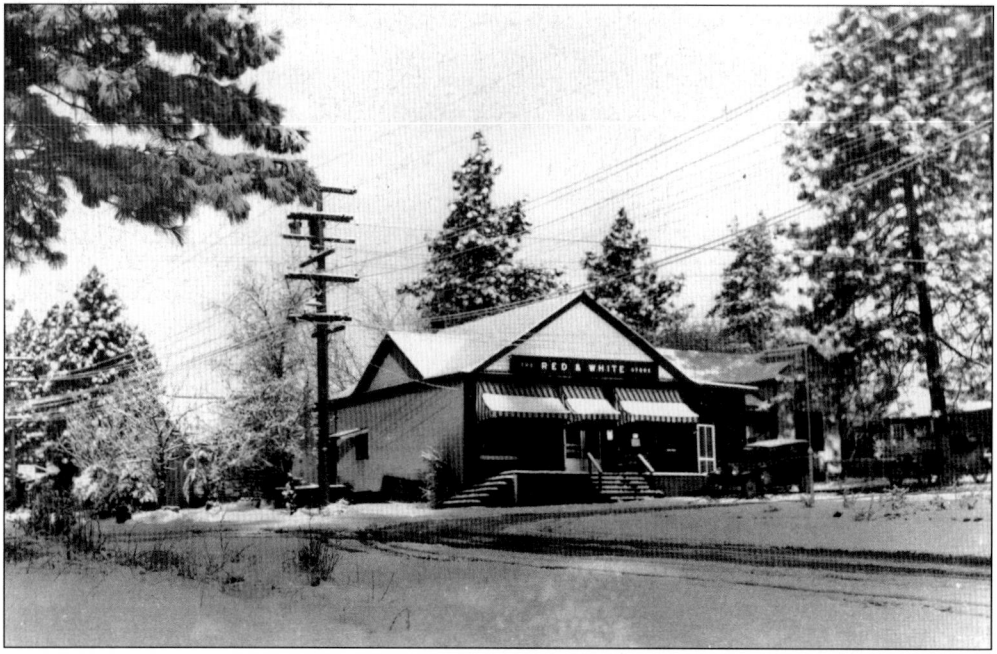

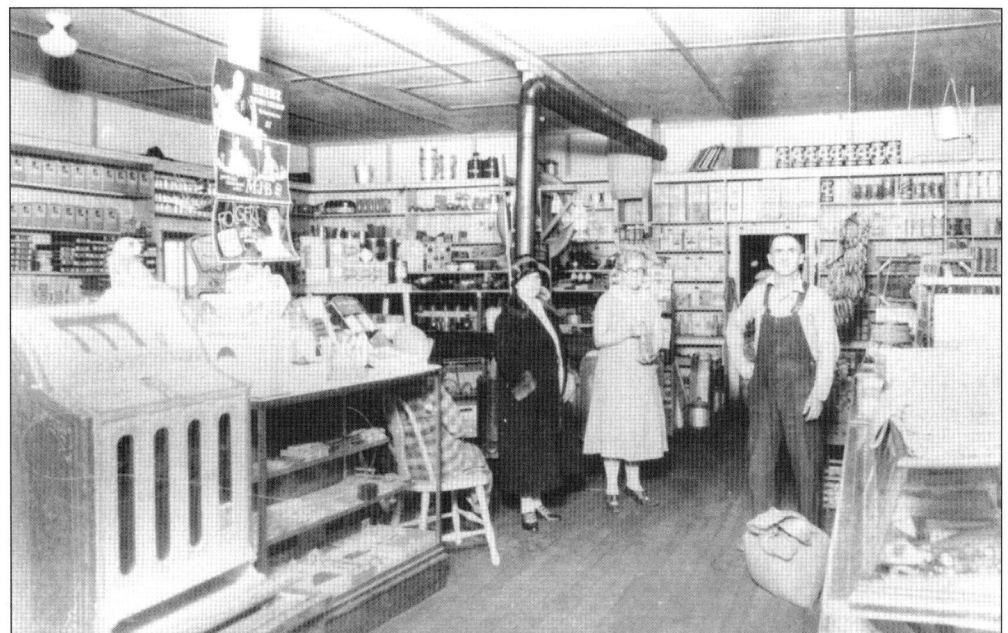

This is the interior of the Hamma's store in 1923. Gertrude Hamma is in the center with a customer on the left, and the man who took care of the lawn is on the right. (Courtesy Paradise Genealogy Society.)

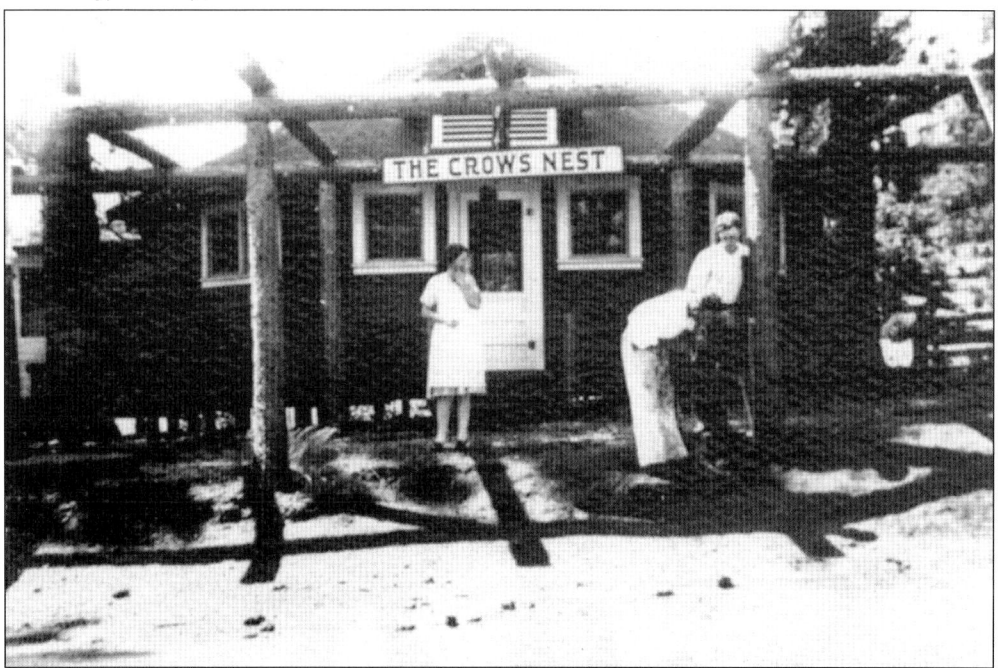

In 1923, H. C. "Bud" Crowfoot built the Crowfoot Sawmill on land below the intersection of Neal and Pentz Roads. That same year, across Neal Road from the sawmill, the Nystrum family built Crows Nest, which served as a restaurant for the sawmill workers. Jane McIvor cooked while her husband, George, worked at the sawmill. This building would eventually become part of the Optimo Lodge. (Courtesy Gold Nugget Museum.)

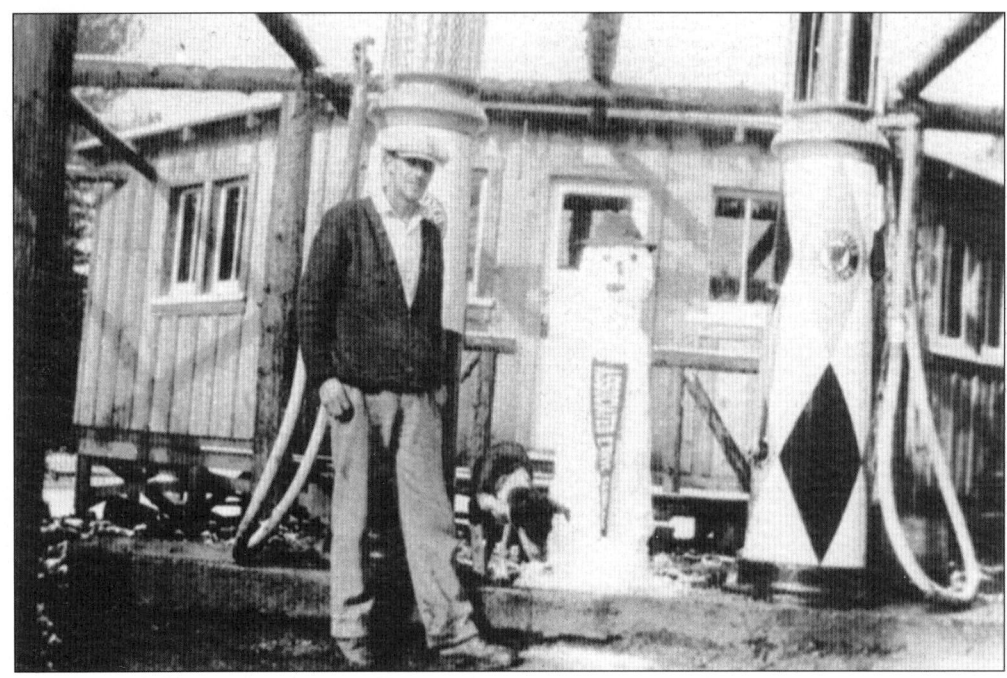

The Nystrum family also sold gasoline from pumps in front of the restaurant. Around 1929, they leased the building to a man who turned it into a speakeasy called the Blue Goose, which specialized in home brew and rotgut booze. The identity of the man and dog are not known, but since the dog is licking a snowman, it must be wintertime. (Courtesy Gold Nugget Museum.)

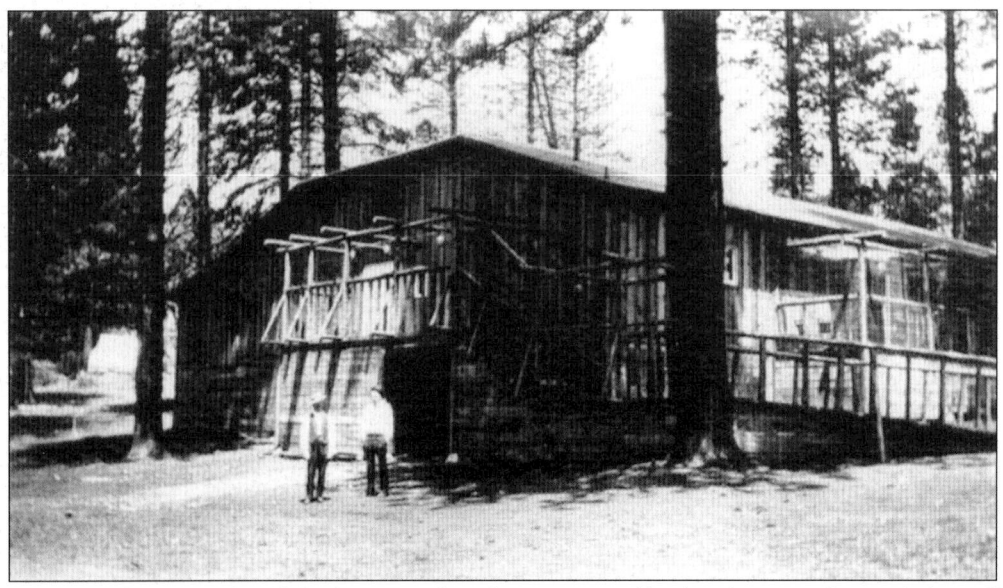

Sierra Gardens Dance Hall, built in 1927 by Al Nystrum and his brother, was about 150 feet off Neal Road and below where the Optimo Lodge is today. It opened in May 1927 and burned to the ground in late October, the night before an American Legion dance. During Prohibition, if one wanted a bottle, the Blue Goose was only a few steps away. (Courtesy Gold Nugget Museum.)

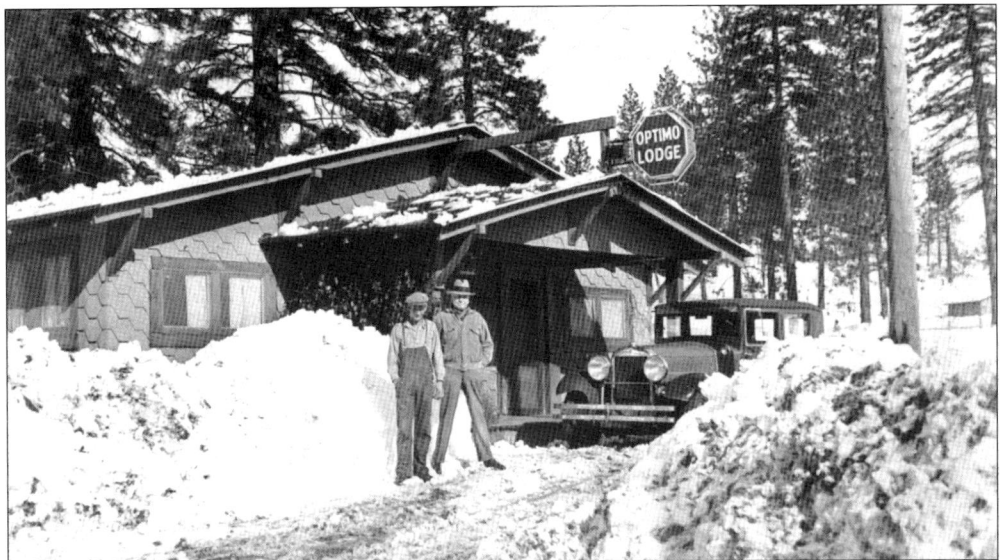

In 1935, Bill and Iva Rankin bought the Blue Goose and served excellent meals and legal liquor. Enlarging the building, they renamed it the Optimo Lodge after the railroad siding into the sawmill. In 1946, they sold to the Linggi family, who operated it until 1965. Since then, several people have owned the lodge, and it operates today, the last remembrance of Optimo. The men in photograph are unidentified. (Courtesy Wayne Stout.)

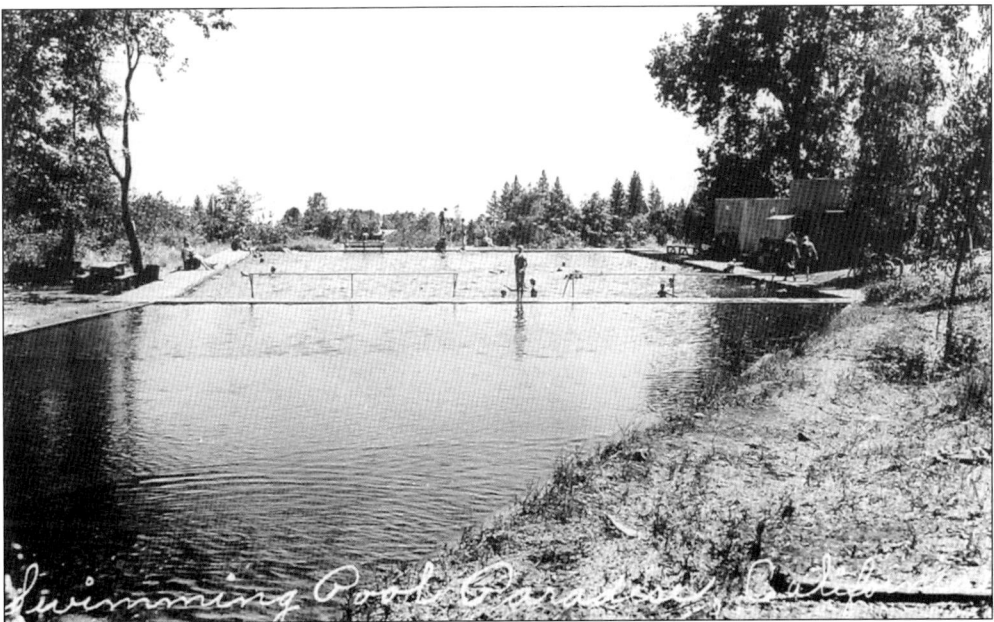

The Paradise Swimming Pool was built below today's Gold Nugget Museum on Berry Creek, which was its water supply. A project of the Women's Improvement Club, it was due to be dedicated in 1928. However, before the ceremony could be held, a herd of cattle headed for summer pasture in the mountains was driven by, and seeing a "watering hole," they dedicated the pool in short order. (Courtesy Gold Nugget Museum.)

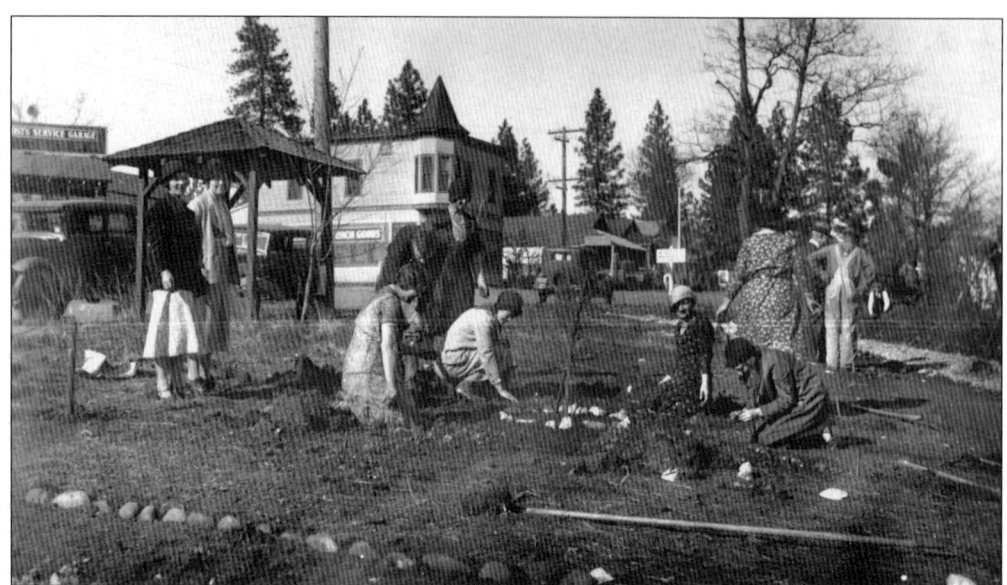

Around 1930, ladies from the Friday Club of Paradise plant a tree to beautify the depot grounds. The town well is behind them to the left and the Thramer building with the cupola is in the background. Pictured here are Helen Pearce, at far front left; Ina Clewett, standing behind Helen; Belle Simkin, at right with her back to the photographer; Belle Samples, at right facing the photographer; Helen Berry, at far lower right; and Flossie Alderson, at middle left kneeling down. The rest of the people are unidentified. (Courtesy Paradise Genealogy Society.)

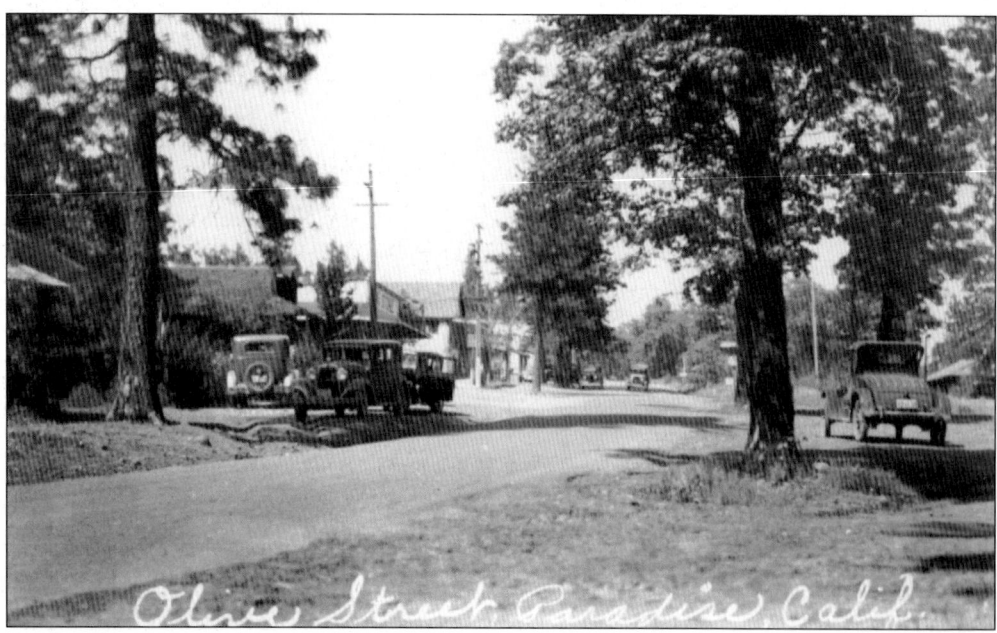

On this day in the mid-1930s, Olive Street had a lot of traffic for a small place like Paradise. The view is to the north, and the depot can just be seen past the automobile on the right. (Courtesy Gold Nugget Museum.)

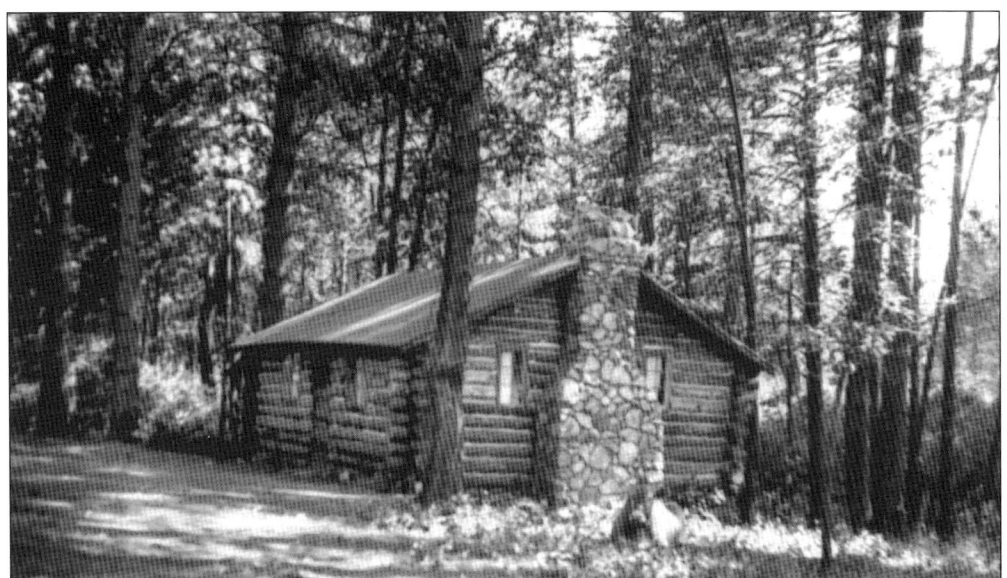

The Boy Scout cabin at Sierra Park Drive and today's Pearson Road apparently was built in the early 1900s; George Bille remembers going to the cabin for Scout meetings around 1931 and his daughter Jerre remembers going there as a Girl Scout around 1961. A Quonset hut eventually replaced the cabin and rummage sales were held in it. Today there is a 1980s vintage A-frame building on the site. (Courtesy Gold Nugget Museum.)

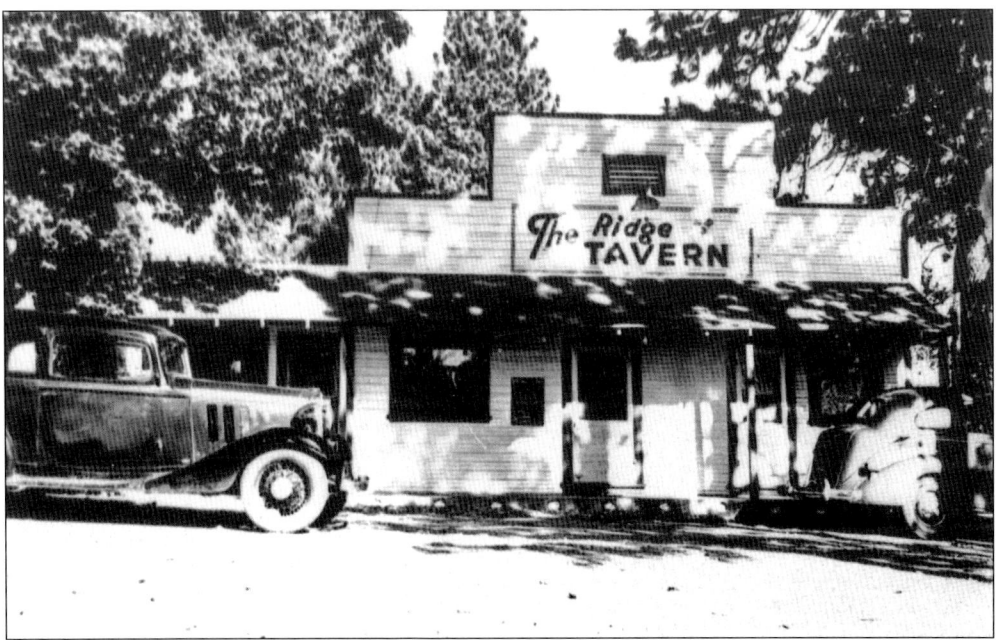

On the east side of Neal Road just above Foster Road, the Ridge Tavern was one of a relative few "watering holes" in Paradise. The photograph was taken around 1933 since the automobile appears to be a 1933 Chevrolet. The building has had many tenants through the years and today houses part of the Back to the Ranch western store. (Courtesy Paradise Genealogy Society.)

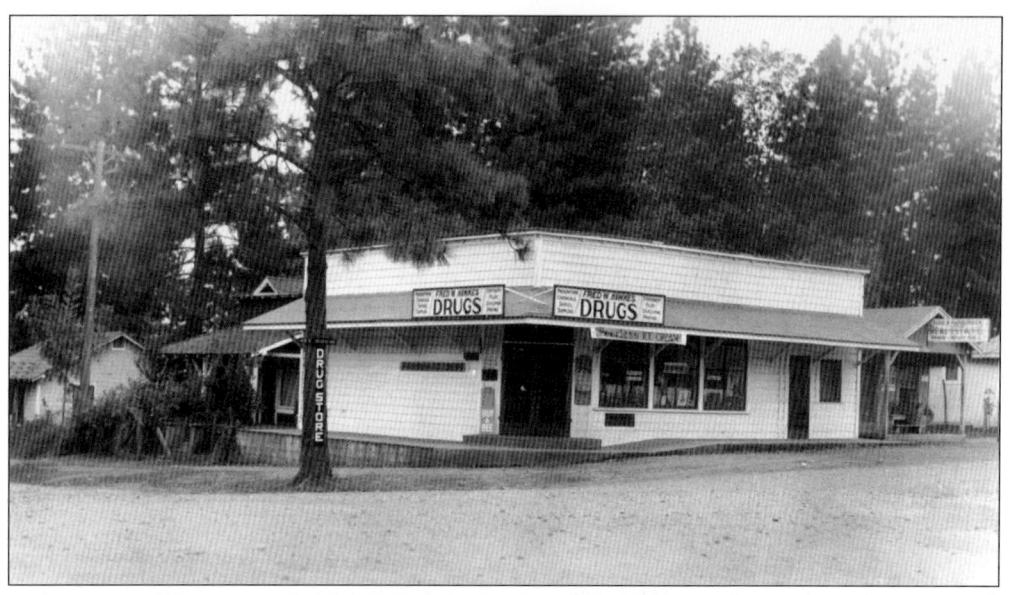

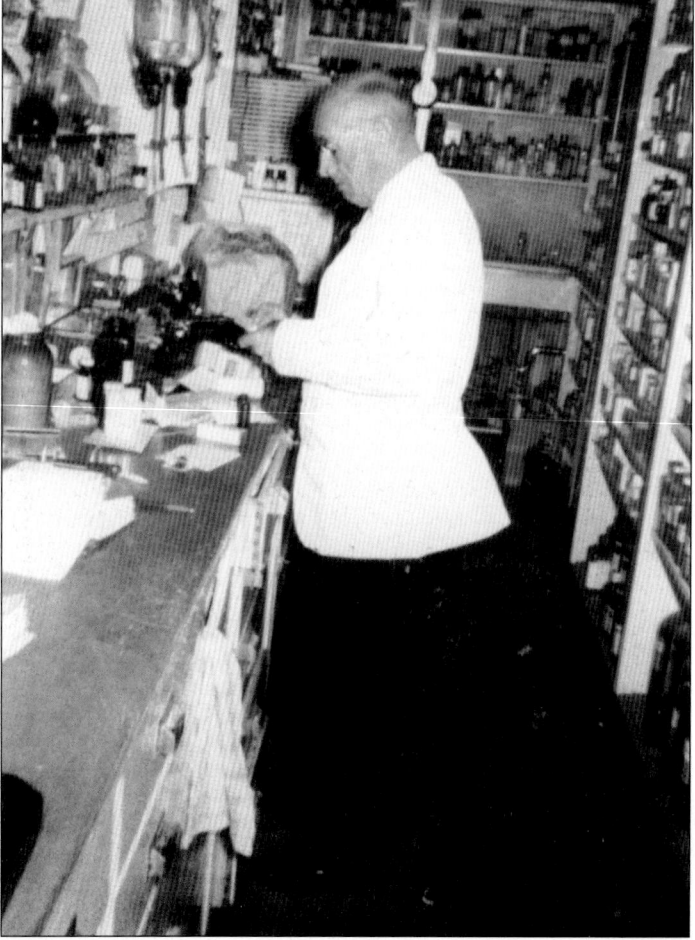

Located on the corner of Pearson Road and Olive Street, this building once housed Young's Trading Post. In 1934, Fred Hawkes bought the property, remodeled it, and opened a pharmacy and drugstore that carried a full line of drugs and cosmetics. Hawkes then added a soda fountain, the first one in Paradise. It was the place to "hang out" to learn the latest news and gossip. Hawkes sold the business to Basil and Alta Gillett in the 1940s. In 1963, Tom McLaughlin bought the business and continued it until 1984, when grocery chains such as Safeway came to town with pharmacies and over-the-counter drugs. Fred Hawkes is working in the pharmacy in the picture on the left. (Above courtesy Paradise Genealogy Society; left Gold Nugget Museum.)

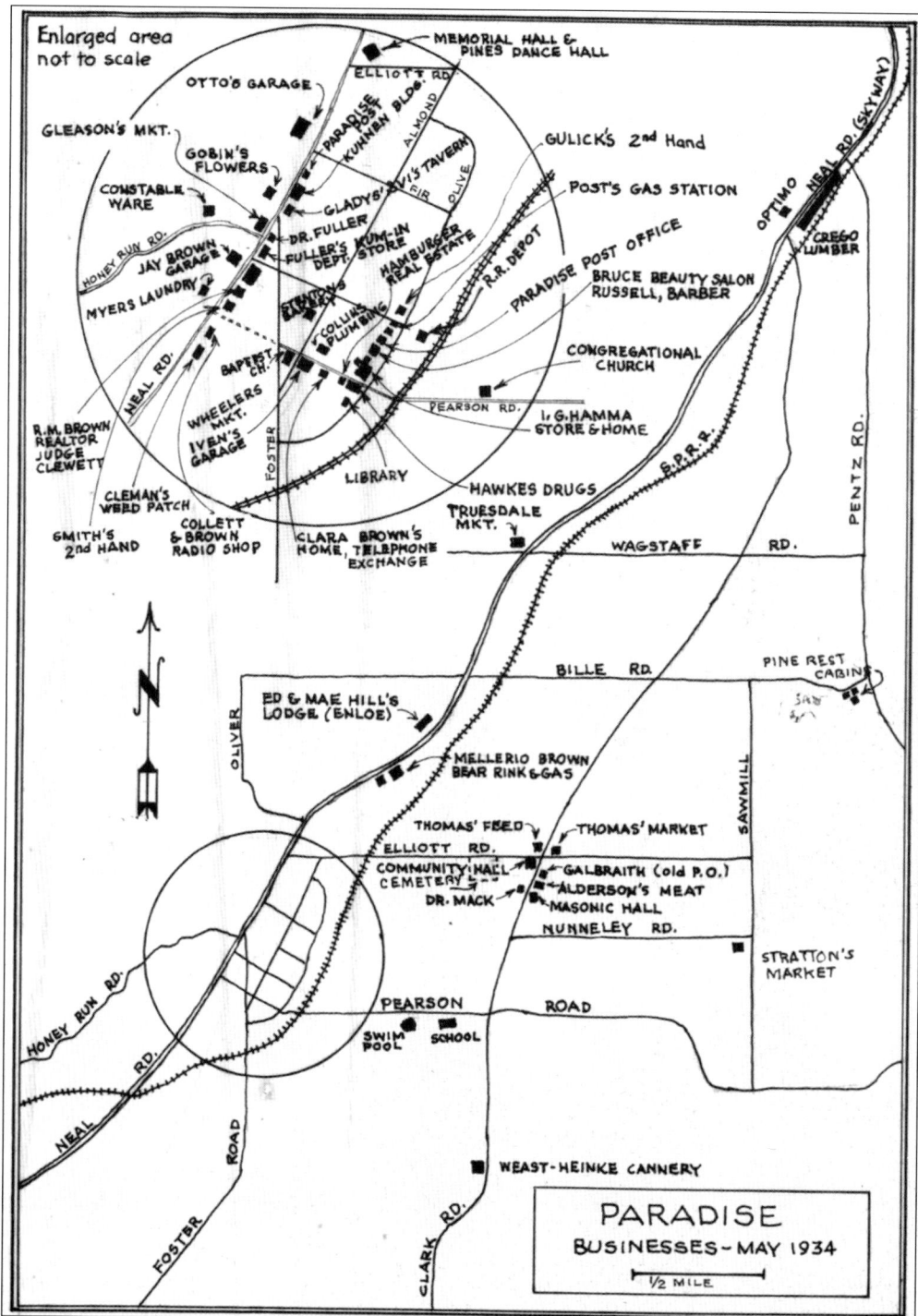

The blown-up section of this map shows the businesses that were in downtown (New) Paradise in 1934. The map also shows businesses around Clark and Elliott Roads in what was originally called Leonard's Mill or Old Paradise. By this time, the entire area was known as Paradise. (Courtesy Lois McDonald.)

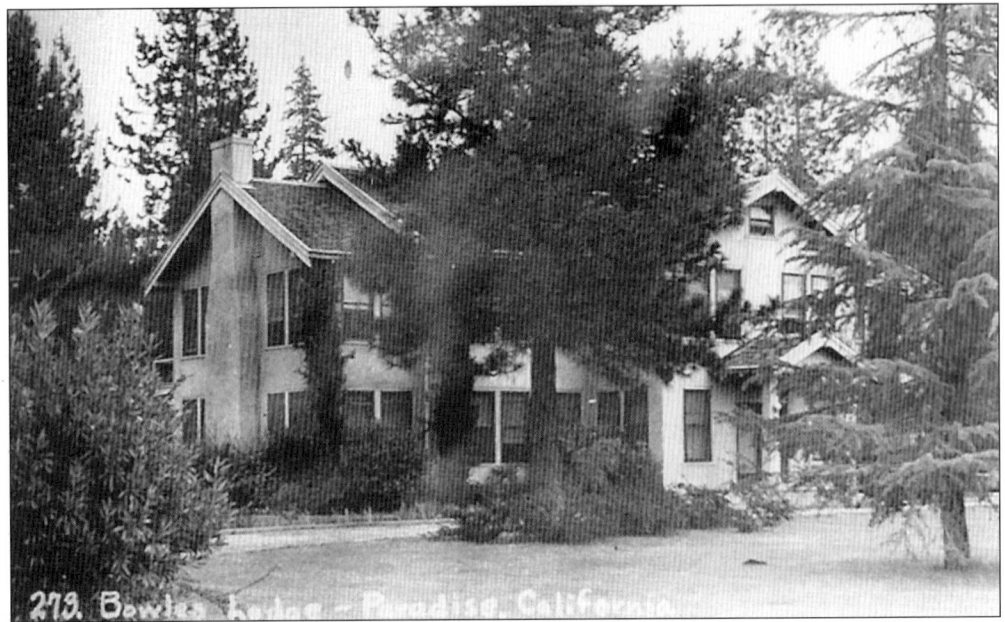

Coming to Chico in 1901, Dr. Newton Enloe practiced medicine and opened two hospitals. Around 1921, he bought the Meline farm on Neal Road and built the first of the two hospitals in Paradise. Within a few years, he closed it and concentrated on expanding his Chico hospital. In 1934, Robert and Laura Boles acquired the old hospital building and opened the Boles Motel, which later became the Evergreen Motel. (Courtesy Gold Nugget Museum.)

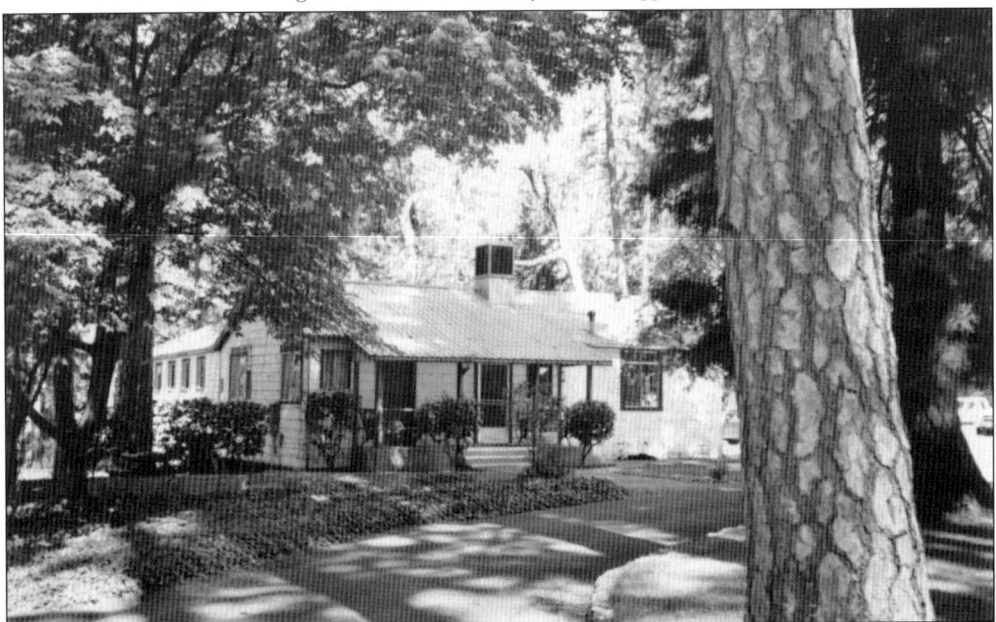

This is the California Division of Forestry/Butte County Fire Station No. 35, originally built for the U.S. Forest Service by the Civilian Conservation Corps (CCC) in 1936–1937 and generally called Paradise Station during its nearly 70 years of existence. CDF took over the station in 1946–1947. This photograph, taken in 2000, shows the original barracks building that was torn down when CDF rebuilt the entire station. (Courtesy author.)

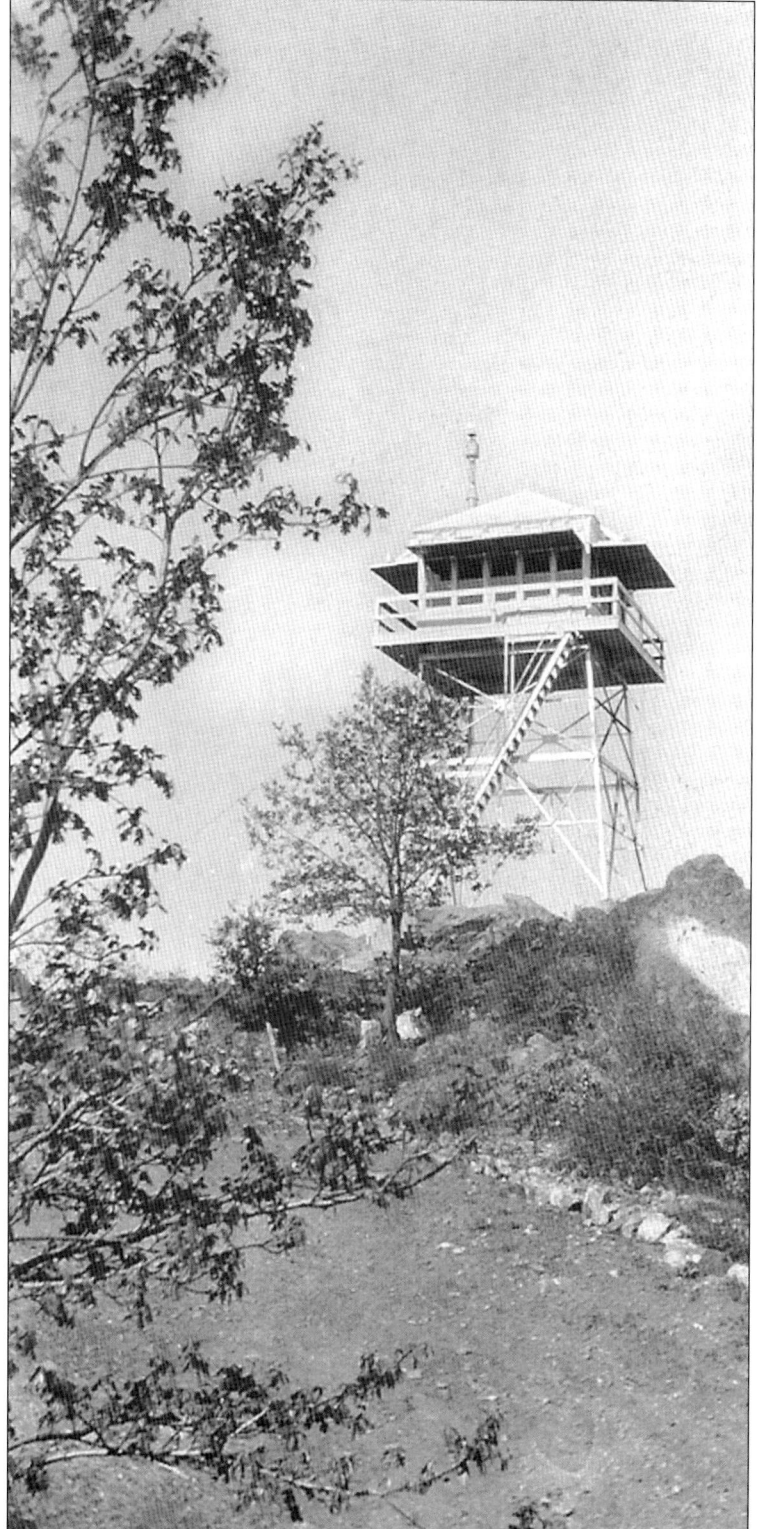

Built in 1929 by the U.S. Forest Service, Sawmill Peak Fire Lookout overlooks Paradise Ridge, protecting it from fires. The California Division of Forestry and Fire Protection (CDF) took over the lookout in 1946–1947. The people of the Ridge have always considered this fire lookout their own, even to the extent of paying salaries for lookouts when CDF cut the staffing budget to zero. (Courtesy Gold Nugget Museum.)

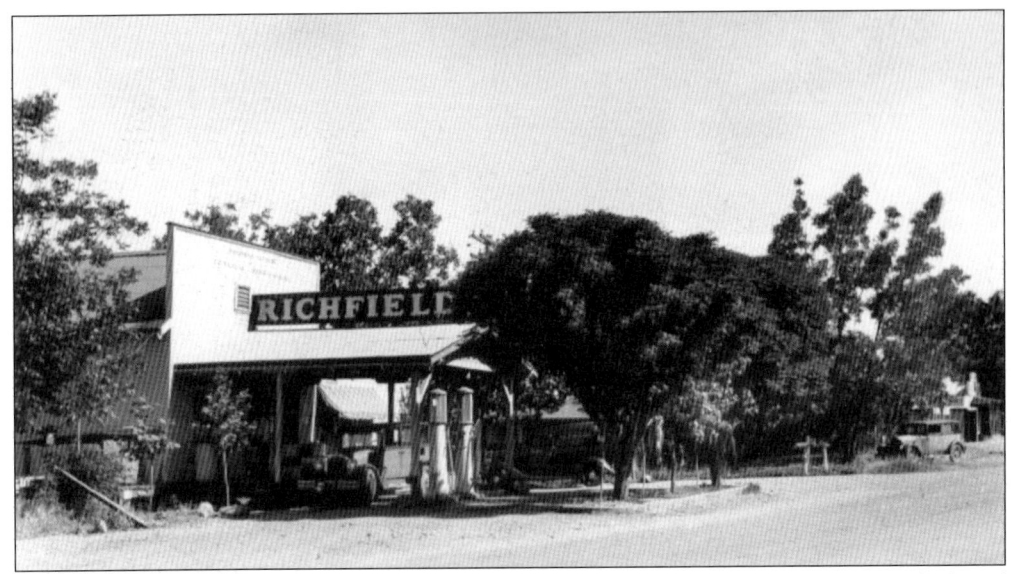

This gas station and grocery store, photographed in 1934, stood at the intersection of Clark and Elliott Roads in what was Old Paradise. In 1927, W. I. Weast sold the station and store to Jim D. Thomas, who sold gas and hardware. After World War II, the gas pumps were removed. The building was destroyed by fire in 1980. (Courtesy Gold Nugget Museum.)

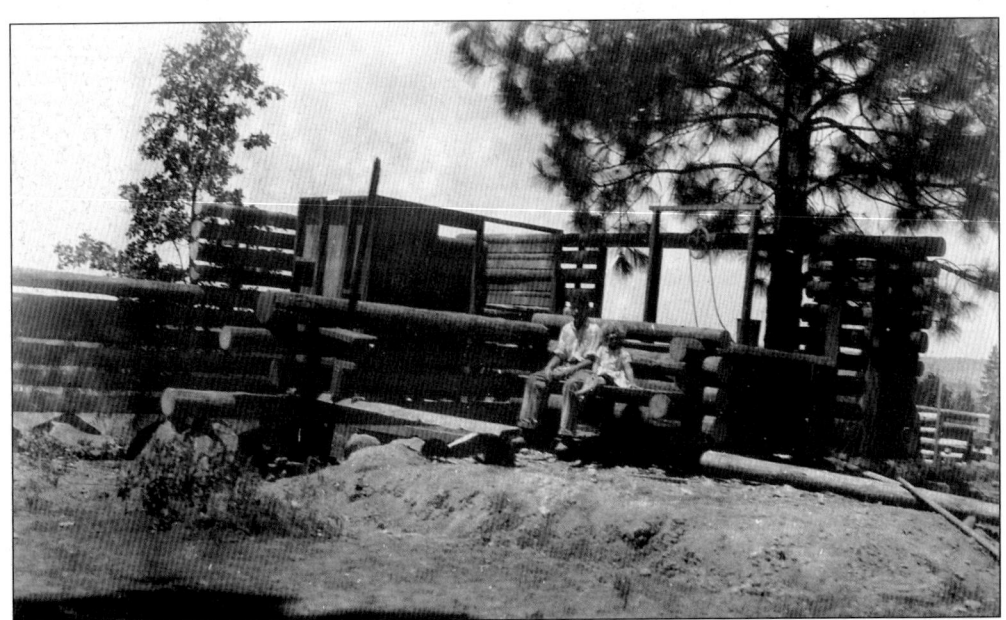

Teenager George Bille sits next to his half sister Martha in this c. 1935 photograph. He was helping build the Bille home on Olive Road, below Bille Road, by cutting notches in all of the logs. The house had a well in the back porch, the head frame and pulley of which are visible behind them. The home still stands. (Courtesy George Bille.)

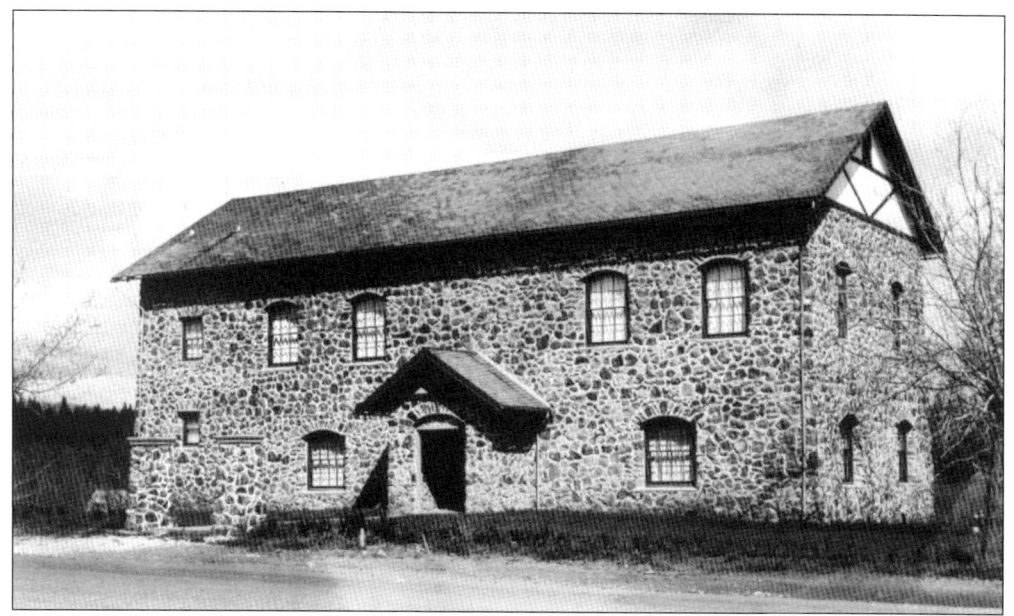

In 1858, the Table Mountain Masonic Lodge formed in Oroville and in 1872, moved to Cherokee. In 1936, the lodge moved to what had been Old Paradise. Dr. William Mack donated land for a lodge just south of Clark and Elliott Roads. In 1937, the new Masonic lodge, made of native stone, opened. In 1963, a new temple was built next to the original building. (Courtesy Gold Nugget Museum.)

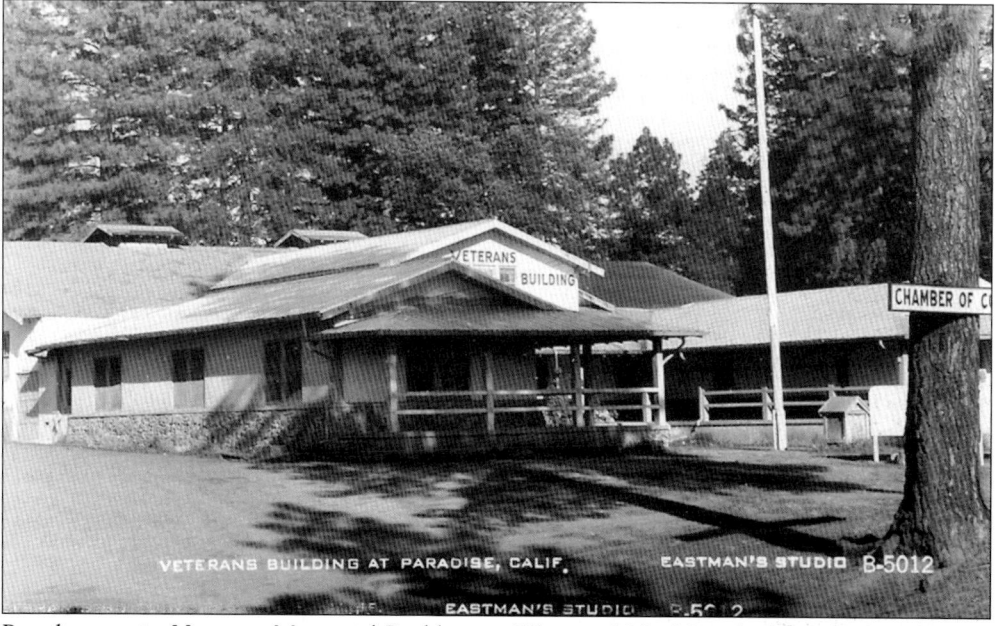

Paradise got its Veterans Memorial Building at Elliot and Neal Roads through the efforts of Max Bille and other World War I veterans. Built by Butte County, it was dedicated in 1927. A large room was added in 1932, and for many years, it was called the Paradise Pines Dance Hall. A number of "big bands" played there, but most of the musical talent was local. (Courtesy Gold Nugget Museum.)

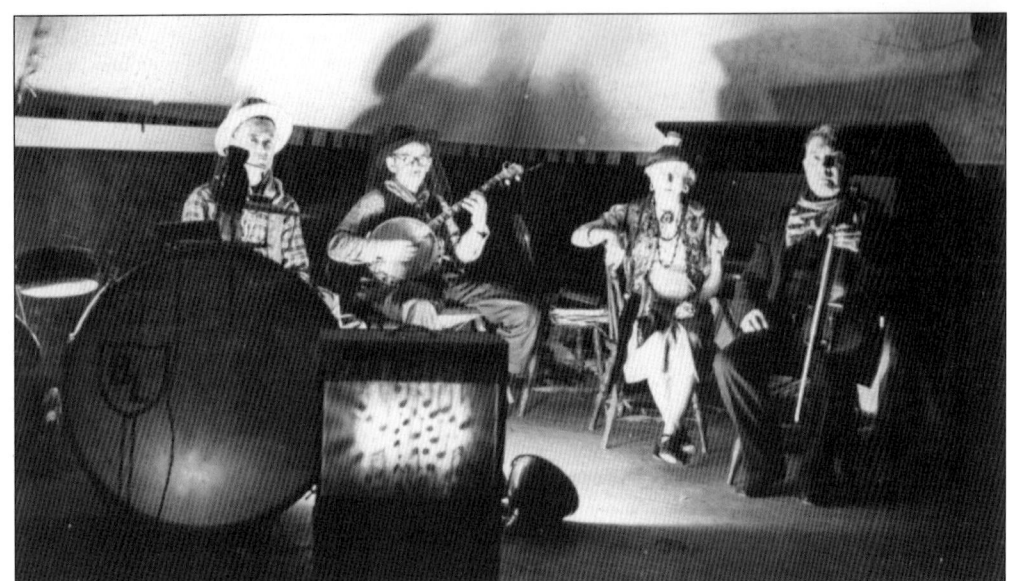

Pictured on the bandstand, the Paradise Mountaineers regularly provided the music for the Saturday night dances at the Paradise Pines Dance Hall. From left to right, they are Bob Lewis, Ray Parks, Mae Richardson, and Walker "Whoopie" Manning. (Courtesy Gold Nugget Museum.)

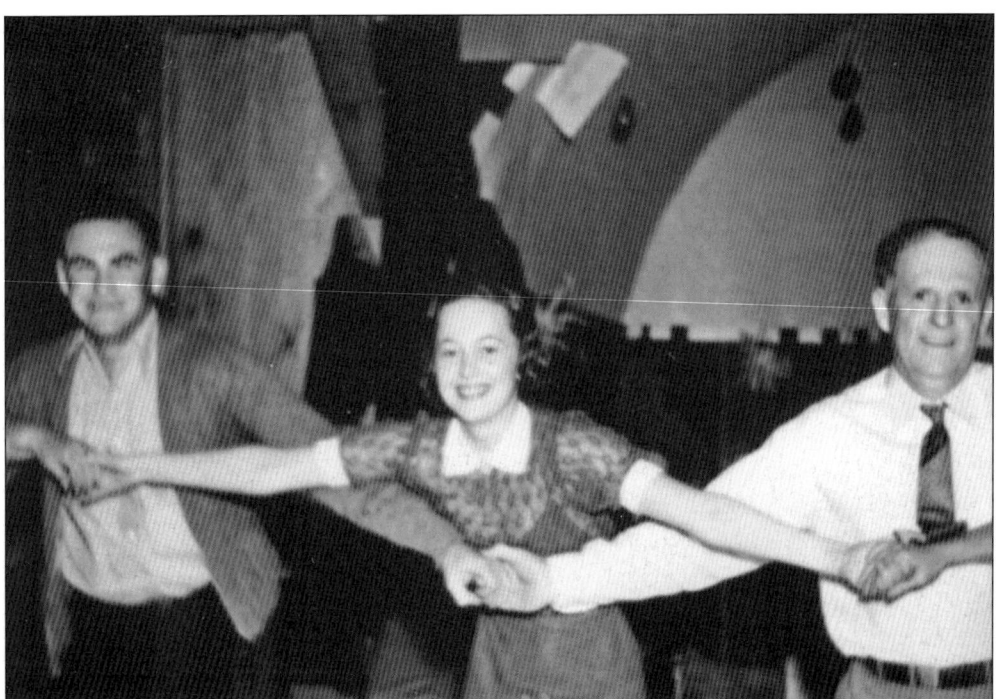

In 1937, Chico's Bidwell Park became Sherwood Forest for the filming of the movie *The Adventures of Robin Hood*. Star Olivia de Havilland came to a Saturday night dance at the Paradise Pines Dance Hall to relax from filming the movie. Here she is with Charles Bader on the left and George Banks on the right. (Courtesy Laura Boles and Gold Nugget Museum.)

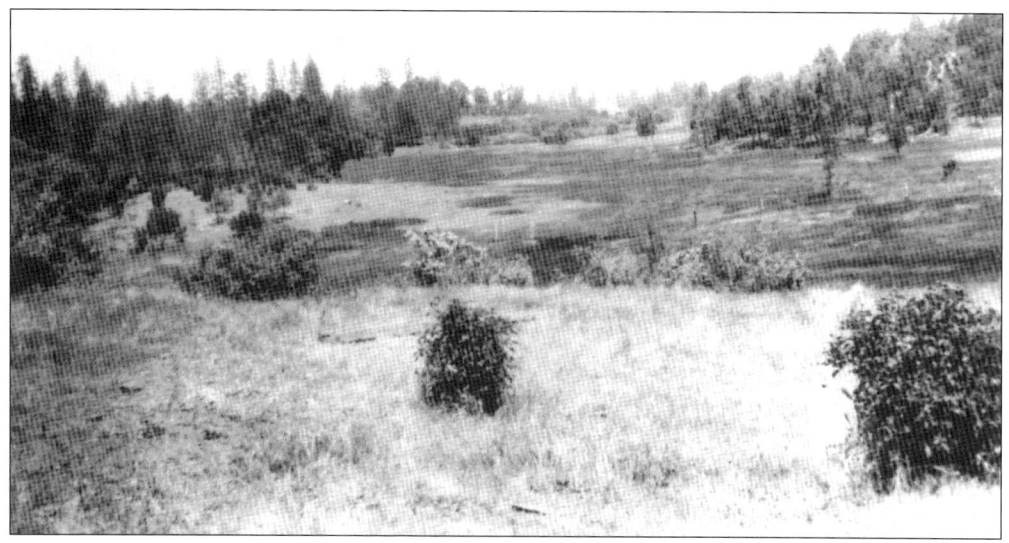

In 1939, scenes from *Gone with the Wind* were filmed in this vacant field on Dr. Nedry's property off Stark Lane, east of Pentz Road. With its red soil and apple blossoms, the land was a good "stand-in" for Georgia during the Civil War. The apple trees were almost through blooming so dogwood blossoms were hung on them, and cotton was attached to the manzanita bushes. (Courtesy Paradise Genealogy Society.)

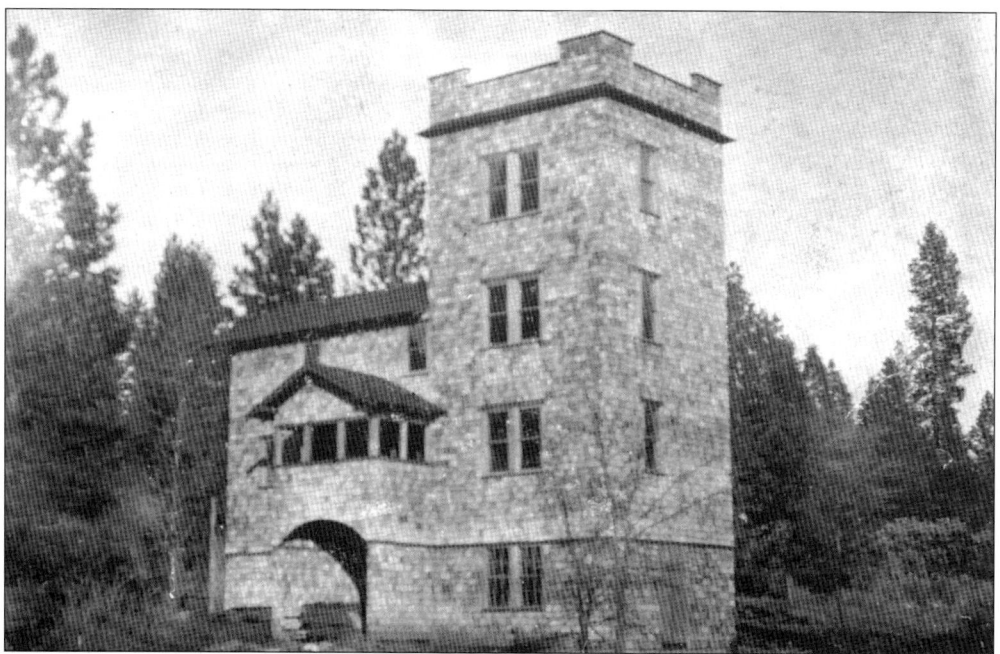

Max Bille built his "castle" on West Wagstaff Road around 1913 before he joined the army and chased Poncho Villa with Gen. Black Jack Pershing. The ground floor housed the well and was separated from a workshop by a drive-through breezeway. Above were a kitchen and dining and living room. Bedrooms were on the upper floors. The castle burned to the ground around 1931. (Courtesy Bernice Abshier.)

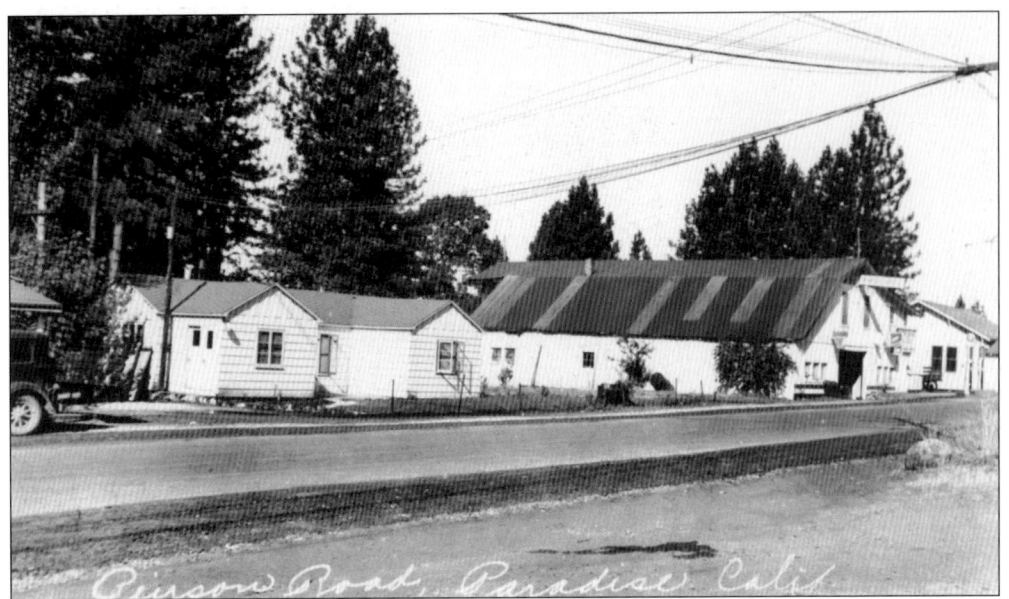

In 1907, Paradise's first telephone system was connected through the phone at the Paradise Depot. The Paradise Telephone Association, formed around 1920, put a switchboard in Wyatt Brown's store. In 1927, it was moved to Clara Brown's home on College Avenue, which can be seen to the left in the 1940 photograph above. Brown operated the switchboard throughout the day until 9:00 p.m., for emergencies, and even on Sunday during fire season. She put through calls for party-line subscribers and got such questions as "how do I make a pie crust?" and "does the store have fresh vegetables today?" The photograph below shows the office and the switchboard. The operator probably is Clara Brown, who manned the switchboard alone until 1940. In 1945, Pacific Telephone took over the system. (Above courtesy Lois McDonald; below courtesy Paradise Genealogy Society.)

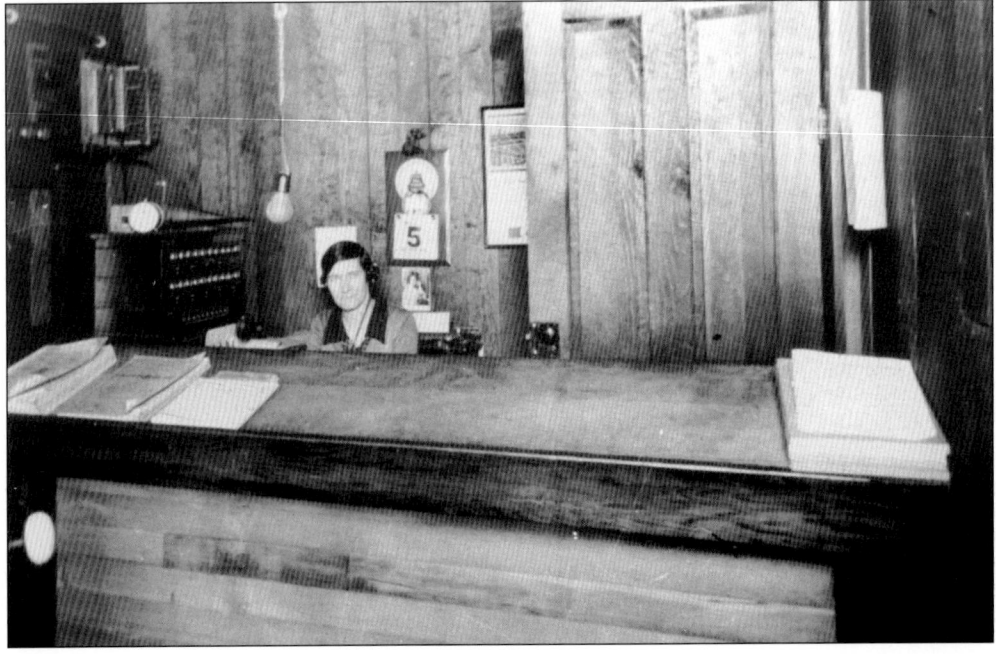

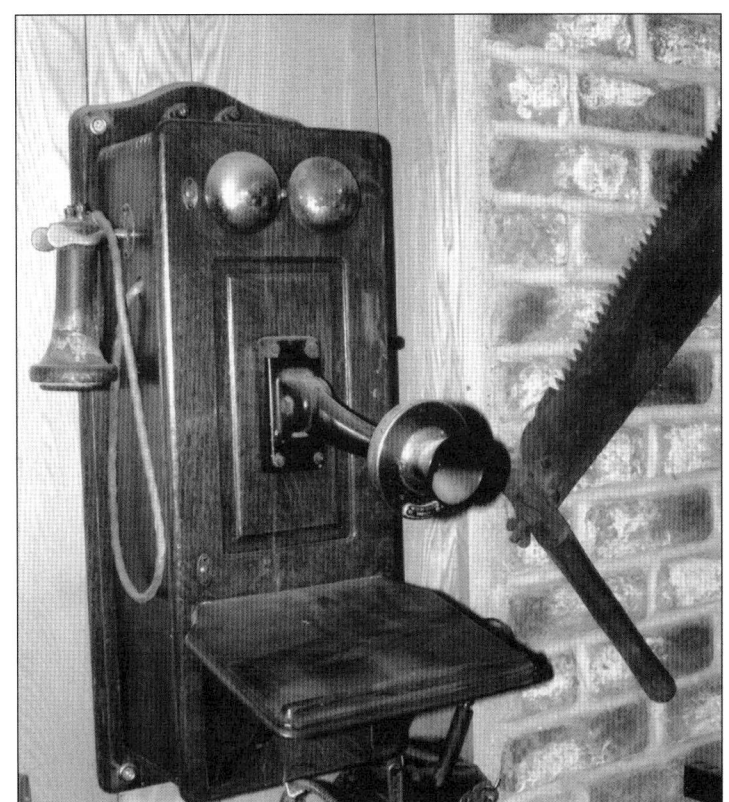

This crank telephone was used by the Bille family in the late 1920s and early 1930s. The Paradise Telephone Association started with 35 subscribers and six or eight phones on a party line. To hear the latest news or gossip, all one had to do was pick up the phone and listen. To reach another party, a person had to give the telephone a crank and talk to Clara Brown. (Courtesy author.)

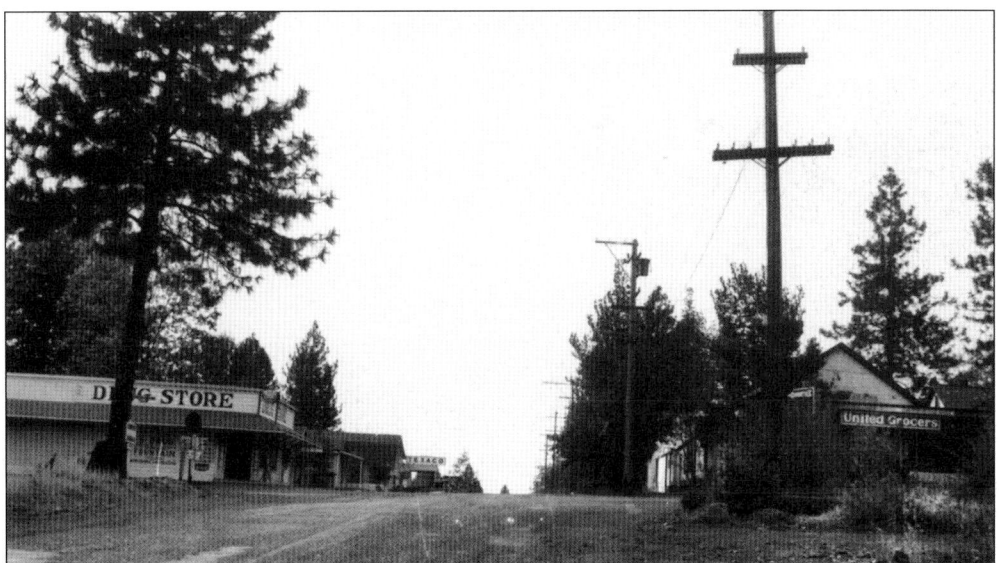

This photograph shows College Avenue (later Pearson Road) in 1937. The Texaco filling station and garage had been a livery stable and would house Paradise Electric and an antique shop before burning in the 1950s. The United Grocers occupied the building that in 1916 housed the PID offices and the post office. Starting with Fred Hawkes, the drugstore had several owners and eventually became Ace Hardware. (Courtesy Lois McDonald.)

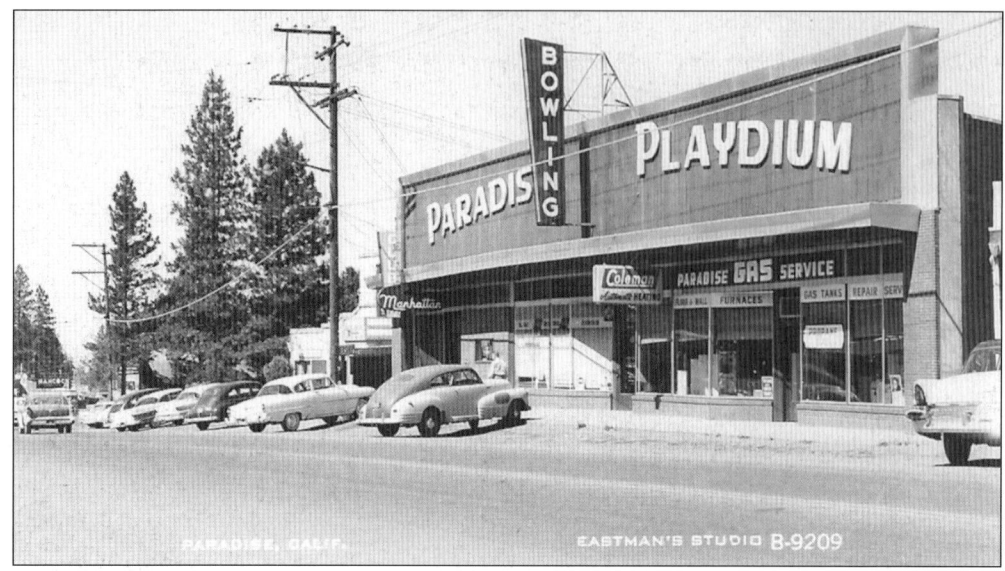

Built in the early 1940s on Neal Road in downtown, the Playdium was the first bowling alley in Paradise. It also had a coffee shop/soda fountain and, although off limits to young people, pool tables. Today the building is home to the Paradise Community Center and its Boys and Girls Club. (Courtesy Gold Nugget Museum.)

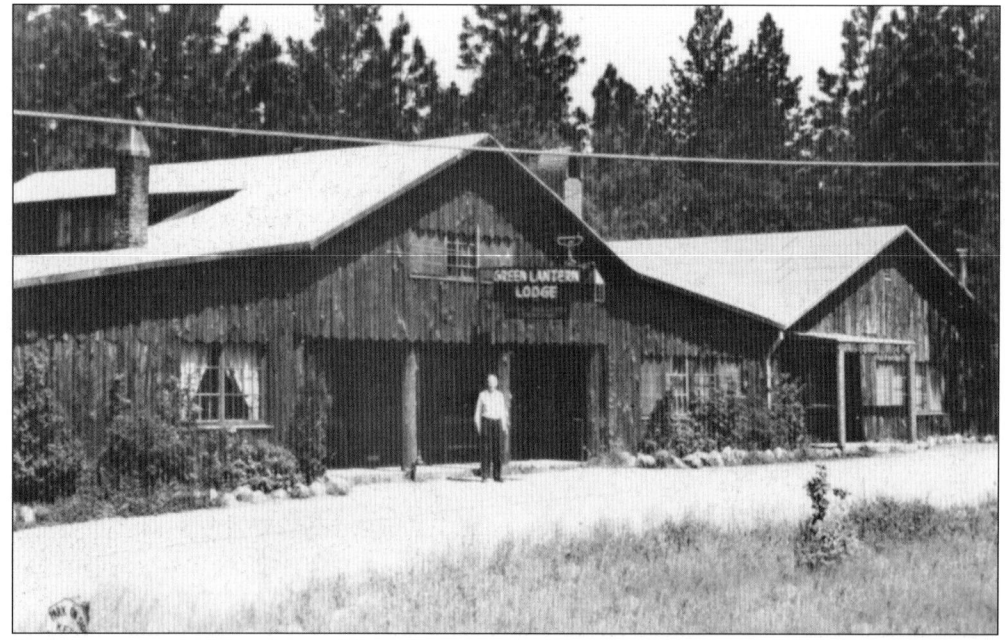

Stan Boquest stands in front of his rustic Green Lantern Lodge on Neal Road in downtown Paradise, where he served delicious meals to local residents and out of towners. The lodge also served as a meeting place for local clubs. In 1945, he had the first neon sign in Paradise. The structure was demolished and replaced with a Bank of America building. (Courtesy Gold Nugget Museum.)

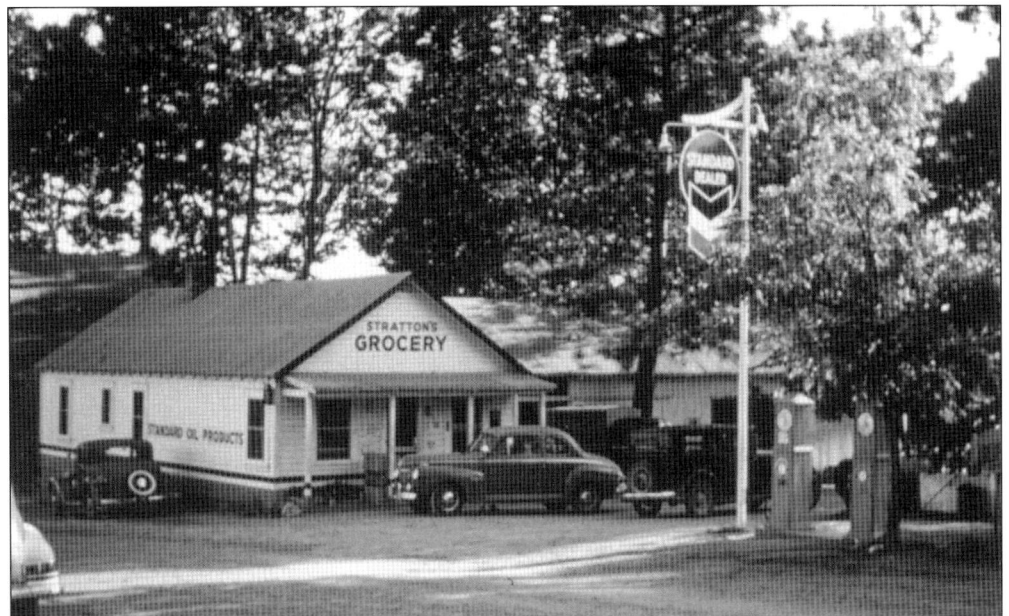

In 1919, the Stratton family bought 50 acres, cleared the land, and planted fruit trees and a garden. They also raised chickens and goats. When William Stratton Jr. was old enough, he started selling eggs and vegetables, and in 1940, opened a store on the southwest corner of Sawmill and Nunneley Roads. This photograph shows the store in 1945, across the intersection from the current market. (Courtesy Gold Nugget Museum.)

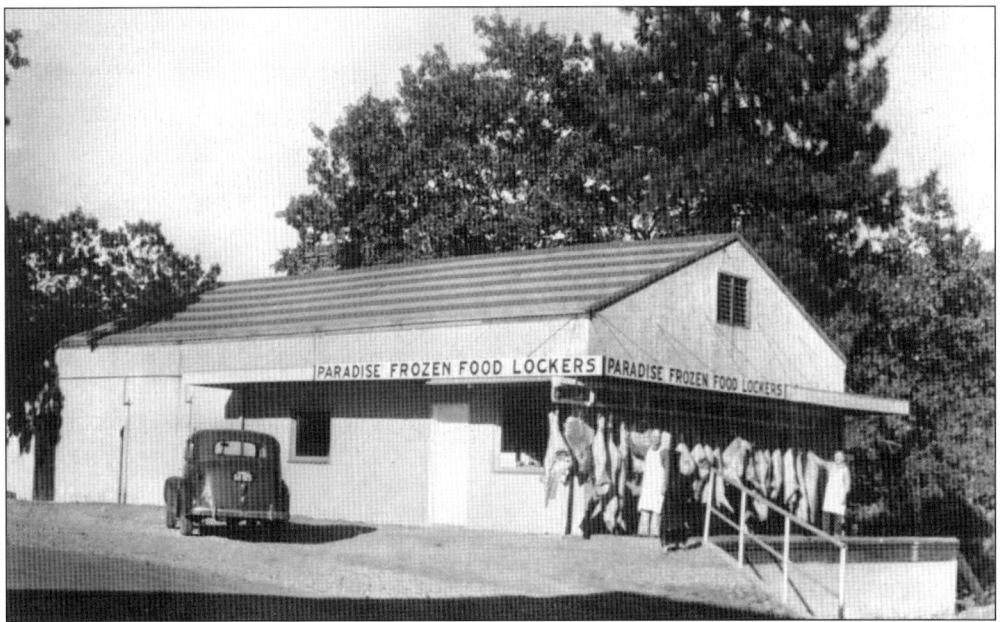

In an era before everyone had a home freezer, a person could rent a locker at Harry Ballew's Paradise Frozen Food Lockers, located just north of the Paradise Depot. Opening in 1946, it offered quick-freezing of fruits and vegetables for commercial and private customers, and patrons could cut and package their own meat or have it done for a nominal charge. (Courtesy Paradise Historical Society.)

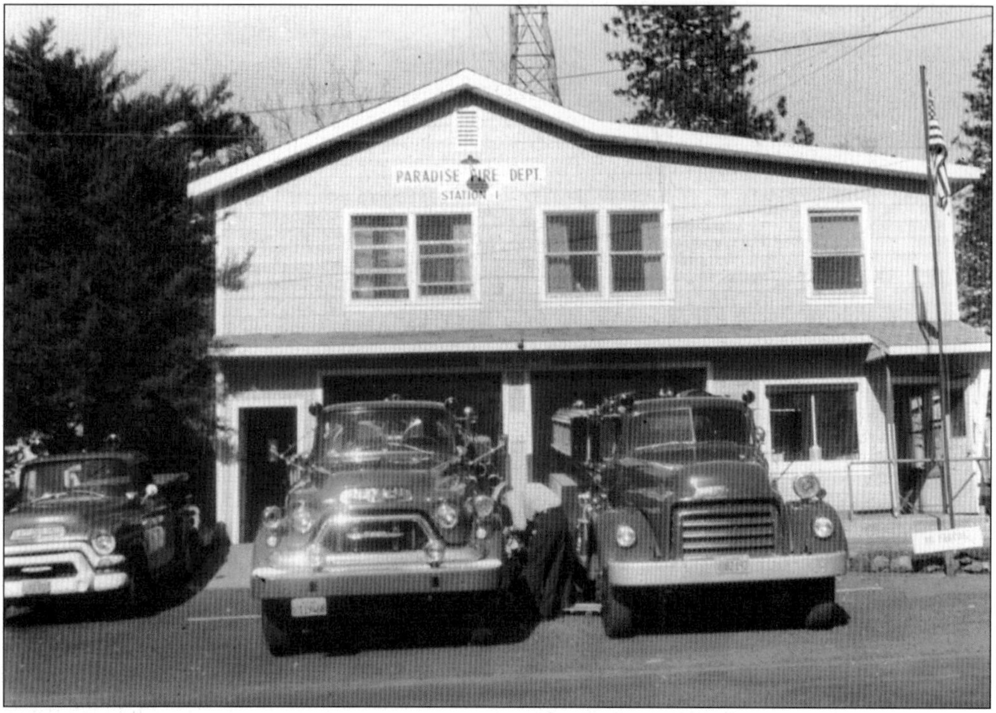

When the Paradise Volunteer Fire Department organized in 1944, Firehouse No. 1 was built on the south end of town west of Neal Road and just above the Pearson Road intersection. In 1947, the town allocated $5,750 to build Station No. 1 on Birch Street, between Olive and Almond Streets, where the current, much larger fire station and headquarters are today. (Courtesy Lois McDonald.)

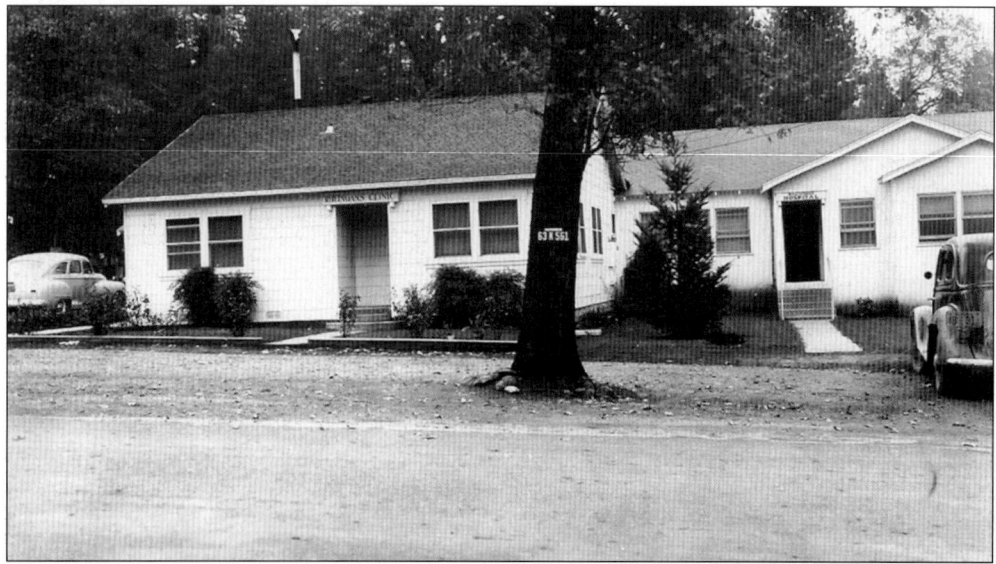

In 1941, Drs. Kenneth and Everina Rheingans opened a medical practice in Paradise, and in 1947, they opened a 10-bed hospital on Olive Street just below Pearson Road. The hospital closed in 1966 and became the Raymar Sanitarium for senior citizens. Since then, it has housed several businesses. (Courtesy Gold Nugget Museum.)

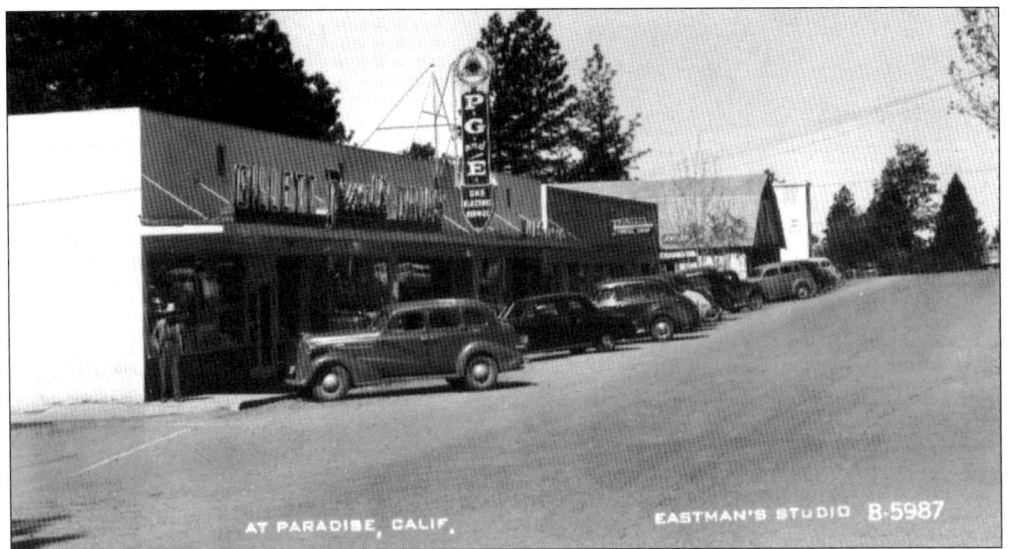

In 1948, Basil and Alta Gillett owned the old Hawkes drugstore on the southwest corner of Pearson Road and Olive Street. Neal Road, to be named Skyway within four years, was rapidly becoming the main business district, but getting the Rexall franchise helped keep business. Having the PG&E office next door also increased foot traffic as people came in to pay their electric bill. (Courtesy Gold Nugget Museum.)

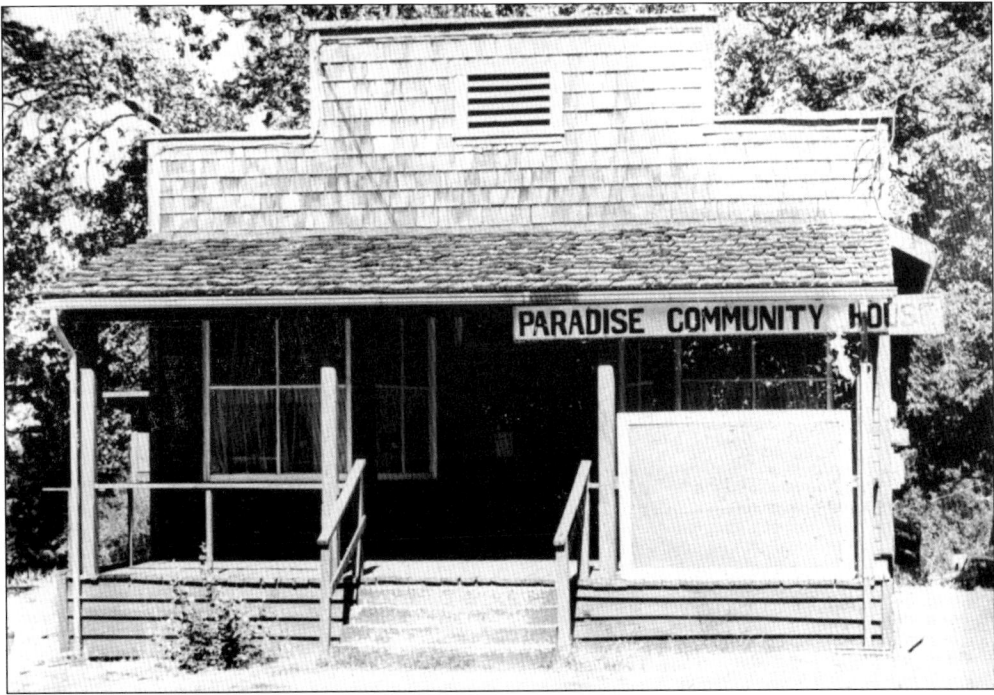

From the earliest days, the people of Paradise stepped forward to help unfortunate families and individuals who needed food, clothing, and other items. In 1948, local citizens formed Paradise Christmas Inc. to distribute Christmas food baskets, clothing, toys, and Christmas trees to those less fortunate. Paradise Community House on Almond Street was the headquarters and thrift store in 1955. (Courtesy Lois McDonald.)

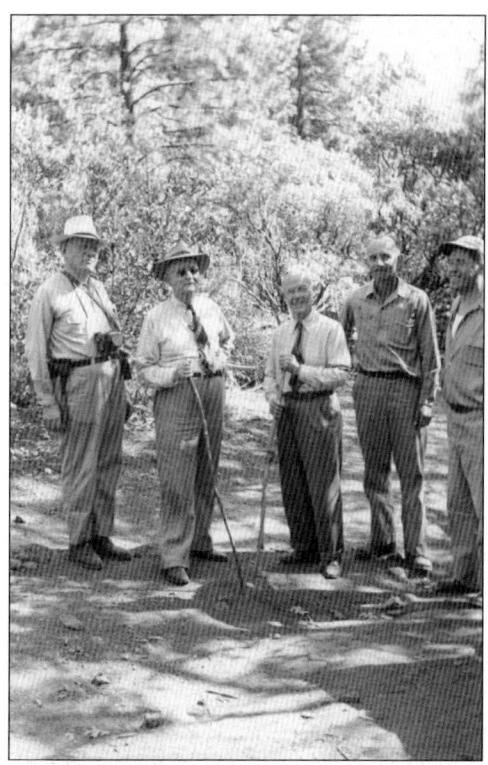

This photograph was taken on October 1, 1947, as the founders of the Feather River Hospital hiked the hillside overlooking the West Branch on an inspection tour of the future hospital site. Pictured, from left to right, are Dr. C. C. Landis, Dr. E. A. Sutherland, Herbert C. White, Jack Bryson, and Dr. Merritt C. Horning. A fourth physician, Dr. Dean Hoiland, took this photograph. (Courtesy Feather River Hospital and Dean Hoiland.)

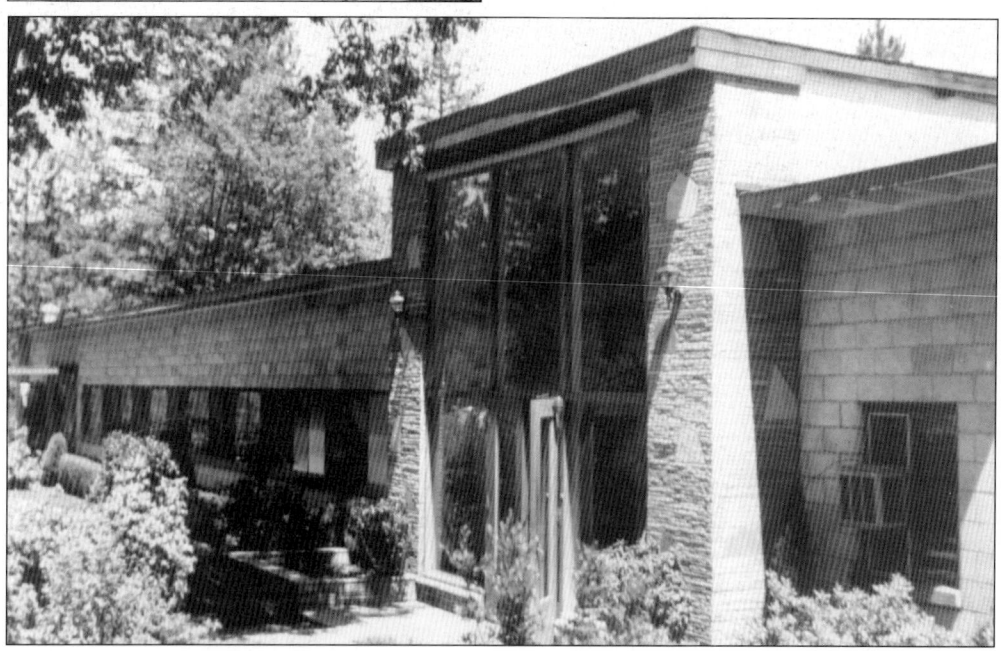

In 1946, Dr. Merritt C. Horning discussed the idea of a new hospital with Dr. Dean Hoiland, Dr. C. C. Landis, Howard Landis, and Jack Bryson. The result was the Feather River Sanitarium and Hospital that opened in 1950 with 18 beds. In 1960, the Seventh Day Adventist Church assumed management. Today the hospital has 122 beds and offers state-of-the-art medical care. (Courtesy Feather River Hospital and J. H. Eastman.)

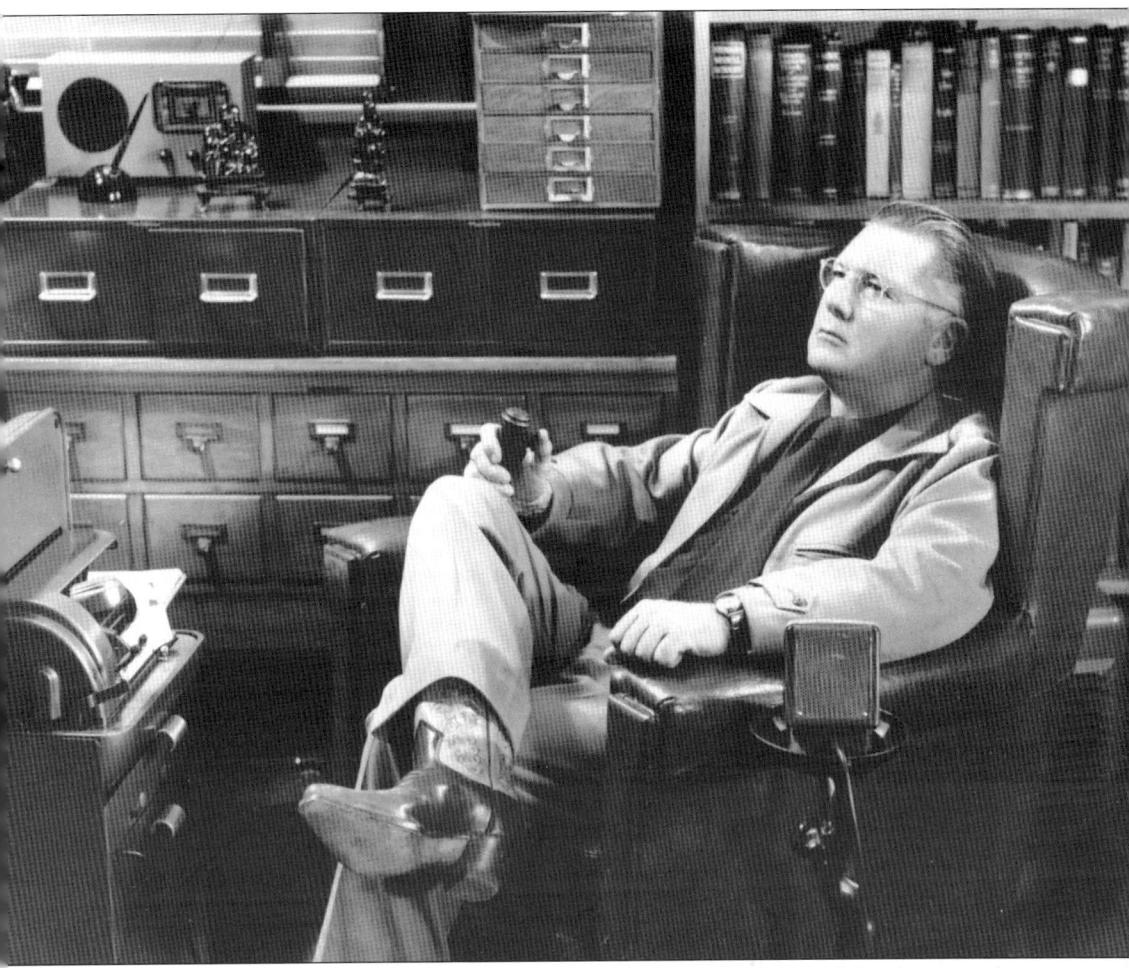

"The address in Paradise is on Crestview Drive. . . . Take the main street through town, then turn left on Oliver Road. At the foot of the grade, make a sharp left turn on to Valley View for a very short distance, then turn left again onto Crestview Drive, and it's the last place on the right-hand side," so wrote Erle Stanley Gardner in his 1954 Perry Mason mystery *The Case of the Runaway Corpse*. Readers did not know that Gardner was describing in detail how to get to his Paradise "hideaway." Around 1952, Gardner bought 20 acres at the end of Crestview Drive. He was no stranger to Butte County, having spent his teenage years in Oroville in the early 1900s where he was suspended from Oroville Union High School for pulling pranks on the principal. He eventually became a lawyer and started writing the Perry Mason novels in 1933. In 1937, Gardner bought a 3,000-acre ranch near Temecula in Southern California. But with fame came fans that intruded on his privacy at the ranch. Only a few of his closest associates knew of his hideaway "somewhere in the mountains of Northern California." Here he could relax, write, and ride his dirt bike. The term "dirt bike" was years in the future, but J. W. Black, a longtime Paradise resident and master mechanic, constructed ones for Gardner and himself to ride in the surrounding mountains. Gardner penned 82 Perry Mason books plus numerous other novels, books, and papers, many of them in Paradise. Prankster that he had been since boyhood, he "pulled one" on his readers when he had a fictional client tell Perry Mason how to get to his secret hideaway. And none of his millions of readers were the wiser. This photograph is of Gardner "writing" to an old Edison Dictaphone in Temecula, a scene that was repeated many times in Paradise. (Courtesy Stan Gardner.)

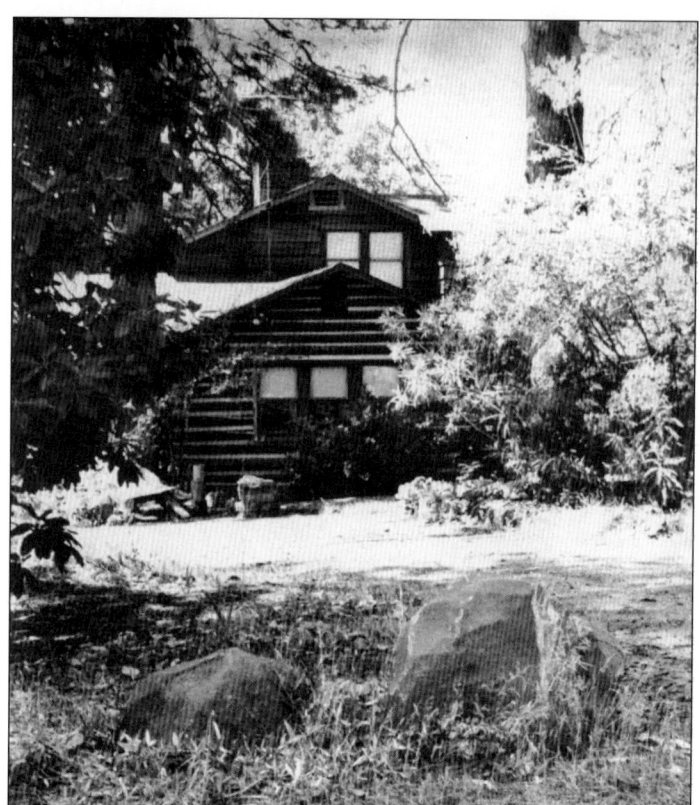

Inscribed on this photograph is "A log cabin on the corner of Bille & Clark." Obviously the Frank Remy home on the northeast corner of that intersection was more than what one usually thinks of as a "log cabin." But log cabins and houses were popular because they were cheap to build and well insulated. The rest of the inscription reads, "Many a time we had our square dance parties here." (Courtesy Lois McDonald.)

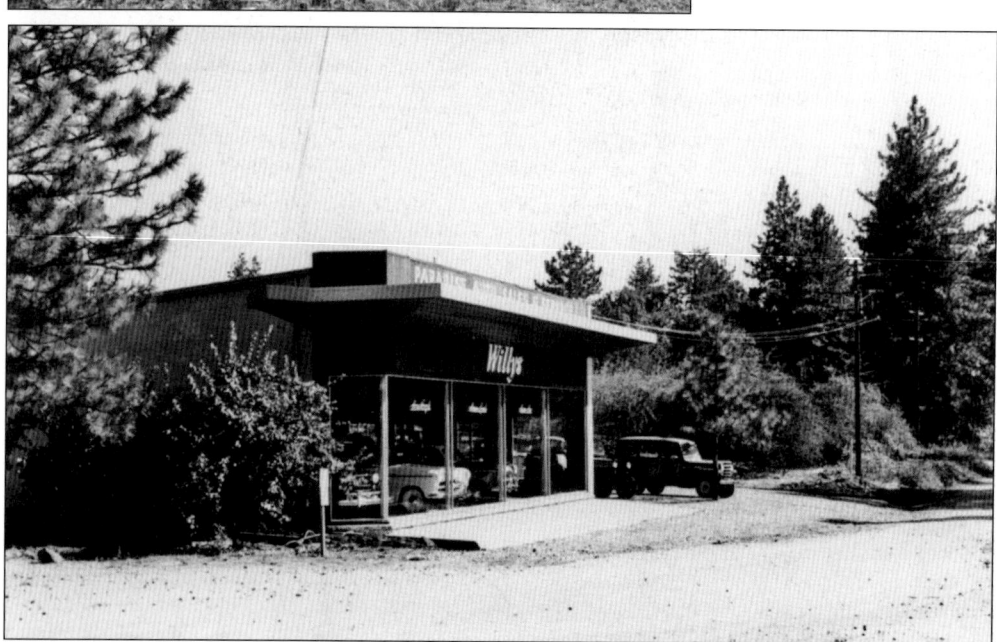

In the mid-1950s, Paradise Auto Sales and Service was Willys Motors dealership, selling Jeeps, Jeep trucks and utility wagons, and the Aero Willys sedan. It was located at Neal and Foster Roads. Owners Harry N. Koehler and Harry A. Mosure advertised in 1955 Chamber of Commerce Community Directory, "Clean Used Cars Bought, Sold or Consigned." (Courtesy Lois McDonald.)

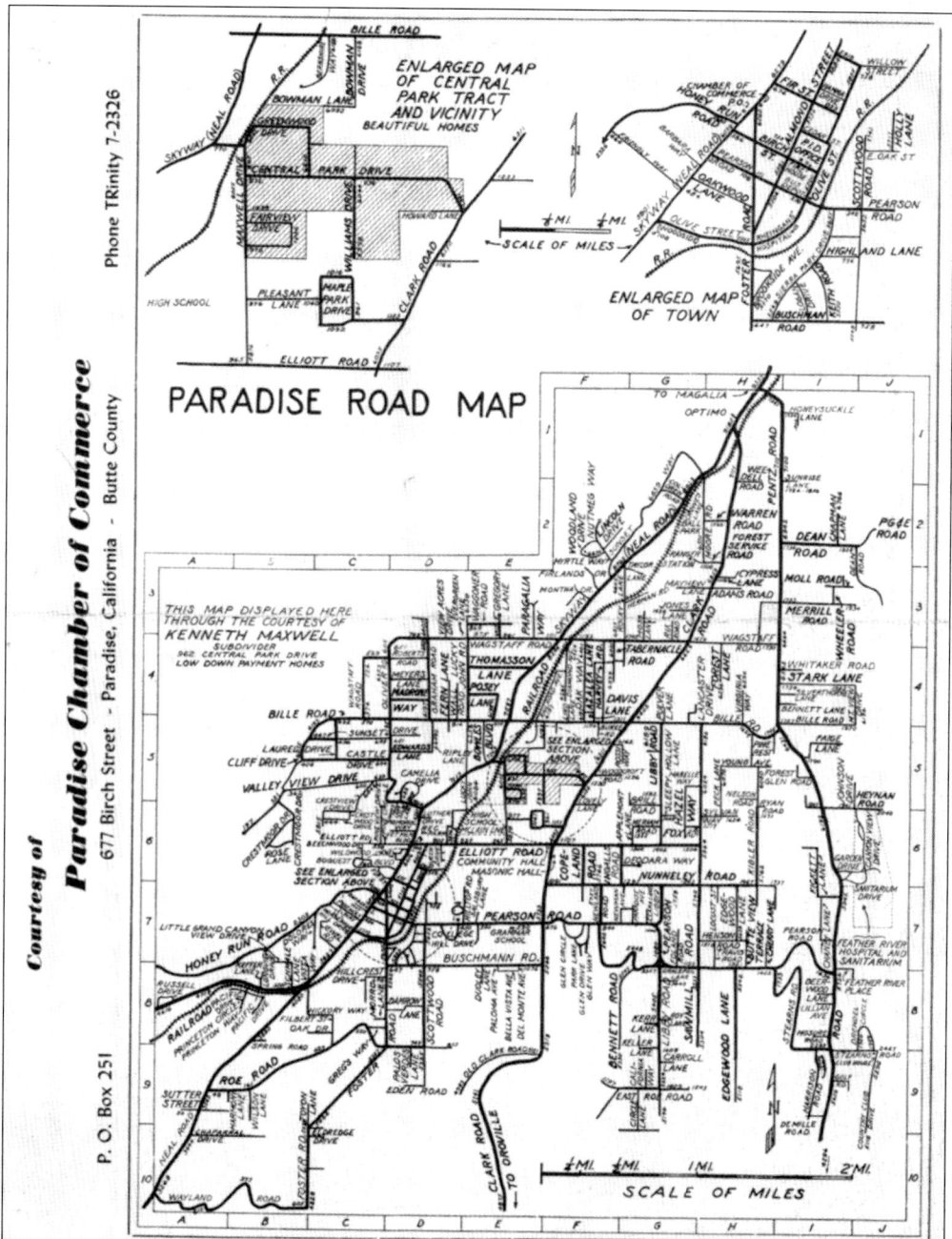

This was Paradise around 1955. The "three-leg A" layout is evident with Skyway (Neal Road), Clark Road, and Pentz Road forming the legs. Except for the addition of numerous streets, the town is much the same in 2006. (Courtesy Lois McDonald.)

Gold Nugget Days celebrates the finding of the Dogtown Nugget in 1859. Tradition has it that the 54-pound nugget set off a three-day binge in Dogtown. Audrey Youngs, who had seen a replica of the nugget in San Francisco as a child, moved to Paradise in 1934 and, in 1959, suggested that Paradise celebrate the centennial of the nugget's founding. This is the program cover for the first celebration. (Courtesy author.)

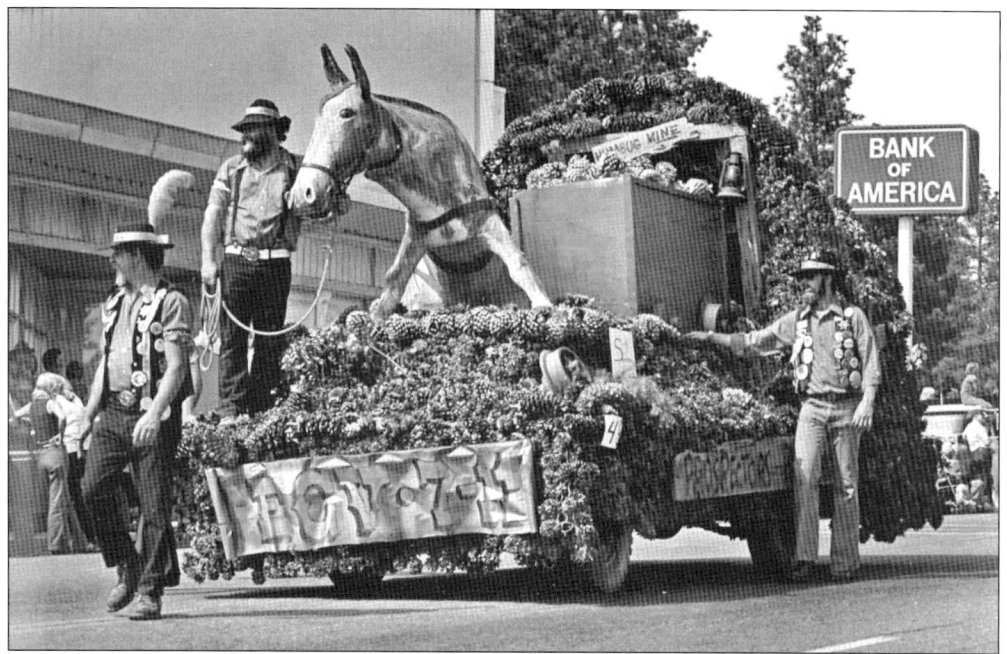

This is the Pair 'O Dice Chapter of E Clampus Vitus float in the Gold Nugget Days parade, probably in 1978. The parade attracts 20,000 visitors. The "Clampers" stage a donkey race every year from Whiskey Flat on the West Branch to Magalia as part of the celebration. Tom Chittick is walking in front of the float, Bob Knowles alongside, and that may be Jerry Heganbart riding. (Courtesy Gold Nugget Museum.)

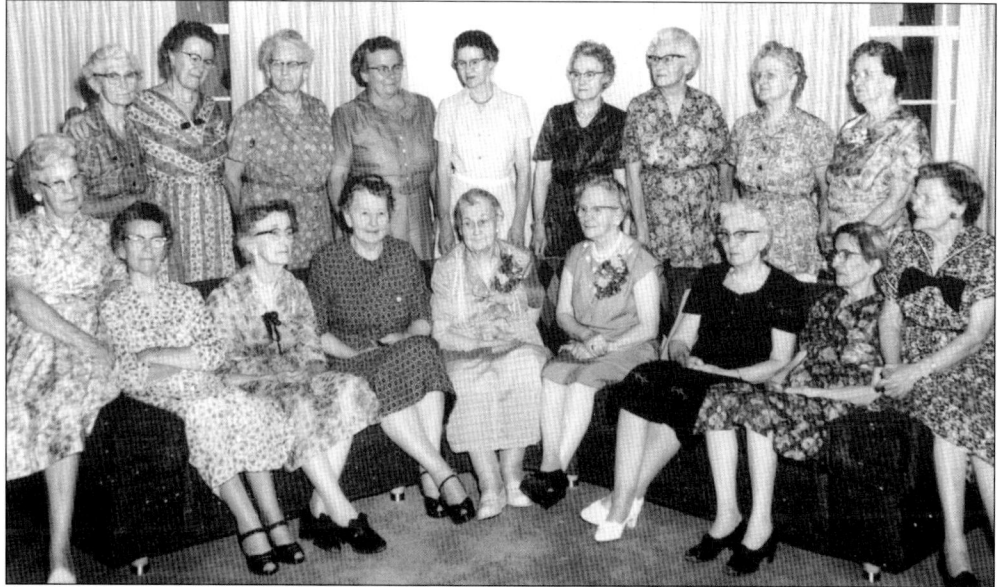

Started in 1921 to ease housework doldrums, the Friendly Friday Club became a community service group. In this c. 1960 photograph, from left to right, are (first row) Alta Slater, Gussie Dudley, Jessie Peck, Mae Bethune, Bell Simkin, Helen Berry, Maude Horner, Bell Sample, and Iva Phillips; and (second row) Mabel Gibler, Ina Clewett, Nell Ingall, Mary Rogers, Helen Pearce, Flossie Alderson, Julia Fontaine, Halycone Stratton, and Iva Collett. (Courtesy Paradise Genealogy Society.)

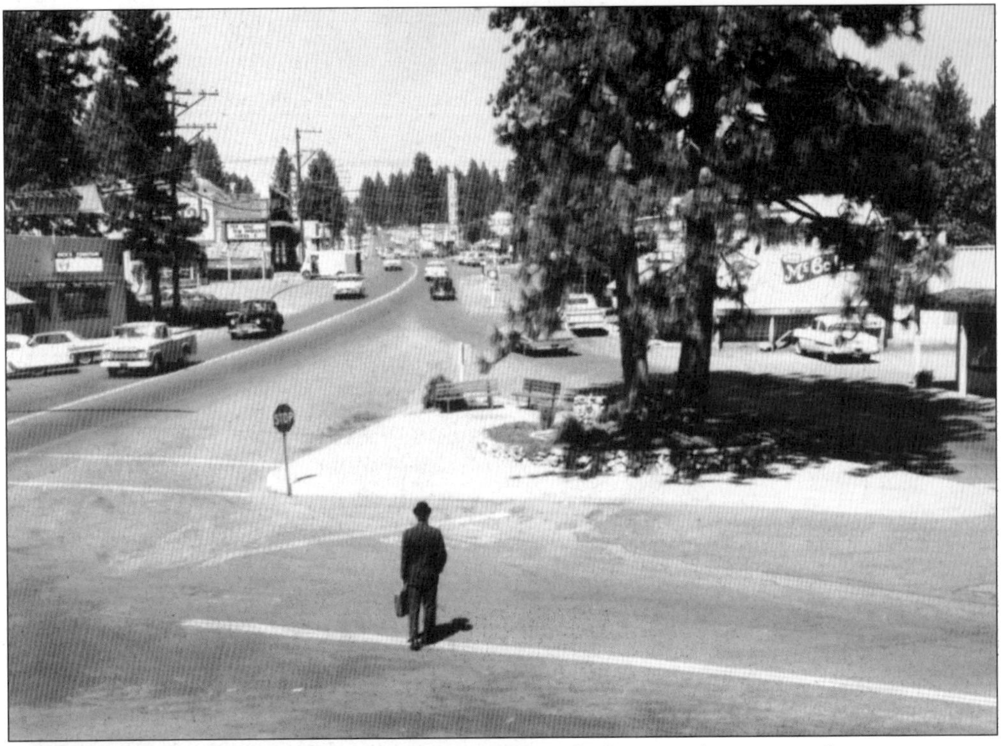

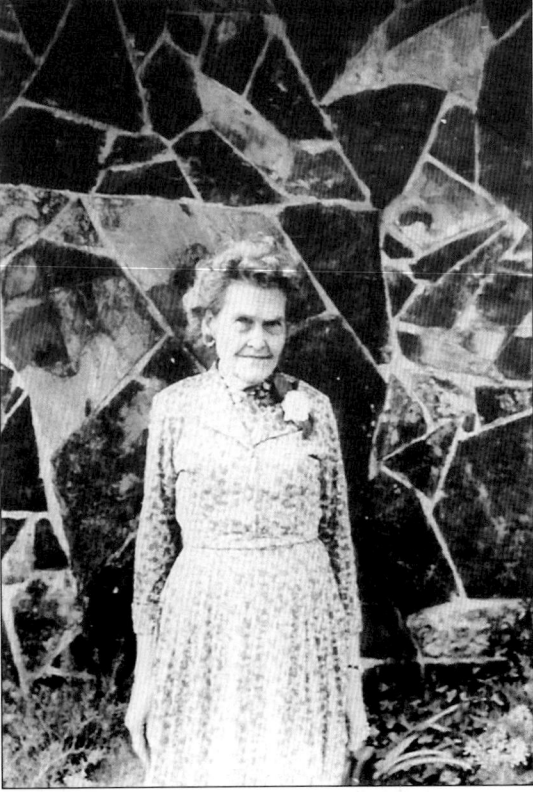

Perhaps a salesman on the way to a call in the 1960s, this solitary soul strolls across Foster Road toward the "Triangle." Originally just a patch of gravel, this mini park, at the intersection with Skyway, was built as part of downtown beautification in 1960. Back then, it provided pedestrians with a drinking fountain and benches, shaded by two trees that later died and were removed. (Courtesy Gold Nugget Museum.)

Elsie Hamburger, pictured here in 1961, had known of Paradise since 1919 but returned for good in 1923 after her husband died. By chance, when she sold a parcel of land to help "make ends meet" for her family, she got into real estate, which became a lifelong career. She was involved in many civic projects, from the Paradise Farm Center to the County Republican Central Committee. (Courtesy Gold Nugget Museum.)

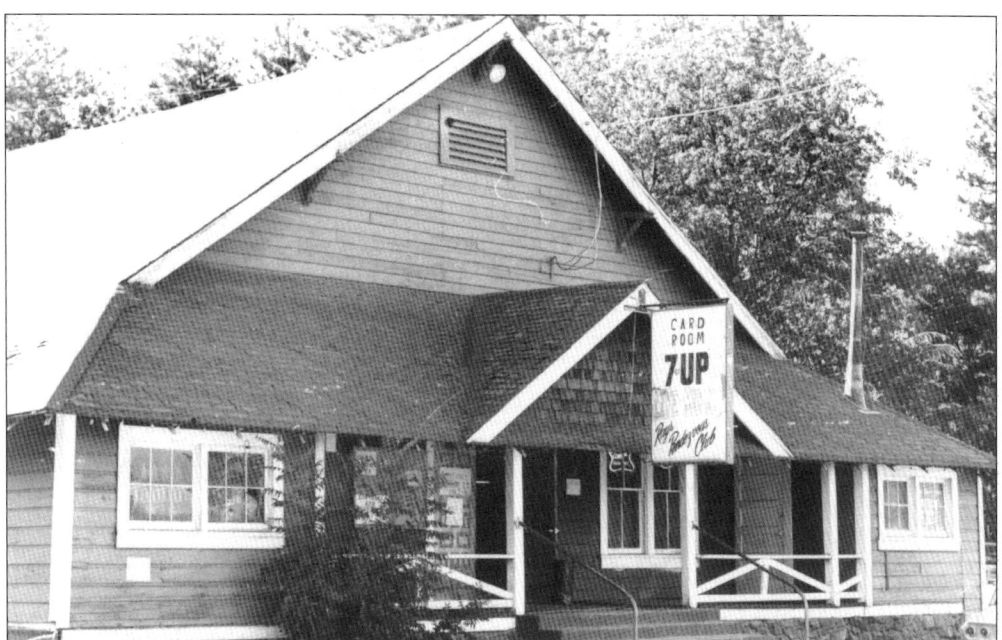

In the 1960s and 1970s, the former Community Center housed Ray's Rendezvous Club, a card room and bar. In the 1880s, the Good Templars Lodge was on this site. Ironically, the lodge is supposed to have been "torched" by a patron of a saloon across the street. Years later, the saloon was moved to the site of the lodge and became the original Community Center. (Courtesy Paradise Genealogy Society.)

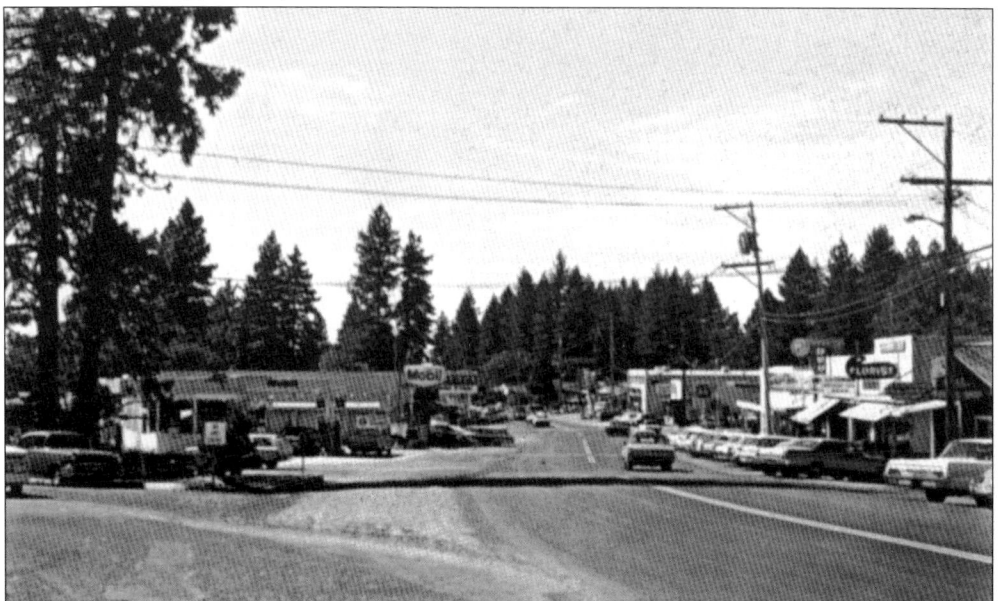

By 1968, Sam Neal's trail, named Skyway since 1952, had a double line down the center of the street and diagonal parking for automobiles, not cattle. The view is to the south with the triangle at Foster Road on the left. This is still downtown Paradise today. Most of the buildings are still there, except for the gas stations, although many businesses have come and gone. (Courtesy Lois McDonald.)

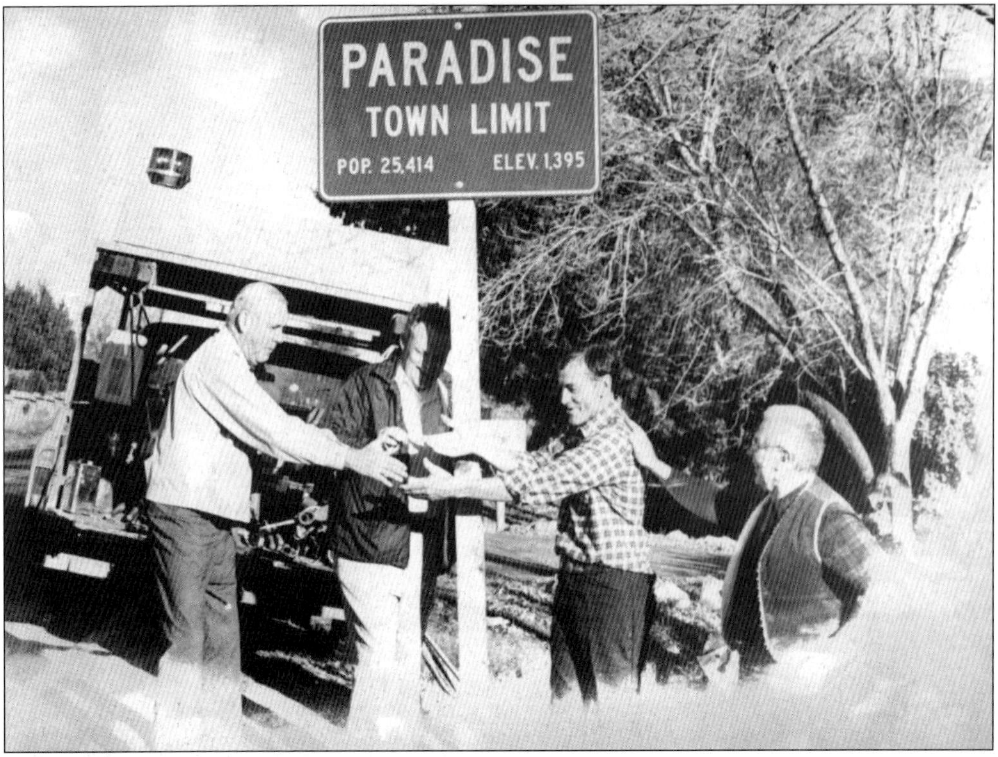

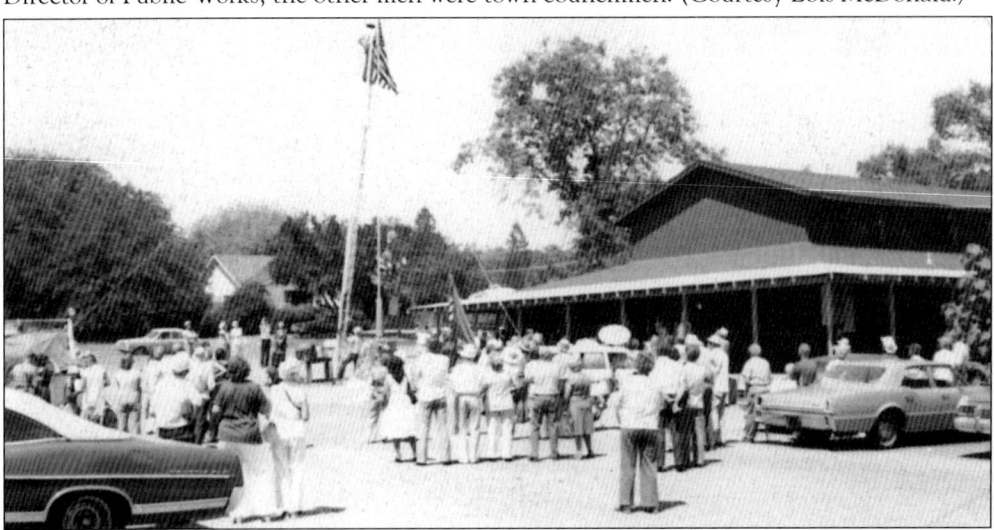

In 1979, the "Town with a Future" finally officially became a town when voters cast their votes to incorporate Paradise. Congratulating each other at the new town limit sign, from left to right, are Bill Holding, Warner Humbert, Clay Castleberry, and Bill Taylor. Castleberry was Butte County Director of Public Works; the other men were town councilmen. (Courtesy Lois McDonald.)

The flag is raised over the Gold Nugget Museum at the April 1981 opening during Gold Nugget Days. Back in 1959, the idea emerged for a museum to house Paradise Ridge historical artifacts and information and to be financed and maintained from the proceeds from the celebration. The museum has grown in size and in the programs offered to the community. (Courtesy Gold Nugget Museum.)

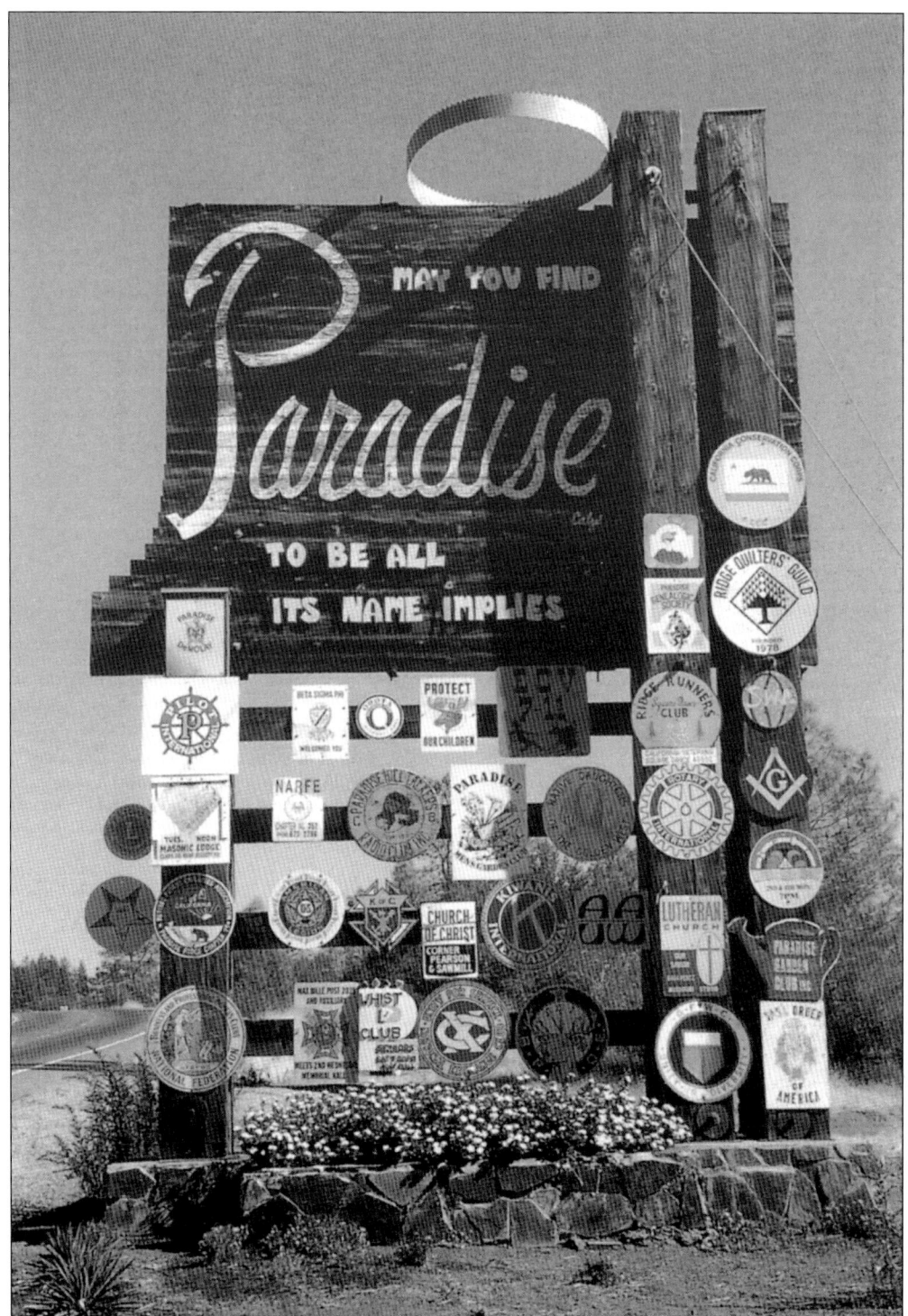

With a halo topping it off, this sign welcomes motorists to Paradise as they drive up Skyway from Chico. The sign was erected sometime in the mid-1980s, shortly after the original two-lane Skyway was made a four-lane divided road between Chico and Paradise. (Courtesy Takao Wakida.)

Across America, People are Discovering Something Wonderful. Their Heritage.

Arcadia Publishing is the leading local history publisher in the United States. With more than 3,000 titles in print and hundreds of new titles released every year, Arcadia has extensive specialized experience chronicling the history of communities and celebrating America's hidden stories, bringing to life the people, places, and events from the past. To discover the history of other communities across the nation, please visit:

www.arcadiapublishing.com

Customized search tools allow you to find regional history books about the town where you grew up, the cities where your friends and family live, the town where your parents met, or even that retirement spot you've been dreaming about.

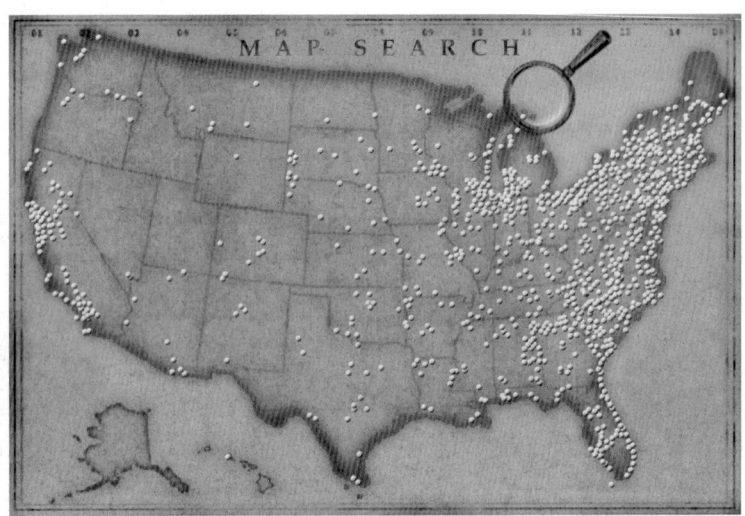